JESUS AND THE PRODIGAL SON

D0168337

JESUS AND THE PRODIGAL SON

The God of Radical Mercy

Brian J. Pierce, OP

ORBIS BOOKS
Maryknoll, New York 10545

ORBIS BOOKS
Maryknoll, New York 10545

Fathers and Brothers
MARYKNOLL

Founded in 1970, Orbis Books endeavors to publish works that enlighten the mind, nourish the spirit, and challenge the conscience. The publishing arm of the Maryknoll Fathers and Brothers, Orbis seeks to explore the global dimensions of the Christian faith and mission, to invite dialogue with diverse cultures and religious traditions, and to serve the cause of reconciliation and peace. The books published reflect the views of their authors and do not represent the official position of the Maryknoll Society. To learn more about Maryknoll and Orbis Books, please visit our website at www.maryknollsociety.org.

Copyright © 2016 by Brian J. Pierce, OP

Published by Orbis Books, Box 302, Maryknoll, NY 10545-0302.

All rights reserved.

No part of this publication may be reproduced or transmitted in any form or by any means, electronic or mechanical, including photocopying, recording, or any information storage or retrieval system, without prior permission in writing from the publisher.

Queries regarding rights and permissions should be addressed to: Orbis Books, P.O. Box 302, Maryknoll, NY 10545-0302.

Manufactured in the United States of America

Library of Congress Cataloging-in-Publication Data

Pierce, Brian J.
    Jesus and the Prodigal son : the God of radical mercy / Brian J. Pierce, OP.
        pages cm
    Includes bibliographical references and index.
    ISBN 978-1-62698-174-4 (pbk.)
    1. Jesus Christ—Person and offices. 2. Prodigal son (Parable) I. Title.
BT203.P5155 2016
226.8'06—dc23
                                                                    2015030012

*I dedicate this book
with my most profound love and gratitude
to my mother and father, Carolyn and Roger.
The words written in these pages flowed into my heart,
having first flowed out of theirs.*

Contents

Foreword

We recall that it was while walking the *Camino* to Santiago in 2013 that Brian told us of his burning desire to write about "Jesus, the Prodigal Son." We thought initially we had misheard him or, perhaps like some politicians, he had just "misspoken." But no! He went on to sketch briefly how the seed had been planted within him and had germinated over time. We should have known it would not end there.

By way of context, we first met Brian in 2007 as part of a group of twenty-eight Christians undertaking a program called *The Fifth Gospel* at the Tantur Ecumenical Institute in the Holy Land. As an older lay Australian married couple (certainly not clerics, scripture scholars, or theologians), we had been excited but apprehensive about this undertaking—a pilgrimage of a different kind. It was Brian in particular who gave us confidence in our faith journey and in our ability to reflect on and share publicly with others our insights about scripture, seen through the lens of our lives as parents and grandparents.

Brian encouraged us to step outside our comfort zone when he gathered a few of us from the group to go with him and witness firsthand the work of a Christian Peacemaker Team (CPT) in Hebron, on the West Bank. This team patiently supported and accompanied the Palestinian people who were facing daily struggles and humiliation by Israeli settlers. Like the prodigal son setting out on his journey into the unknown, the members of the CPT team had left behind their comfort zones, taking risks without counting the cost. They had put themselves in danger "in a foreign land" in order to serve those suffering injustice and abuse. In "emptying themselves," they both identified with and bore witness to the suffering of the poor.

Through our time shared in the Holy Land and on the *Camino*, our friendship has grown and our faith has been strengthened through this friendship. We were surprised when, in a 2014 email, Brian invited us to read some draft chapters of his planned book and give him feedback from our perspective as ordinary Catholic Christians "active in parish

life." Like our friendship with Brian, our involvement with this book
has grown.

Without doubt, after having read this book we know we will not
see the parable of the Prodigal Son in quite the same way again. And it
is no exaggeration to say that we will never again see God's unconditional love for us, fully alive in and through Jesus, quite the same way.
We are now starting to see the wonderful grace that Brian sees in and
draws on so passionately and insightfully in the parable. We discover
Jesus' real humanity and it becomes more real as we read on. We are
human beings greatly and totally loved "into being" by God, graced
with the hope and the courage to act for the love of God in the service
of the least of his people.

Brian's gift is not only to place himself in the parable but to draw
us in with him, often in challenging and unexpected ways. Brian is a su-
perb storyteller, which allows him to present us with scripture and
scriptural events wrapped in the idiom and images of our own time, not
least those of "the family" and "the table" (home and Eucharist). He
closes any apparent gap between Jesus' life "then" and "now" as we
journey together. His own personal experiences, sometimes tragic, always compelling, and recounted humbly, bring life and meaning to
God's great and merciful love for us, in and through Jesus. What is
transformative for him through his writing becomes so for us too.

Amidst all the sin and suffering and evil in our world, Brian's book
offers us an understanding that no matter what or how we suffer, Jesus
is there in the midst of it, embracing the outcast and rejected, truly one
with us, transforming us and our world. On the *Camino* to Santiago
there is an intriguing crucifix in a small church in the hamlet of Furelos,
in Galicia, which we discovered after taking shelter there because of
threatening rains. It is an image of Christ crucified, nailed by one hand
and reaching down and out to us, and our world, with his other hand.
For us this image is the Jesus of Brian's book. Jesus descends into our
brokenness and loves us, and he invites us to do the same with "our
neighbor." That we are loved unconditionally, that it is a "story" of
friendship and love, that we hunger for God's mercy and compassion,
are all burning realities for Brian.

Kevin, a *Camino* pilgrim whom we met on the Portuguese *Camino*,
enthusiastically urged us to go somewhat out of our way the next day
in order to stay at Casa Fernanda, a pilgrim hostel somewhat off the
beaten path in a place called Lugar do Corgo. We took up Kevin's sug-
gestion and, as it turned out, experienced such *Camino* hospitality as
we'd not known before. We were pilgrims from different nations with
diverse backgrounds and beliefs, meeting for the first time, yet we were
all equal and welcome without exception. We sat round the family

table, sharing Fernanda's homegrown food, Jacinto's homemade wines, and much laughter and conversation. A wonderful internationally inspired sing-along rounded off the evening.

A large home-cooked breakfast greeted us in the morning. With something akin to sadness we embraced our hosts as we said farewell to continue on our travels. We tell this story because it mirrors what Brian so eloquently explores in this book: a journey, something akin to a pilgrimage, a story of generosity and love. He opens us up to the heart of Jesus who broke bread and shared fellowship with others. Our lives are shaped around the table, literally, and in the Eucharist, where we are loved unconditionally. Brian challenges us to "give ourselves permission to believe this marvelous truth" and to act accordingly.

This book explores "what it means to follow Jesus today in an imperfect, complicated, and beautiful world." It leaves us with a challenge and a gift. The author's reimagining of the first Eucharist, the significance of the crucifixion and suffering, the paradox of victory and failure, and the mandate of the resurrection are gifts to us, inspiring us in our incompleteness to follow Jesus right into the heart of our world.

Brian makes a compelling case for our need to live in community and as church, no matter how imperfect, stumbling, or stuttering. We discover that it is not possible "to see the face of God" alone, without being accompanied by our brothers and sisters.

We would like to reveal more about the journey of "Jesus, the Prodigal Son," and to tell you about Louie, Roger, the Guatemalan woman with the two bananas, and all the grace-filled people who inhabit this book and bring it alive for the reader. But you will have to make that journey yourself. For our part, we are glad to be here to open the door for you!

Peter and Carmel Cowan
Mt. Evelyn, Melbourne, Australia
April 2015

Introduction

The parable of the Prodigal Son, sometimes called the parable of the Merciful Father (Lk 15:11–32), is undoubtedly one of the most beloved stories of all the Christian scriptures. Great artists have painted masterpieces depicting this story, Rembrandt's being among the most well known. It is a story that children can understand and one that still moves adult hearts, even those that have given up on religion.

As the title suggests, I will be looking at this ancient story through a different, somewhat unconventional lens. I hope to share my own insights into this beautiful text and will do so with the same conviction with which they have come to me through prayer, study, and reflection. I am *not* a biblical scholar; I am a preacher, schooled in the ancient practice of *lectio divina*—the prayerful reading and pondering of the Word of God. I share these reflections with the hope that they might add to the *life* that this text has generated for so many friends of God over the centuries.

I have come across the parable of the Prodigal Son at different points in my life. There was one particular instance, about fifteen years ago, that shook the very ground beneath me. On that day, the seed of this book was sown in my heart. The experience was shocking and unsettling for me at first. I was praying with the text in preparation for a Sunday preaching, when suddenly I found myself caught completely by surprise, almost paralyzed by the words of the father, "This son of mine was dead and is alive again" (v. 24). My encounter with these words that day sent a seismic shock through my entire being. Shaken and sensing in that very moment that it was a dangerous question, I asked myself, "Could Jesus be the prodigal son? After all, is not Jesus the son who was dead and came back to life?"

I was living in a small community in Honduras at the time. One of the friars in the community, a Dutch Dominican brother, named Alberto, was a great scripture scholar. Though I was somewhat embarrassed to mention my insight to someone of his stature, I ran as fast as I could to his room to share my good news with him. I was hardly surprised when his reply came immediately and unequivocally: "Impossible!

The prodigal son in the parable is a sinner and Jesus was without sin." Alberto had a way of speaking with such conviction that it left one speechless. I must say, though, that I was almost relieved. I decided immediately to drop such a strange and ridiculous idea.

As one might suspect, it never really dropped out of sight completely. It kept coming back, almost as if it were pursuing me. I am the first to admit that this particular reading of the ancient text is rather unusual. To suggest that Jesus *might be* the prodigal son will, I am sure, provoke some raised eyebrows. Edward Schillebeeckx reminds us, though, that we are supposed to leave our encounter with a parable somewhat disoriented, which frequently serves as the first step toward conversion:

> A parable turns around a scandalizing center...[and] often stands things on their head; it is meant to break through our conventional thinking...Parables open up new and different potentialities for living, often in contrast with our conventional ways of behaving...Parables point to...a new potentiality... a real possibility of coming to see life and the world...in a way quite different from the one we are accustomed to.[1]

I share my insights because *not* to share them is no longer an option for me. They burn inside me as good news and, as St. Paul said after the radical transformation that followed his encounter with the Risen Christ, "If I preach the gospel, this is no reason for me to boast...woe to me if I do *not* preach it" (1 Cor 9:16).

Since that unforgettable day, I have frequently stumbled upon many treasures that have reassured me that my original intuition was not completely heretical after all. At some point several years ago, I decided to take the risk and follow through with my initial intuition, even after having heard Brother Alberto's emphatic "Impossible!" Trusting my intuition was an important step for me spiritually. I was much younger then and not accustomed to disagreeing with the views of a biblical scholar whom I so greatly admired.

Today I am convinced that this parable is broad enough to embrace my original, "crazy" insight. Of course, it is only one of many lenses through which we can reflect on this treasure of good news that St. Luke has given us. No single interpretation can exhaust a parable's potential; that is why the parables are such an important part of Jesus' preaching. I do not ask you to agree with all of my insights. I do, however, hope that they will encourage you delve into this great biblical treasure with your own questions and with the same joy and enthusiasm that have motivated my exciting journey.

I am quite sure that my brother Alberto has by now had a good laugh with the prodigal Son himself, up in the heavenly realms, as they both smile down upon this rather audacious project. In honor of dear Alberto and all those who dedicate their lives to hearing and interpreting the *living* Word of God, I will attempt to share the journey that I have undertaken during these years, sitting at the feet of Jesus, trying to learn from this magnificent story.

The possibility that Jesus, in telling the parable of the Prodigal Son, could actually have in some sense been speaking of himself may be a wild idea ... and yet it just may be true. There is no doubt that he lived his life deeply conscious of being the beloved Son of God. Is this not what he wanted to announce to the world—that we are *all* beloved children of God, loved unconditionally?

As I said, my first powerful experience with this parable happened as I was preparing a preaching. Here I am many years later, still working on that same preaching. Unable to hold it in any longer, I finally asked my Dominican brothers for some sabbatical time to organize and put to paper these insights that I have collected in my heart over the years. I thank them for this gift of time and space to reflect and write. I hope that I can accomplish in this book what our founder, St. Dominic, asked us to do: to contemplate and then to share with others the fruits of our contemplation (*Contemplari et contemplata aliis tradere*).

Even before thanking my Dominican brothers and sisters, I want to thank God, who, through the unconditional love and example of my parents, showed me from very early on what it means to be loved unconditionally. I have known the meaning of *mercy* and *compassion* from a very early age; they form the ground of everything I want to express in these pages. I also thank Santa María de Guadalupe, the mother of Jesus, venerated by the people of Mexico and the Americas. She welcomed me into her open arms when I was a young college student, and her universal heart and love for the poor have never ceased to teach me the secrets of the gospel of Jesus.

When we make profession in the Dominican Order we place our hands into the hands of the prior or prioress, who asks, "What do you seek?" Our response is simple and to the point: "I seek the mercy of God and yours." I write these pages in the thirty-third year of my pilgrimage as a Dominican preacher. I want to thank the last three Masters of the Order of Preachers, who have offered me great fraternal love and support over the years: Timothy Radcliffe, OP, Carlos Azpiroz, OP, and Bruno Cadoré, OP. Their example of humility, compassion, and mercy has been bread for my journey. I also give thanks to the brothers of my province of St. Martin de Porres, in the southern United States, and especially to my community in Irving, Texas, as well as to the many friars, sisters, laity, and friends who have been a tremendous source of support in my journey. In a very special way, I thank the contemplative nuns who live at the heart of our Order. It was through these women of faith that I first stumbled upon this "Way of the Preacher." Thank you, my dear sisters, for being faithful companions these many years, and for your prayerful support in the writing of this book.

Many people have given me support and a quiet place to write these pages this year, and I thank them: the Trappist monks of Genesee and Mepkin Abbeys in the United States, the nuns of Queen of Peace Monastery in the Squamish Valley in Canada, and the Benedictine nuns at Hesychia House of Prayer in Arkansas. Thank you for welcoming me into your beautiful oases of contemplative silence. I especially thank Fr. Isaac Slater, OCSO, of Genesee Abbey, who was constantly finding hidden treasures in the Abbey library for me to consult, and then leaving them at my door in perfect monastic silence. What would we itinerant preachers do without our monastic brothers and sisters who invite us to slake our thirst and refresh our hearts at their deep wells of contemplative silence?

Thanks also to my dear friends Carmel and Peter Cowan; Mary McNamara; Barbara Pegg, OP; Joe "Chepe" Owens, SJ; Beth Clary; Sr. Jean-Marie Dwyer, OP; Sr. Claire Rolfe, OP; Sr. María del Salvador, OP; and Ed Kinerk, SJ. I thank each of you for lovingly and patiently listening to this story, reading the drafts, and offering fruitful feedback. I am especially grateful for your prayers on behalf of this project and for this poor, itinerant preacher. I am also grateful to the Vatican Library and Radio for providing access to a number of papal quotes.

Now, my fellow pilgrims, I invite you to strap your sandals on your feet (or buckle your seatbelt, whatever feels best for you), grab a piece of bread and a walking stick, and prepare to set off on a journey—with Jesus. I warn you ahead of time: there will be some unexpected turns and maybe even a few bumpy roads along the way. As Jesus said, "Courage . . . Do not be afraid!" (Mt 14:27).

A note on quotations: Except when a different source is cited, all scripture quotations in this book are from the New Revised Standard Version. I have added italics to scripture quotations for emphasis. In the case of all other quotations, italics are in the original unless otherwise indicated.

A note on inclusive language: Since this book is based on the parable of the Prodigal Son, it would take an acrobat from the renowned Cirque de Soleil to get us through these pages without using language that does not rely in large part on the words *father/abba* and *son.* I am most conscious of the need to be inclusive with regard to language, and do so whenever it is possible. At the same time, I have not wanted to turn Jesus' simple and powerful story into a dizzy maze of complicated sentences. My hope is that we can all enter deeply into this masterpiece of a parable and discover in it a love that knows no boundaries. I thank you for your patience and understanding in this area.

GOOD NEWS IN PARALLEL

Mapping the Journey

Jesus, the Prodigal Son —————————— Jesus, the Beloved Son

The Son leaves home and sets off for a distant land.

The *Abba* gives him his inheritance, his very own life.

The Son lives among the poor and rejected in the faraway country.

He breaks his bread with the hungry,

befriends prostitutes and sinners,

squanders / gives away everything

and knows utter destitution and desolation.

My God, my God, why have you abandoned me?

I thirst.

I will get up and go to my Abba.

Come follow me.

Open arms.

We have to celebrate and rejoice;

This brother of yours was dead and has come to life.

He was lost and has been found.

We are home.

1

Incarnation
The Journey to the Distant Country

In the beginning when God created the heavens and the earth,
the earth was a formless void and darkness covered the face of
the deep, while a wind from God swept over the face of the waters. Then God said, "Let there be light," and there was light.
God saw that the light was good...There was evening and
...morning, the first day. (Gen 1:1–5)

The first book of the Bible begins by describing, in vivid imagery,
the birth of the universe, the great *flow* of creation from its Source,
from God, from God's dynamic and living word. Everything—from
wind and word, to wild animals and water—*flows* like a great river
from this eternal Wellspring in God, manifesting itself in a magnificent
display of form and color, of energy and mystery. It is impossible *not*
to experience the creative power and dynamism present in the story of
the universe, which is the story of God, and which is our story, too.

In the day that the Lord God made the earth and the heavens,
when no plant of the field was yet in the earth and no herb of
the field had yet sprung up...a stream would rise from the
earth, and water the whole face of the ground. Then the Lord
God formed Adam from the dust [*adamah*][1] of the ground, and
breathed into his nostrils the breath of life; and Adam became
a living being. (Gen 2:4–7)

Our human story begins with this flowing stream that moistens
and waters the earth, preparing the wet clay with which God will
mold and fashion the first human being with gentleness and love. This
is *our* story. We are the clay that has been softened by the flowing

1

stream, fired with the Spirit and enlivened with the breath of God. A number of years ago a lovely film appeared, entitled, *A River Runs through It*. It ends with these words: "Eventually all things merge into one, and a river runs through it." *That* river—call it what we may—is the river of life, born from deep within the very heart of God. It flows outwardly and eternally in every direction, carrying in its waters the gift of life.

The medieval Dominican mystic, Meister Eckhart, inspired by his teachers Thomas Aquinas and Albert the Great, frequently spoke of the universe as a dynamic energy of love that flows out from God like a great river, only to return, as if completing a circle, to the eternal Wellspring from which it was born.[2] In other words, for Eckhart and his companions, being *flows forth* from God, the Ground of God, and it returns, *flowing back* into its infinite Source. Says Eckhart, "All creatures...flow forth from the superfluity of God's goodness."[3] Eckhart's disciple, John Tauler, follows up on this *flowing* image in one of his Christmas sermons:

> God rests...in the unity of essence and flows out in the distinction of persons...in perfect self-delight. And this self-delight *streams forth* as ineffable love, and that ineffable love is the Holy Spirit. Thus God turns inward, goes outward, and returns...Hence the celestial orbit is the noblest and most perfect, for it constantly returns to the origin and source from which it emerged.[4]

Theologian Robert Barron, in a thought-provoking reflection on the theology of Hans Urs von Balthasar, points to this same dynamic and creative energy, noting that, "God's creation is nothing but the ecstatic *overflowing* of God's...tendency to *other* himself...The entire universe is a sort of image of the Trinity."[5] This makes perfect sense, for if creation flows forth from the very Ground of God, then that which flows out is an image of its Source. The entire universe, then, is a kind of *Imago Dei*.[6]

These mystical theologians remind us time and time again that at the heart of this divine flow is the energy of *love*, the same energy that we find at the heart of our parable of the Prodigal Son. Barron highlights this idea in a delightful way, reminding us that "God is a community, a play of contrast, an energy of love or, to use Balthasar's favorite image, a drama. The Father goes out from Himself in the Son and returns in the Spirit, allowing for the playfulness and theatricality of *love*."[7]

The house of bread

> Now the birth of Jesus the Messiah took place in this way.
> When his mother Mary had been engaged to Joseph, but be-
> fore they lived together, she was found to be with child from
> the Holy Spirit. Her husband Joseph, being a righteous man
> and unwilling to expose her to public disgrace, planned to dis-
> miss her quietly. Such was his intention when, behold, the
> angel of the Lord appeared to him in a dream and said,
> "Joseph, son of David, do not be afraid to take Mary your wife
> into your home. For it is through the Holy Spirit that this child
> has been conceived in her. She will bear a son and you are to
> name him Jesus, because he will save his people from their sins.
> (Mt 1:18–21)

"This is my commandment," Jesus says, "that you love one another as I have loved you" (Jn 15:12). Jesus is God's love flowing out
into the world in human form. Matthew, the evangelist, reminds us of
this when he associates Jesus with the ancient name *Emmanuel*—"God
with us" (Mt 1:23). In other words, Jesus shows us the human face of
the God who has chosen to *be with us*, to *live with us*, and even to *suffer with us*. In fact, not only does Jesus speak of this *Emmanuel-God*;
he lives it and embodies. Jesus *is* Emmanuel.

There are different versions of the story of Jesus' conception and
birth, each emphasizing important theological insights. The two gospels
that provide most of the details, namely Luke (1:26–2:7) and Matthew
(1:18–2:23), both tell us that Jesus is a descendant of King David, born
in the town of Bethlehem. Both also point to the fact that the first visi-
tors to witness Jesus' birth were *outsiders*; in Matthew's gospel, some
were even pagans. Strangely, none of the gospels mention anything
about Jewish rabbis or temple authorities coming to pay their respects
to the newborn baby. The only *Jewish* authority who shows any inter-
est at all in the child's birth is Herod, and his desire to "pay homage"
to the newborn child (Mt 2:8) is nothing but a murderous plot hidden
behind a mask of false piety.

The Hebrew word *bethlehem* literally means "house of bread."
Given that the parable of the Prodigal Son is told in response to contro-
versies regarding Jesus' frequent sharing of meals with sinners (Mt
9:10–11), it is no small detail that he was born in a town called "House
of Bread." Breaking and sharing bread will be no minor detail in this
child's life.

In Luke's story of the birth of Jesus, the first people who arrive to
celebrate and pay homage to the newborn baby are not great dignitaries,

but ragged, socially despised shepherds. They have very little in common with the angelic shepherds that we are used to seeing in our traditional nativity scenes, with "O Little Town of Bethlehem" playing in the background, but what would Christmas be without them? In Jesus' day, shepherds were loved about as much as tax collectors and sinners, given their regular contact with the animal blood (rendering them impure) and the fact that they were often looked upon as thieves (an accusation backed up by a fair amount of truth). On that particular day, though, when they stumbled into the cave where the newborn baby was, they were exuberant with joy, hungering for a piece of the bread of life that this newborn child was destined to break and share with the world.

Matthew's story of the birth of Jesus presents a somewhat different though equally symbolic scene. In this version of the birth story, Jesus is visited not by poor shepherds, but by three foreign (i.e., *pagan*) astrologers from the East, who have been guided to the baby by a star in the sky. Also part of our traditional Christmas iconography, these *magi* symbolize the pagan nations that come to pay homage to the newborn child. The gospel writers are very intentional in crafting these birth narratives, announcing from the very beginning that Jesus' heart and house are open to all, and especially to those who normally would be excluded. Donagh O'Shea, reflecting on Luke's version of the story, offers this insight: "Jesus was born in a stable—a cave, really. A cave has no door to keep people out; he was *accessible* from the start. St. Thomas Aquinas said that the Word became flesh in order to be accessible to us."[8]

The stories of Jesus' conception and birth point to themes of crucial theological importance. They show us the rich intermingling of human and divine love, reminding us that God's world and ours are not as far apart from each other as we often imagine. Luke's version of the story, which begins with a very unusual pregnancy, is filled not only with God's incredible tenderness and grace, but also with tension, questions, and probably a fair bit of local gossip. After all, virgin births are not everyday news, and we must not forget that this is small-town Galilee. There is enough unexplainable mystery surrounding Mary's pregnancy and birth to suppose that serious questions (and more than a few eyebrows) would have been raised. This is *not* just another baby being born at the local hospital.

How does all of this affect Mary and Joseph? Do people talk about the unusual details surrounding the birth? How do they react to the idea of a virgin birth? How would *we* react? We who live two thousand years after the fact have had time to get used to this story, a story that gives deep meaning to our faith. It is important to look back and ask ourselves, though: how does this play out in small-town Galilee? We must not forget that the birth of Jesus happens in *our world*, in real circumstances, surrounded by real people.

And Jesus? How does he grow into his own unique story? Is he ever questioned or teased about the "mysterious details" surrounding his birth? It is helpful to try to imagine a similar story unfolding in our own times, for *not* to do so makes Jesus' birth seem like a make-believe children's story or, worse yet, a fairy-tale. What would *we* say if we were told that the young teenage girl down the street is pregnant, but that we are not to worry, because it happened through the intervention of an angel?

In Matthew's gospel, an angel appears to Joseph in a dream and tells him: "Joseph, son of David, do not be afraid to take Mary as your wife, for the child conceived in her is from the Holy Spirit" (Mt 1:20). Reflecting on this, Pope Benedict XVI notes that "the message conveyed to Joseph is overwhelming, and it demands extraordinarily courageous faith. Can it be that God has really spoken, that what Joseph was told in the dream was the truth? . . . We can well imagine his inner struggle now to make sense of this breathtaking dream-message."[9]

One of the things that Joseph is told in his dream is that the son to be born "will save his people from their sins" (Mt 1:21). Even before Jesus' birth, the fact that he will come to be with sinners is announced. As we will see, it is a journey that will meet with great opposition, leading ultimately to his violent death.

It is important to remember that before hearing the angel's message Joseph had to face and deal with the complicated and unexpected news of Mary's pregnancy. Accepting God's mysterious plan was no simple step for him, just as it is no simple step for us. Perhaps he confided in friends and relatives as he tried to figure out what to do, even weighing the possibility of ending his relationship with Mary (Mt 1:19–25). It was hardly a decision that one would make lightly. Maybe he and Mary went to speak with one of the trusted elders in the community as they discern how to respond to God in faith. Was this not one of the biggest moments of their lives?

Because the story is so *human*, it can help us on our own journey to God. Does divine light not frequently shine most brightly in the midst of our human struggles, in the midst of darkness? Joseph was finally given the grace he needs to say "yes," but not without his own nighttime struggle with God's angel, as had happened generations before with his ancestor, Jacob (Gen 32:22–31).

We too must struggle, and this keeps our feet planted firmly on the ground, thus facilitating our own process of *incarnating* God's good news. Our story, like Jesus', is *real*. Jesus does not grow up in some fantasy world. His story is not taken from Aesop's fables. Jesus was born in *this* world, this very real world, and because of that, we must be careful not to rob him of the journey that leads him—step by step— into his full human awakening as the anointed and beloved son of God. He is an ordinary kid from small-town Galilee learning about life while carrying within the depths of his being the pain and bliss of the mystery of God. He responds to the call of his *Abba* with a mind and heart that are fully human and fully divine. Though he is enlightened he also struggles. He is obedient, and yet knows the darkness of faith. He has clearly been given a unique and challenging grace, to live *in God*, while being fully human. Says Donald Goergen:

> To be human is to be finite and to develop within limits . . . our capacity is limited. I shall never know all there is to know. Likewise, Jesus' participation in human modes of knowing and human intellectual activity indicated that he too needed to learn what he knew, that he learned from experience and re-flection. This is also true in the area of self-knowledge. He grew in an understanding of his mission or vocation. He had to trust in God and live at times by faith.[10]

Jesus comes to understand little by little, deep down in his guts and probably long before he can put it into words, that he is the beloved son called by his *Abba* to speak a word of good news that will trans-form the world. His *yes*—freely embraced—is both human and divine, and in some mysterious way, it is the "yes" that each of us is called to speak as well.

The English Benedictine nun Maria Boulding has captured beauti-fully this delicate interweaving of the human and divine threads of Jesus' life. She reminds us that, like us, Jesus had to *find his way* through life's ambiguities, attentive always to the inner voice of God. Her insights help us glimpse the human face of Jesus, a reminder that the great river of mercy and compassion that flowed from Jesus came from a heart as human as our own:

> Jesus was fully human, not only in body but also in mind and spirit, and to be human is not a static condition but a process of growth. [His] birth . . . was the gateway to an open-ended ad-venture, a life project. He was confronted in his dawning under-standing with the task confronting us all: to become maturely human through discovery, growth, interaction with other people, and risk . . . He began to listen, from within his human condition and with the unfolding resources of his human mind, to [God's] word of love. Within our race, amid the opaqueness of the "sit-

uation, there was someone saying 'Abba' with a human voice, mind and heart, someone struggling to meet the love that called to him in prayer, in people and in every experience . . ."[11]

How important it is for us to pause and truly hear these words, to remember that the incarnation of the eternal Word of God in the person of Jesus *really* happened. Mary and Joseph's "yes" to God brings eternity into time. Heaven has *come down* to earth, allowing us to glimpse the face of God. Jesus lives his life with limitations and struggles, choosing time and time again to respond to the voice of love in the midst of "the sin-situation." Is this not what all of us are trying to do, as well? Are we not all trying to respond, to the best of our capacity, to that voice that beckons us to live with human dignity and love?

> The issues of the humanity of Jesus and his identity with us really come down to one question. We want to know whether it was really as tough for him as for us, whether his search and struggle were real, whether he really knew what it is like to be one of us . . . The question is not whether his core human nature was like ours, but whether his existential condition was. And it is his identity with this condition, our condition, to which the Scriptures give witness.[12]

Jesus' humanity, his coming into the world as a tiny baby, is filled with a symbolism that reveals much as the gospel unfolds. Luke's gospel, the same gospel from which our parable of the Prodigal Son comes, offers us very powerful and symbols hidden in the details surrounding the birth of Jesus. We are told that after his birth Jesus is wrapped in "swaddling clothes" and laid in a *manger*, a feeding trough. As children, many of us grew up singing the Christmas hymn "Away in a Manger." It was not until I lived in Italy as an adult that it finally dawned on me that our English word "manger" comes from the Italian word *mangiare*, which means "to eat." The tiny baby Jesus was placed in a trough where the animals ate. Pope Benedict XVI, in his book, *Jesus of Nazareth: The Infancy Narratives*, highlights the important theological significance of these two very important symbols:

> The child stiffly wrapped in bandages ["swaddling clothes"] is seen as prefiguring the hour of his death: from the outset, he is the sacrificial victim . . . The manger, then, was seen as a kind of altar . . . the place where animals find their food. But now, lying in the manger, is he who called himself the true bread come down from heaven, the true nourishment that we need in order

to be fully ourselves. This is the food that gives us true life, eternal life. Thus the manger becomes a reference to the table of God, to which we are invited so as to receive the bread of God. From the poverty of Jesus' birth emerges a miracle in which [humanity's] redemption is mysteriously accomplished.[13]

In Luke 15 Jesus tells three parables—the lost sheep, the lost coin, and the prodigal son—in response to criticisms regarding his spontaneous practice of eating with a rather disreputable group of friends. In light of this, the simple fact that his first bed as a newborn baby was a feeding trough for animals is quite symbolic. It seems that from the very beginning Jesus has associated with a pretty unusual group of "friends." The symbolic imagery in Luke's infancy narrative is already announcing to us that Jesus has come to be bread and sustenance for the world. He has come to feed the lowly, the poor, the sinners, even the four-legged friends of God. Luke's imagery also tells us that this child, who has come to nourish the poor and the outcast, will end his life wrapped in a shroud, put to death for daring to let his life—his very own body—become the bread of life, the bread of hope for sinners and for the poorest of the poor.

The journey of salvation

> There was a man who had two sons. The younger of them said to his father, "Father, give me the share of the property that will belong to me." So he divided his property between them. A few days later the younger son gathered all he had and traveled to a distant country... (Lk 15:11–13)

Jesus, the Son of God, *flows out from the eternal Source*, from the house of his *Abba*, setting into motion a faith-filled "journey of salvation," a story of light and darkness, of life and death—the latest segment of Israel's long journey of faith. Traveling from one land to another, often in desperate situations, Israel has tried to respond in obedience to God. The good news behind this long story, of course, is that beneath every step of Israel's pilgrim journey one finds God's footprint and God's promise, *"I am with you."*[14] This is what we call "grace."

This faithful, *grace-filled* presence of God has guided Israel from the very beginning. As Moses stood barefoot and transfixed before the burning bush at the base of Mt. Horeb, he heard God speak: "Thus you shall say to the Israelites, 'I AM has sent me to you'" (Ex 3:14).

This face-to-face encounter with the holiness of God has marked Israel's entire history. The God who *is* can never be separated from us.

Moses is the quintessential pilgrim of God, a worthy descendant of his spiritual ancestors, Abraham and Sarah, who are clearly the "patron saints" of Israel's faithful history of pilgrimage. Barely has tiny Moses been born when he is already on the move, thanks to his mother who, realizing that her son's life is in danger, places him into a small papyrus basket and sends him down the river. Little does she know it at the time, but God makes use of her maternal instincts and her gut-wrenching act of heroic love to prepare the journey of liberation for the people of Israel. She surely deserves to be remembered as a kind of *grandmother* of Israel's liberation from oppression. In the meantime, while all of this drama is unfolding, baby Moses floats down the river with no idea of what is going on. Who would have ever thought that his first voyage on the *river of life* would seem like nothing when, years later, he and the people of Israel cross the Red Sea, followed by years of wandering through the desert in search of God's land of promise.

In the end, the story of Moses and the people of Israel is our story; it is the universal story of humanity. We all, in one way or another, flow out from the eternal Source, from the womb of God, from our parents, in order to set off on a journey that carries us to places we would never have expected to go, and frequently to places we would have preferred *not* to go. Given all of the surprises and unexpected sufferings along the way, though, we eventually discover that at no moment have we been very far from God's tender care and grace.

Then comes that point in most human journeys, usually unexpected, when we awaken to the harsh reality that our pilgrimage has taken a detour, leaving us stranded on some dark street corner in the "distant country."

> When [the younger son] had spent everything, a severe famine took place throughout that country, and he began to be in need. So he went and hired himself out to one of the citizens of that country, who sent him to his fields to feed the pigs. He would gladly have filled himself with the pods that the pigs were eating; and no one gave him anything. (Lk 15:14–16)

This exile from home has been the story of all of our ancestors: Abraham and Sarah, Moses and Ruth, Jeremiah and the Babylonian exiles, Jonah and Jesus, and of course the prodigal son. Though in the end the distant country reveals itself as a place of blessing and wisdom, it first appears as nothing but a dark night of alienation, loneliness, exile, and sin—a place void of beauty and peace. Like John of the Cross, we are plunged into a dark empty nothingness—*Nada*—only to be surprised once again by God's grace. Most of us can testify that *eventually* we are embraced by God's unconditional love, but not until we have faced our fears and walked barefoot through the inward deserts of our heart.

Jesus: God's pilgrim of love

> In the beginning was the Word, and the Word was with God, and the Word was God...The Word became flesh and made his dwelling among us... (Jn 1:1,14 NAB)

God's eternal Word, the very Word that has been manifesting itself in creation and in history since the beginning, surprises us by taking on a human face in Jesus.[15] "We declare to you what...we have heard, what we have seen with our eyes, what we have looked at and touched with our hands..." (1 Jn 1:1). Jesus is God's Word with a human face, the beloved Son through whom we see and touch the mercy and love of God. This powerful mystery never stops surprising us.

Jesus is *sent* from the safety and eternal bliss of the heavenly abode to be born in our small, limited world, here in this unfinished and fragile "distant country." Becoming small, weak, and poor, he "pitches his tent"[16] among us. Why, though, would someone be willing to leave the eternal bliss of God's love and come into this broken world? Why would this Son who has *everything* choose to set off on a dangerous journey into a world filled with suffering and sin? The only answer we can muster up, as Eckhart and the Rhineland mystics pointed to above, is because of *love*.

The birth of Jesus in our world makes manifest the *ecstatic overflowing* of God's love. God wants to come into our world, and does so by sending the beloved Son. Says Kathy Coffey, commenting on the medieval philosopher and theologian, John Duns Scotus, "God would've become human even if Adam hadn't sinned, because God has fallen irretrievably in love with us. The driving motive of the incarnation ...wasn't to blot out the effects of sin, but was a free act of the Creator to move closer to the creatures."[17] In other words, Jesus *flows out* from God for no other reason than to show us that God is passionately in love with us, for "God so loved the world that he gave his only Son, so that everyone who believes in him may...may have eternal life " (Jn 3:16).

Like Jesus, we too are an incarnation of God's love, sent on a mission into the heart of the world. Is this not what it means to be a disciple?

The prodigal Christ, who *leaves home* and plunges into our world, then turns toward us, calling out, "Come, follow me" (Lk 18:22). We cannot remain closed in our small, comfortable nest and call ourselves followers of Christ. When I was in college, I met a contemplative Dominican nun who had spent many years confined to a wheel chair. Other than her occasional visit to the doctor, she never left her monastery. I was shocked when I discovered that Sr. Mary Michael had dedicated her whole life to corresponding with prisoners, especially those on death row. Her wheelchair and her life of prayer were not impediments at all to her missionary spirit. Her quiet life of prayer was the pulpit from which she proclaimed Jesus' unconditional love to those whom the world easily forgets. She was a fountain of love that flowed out into the world.

"You are the salt of the earth...the light of the world," says Jesus to each of us (Mt 5:13–14). Our proper place is right in the heart of this wonderful and complicated world, living out the drama of the incarnation. Worldly realities are good and important for us precisely because the world has been created by love, in the image of God. We are not afraid to embrace the world. In fact, we are anointed to be salt and light precisely because God is passionately in love with the world. This is what it means to be *Church*: to stand in the middle of our beautiful and broken world, with our baptismal candle held high, and be God's presence and God's light right here and now in the midst of it all. As Pope Francis reminds us, we are sent as bearers of God's healing love and mercy:

> The thing the church needs most today is the ability to heal wounds and to warm the hearts of the faithful...it needs nearness, proximity. I see the church as a field hospital after battle. It is useless to ask a seriously injured person if he or she has high cholesterol...You have to heal [the] wounds. Then we can talk about everything else.[18]

"*Nearness, proximity*"—these are powerful, beautiful words that lead us right into the heart of Jesus' incarnation. Pope Francis challenges us to make these words part of the vocabulary of our daily lives. To really be disciples of Jesus, we must be prepared to draw near to those who live on the periphery of human existence, those who have been excluded for one reason or another from a full life. In this way we practice *proximity*, releasing Christ's healing love into the universe. Pope Francis continues, "We Christians remain steadfast in our intention to...heal wounds, to build bridges...to bear one another's burdens (Gal 6:2)."[19]

Jesus is sent into the world to be a bridge of love that unites us with God, our original Source. In her mystical dialogue with God, St. Catherine of Siena was told, "The body of Christ has been made a bridge by the union of the divine nature with the human."[20] Christ, "the firstborn of many brothers and sisters" (Rom 8:29), bridges the chasm of separation so that we might see the face of God here and now in our midst.

The inheritance and the prodigal's journey

In the parable of the Prodigal Son, the younger son does not *trip and fall* into the distant land of sin and suffering (like most of us). The fact is, he *chooses* to set off down this road. Before leaving on his journey he asks his *Abba* to give him his inheritance. The Greek word that is used, *ousia*, usually translated as "property" in this parable, is more properly translated as "being," "nature," or "substance." The Greek text reads, "*Abba,* give me the share of the *ousia* that will belong to me" (15:12). The son is clearly asking for something more *substantial* than money or property. It seems that he is asking for a portion of his *Abba*'s *being*.[21] He wants it to be his, and he wants it now. With it he can set off on his journey, self-suffucient and alone, to discover what it means to be free—free to follow his desires, unfettered by responsibility, answerable to no one but himself.

Scripture scholars rightly point to the fact that, in the socio-cultural world in which Jesus lived, the son's request to be given his inheritance while his father is still alive would have been unheard of, almost impossible, a real slap in the face to the father and the rest of the clan. "Loyalty to kin [is] crucial for survival."[22] In fact, in Palestinian culture, members of a family "understood themselves only in relation to their family, their kin, village, and religious community."[23] To make such a request is to treat the father as if he were *dead*. Barbara Reid points to a text from the book of Sirach, which clearly advises against assenting to such a request, so as not to bring shame on the family:

> Hear me . . . you leaders of the congregation, pay heed.
> To son or wife, to brother or friend,
> do not give power over yourself, as long as you live;
> and do not give your property to another,
> in case you change your mind and must ask for it.
> While you are still alive and have breath in you,
> do not let anyone take your place.
> For it is better that your children should ask from you
> than that you should look to the hand of your children.
> Excel in all that you do; bring no stain upon your honor.
>   (Sir 33:19–23)

In his book, *Jacob and the Prodigal*, Kenneth Bailey reminds us that, "The prodigal breaks his relationship with his father by his blunt request...[and] when [he] sells the property given to him...the unspeakable insult to his father then becomes public knowledge in the community."[24] The story is even worse than it seems, given that in Jesus' day the Jews severely punished any young Jewish man who had lost his family's inheritance to *Gentiles* (which is clearly the case in the prodigal son's situation):

> To discourage any thought of committing this heinous offense, the community developed what was called the *kezazah* ceremony... Any Jewish boy who lost his inheritance among the Gentiles faced the ceremony if he dared return to his home village. The ceremony itself was simple. Fellow villagers would fill a large earthenware pot with burned nuts and burned corn and break it in front of the guilty individual. While doing this, they would shout, "So-and-so is cut off from this people." From that point on, the village would have nothing to do with the...lad.[25]

As Bailey makes clear, the son's return would have been the ultimate humiliation for the father and for the whole family; he would have been shunned forever.

I recently spent some time in a community of monks where the reading during meals was taken from a book entitled *A Price to Pay: A Muslim Risks All to Follow Christ*.[26] It is a gripping story of tragedy, revenge, and family division, but this time within an Iraqi Muslim family that faces the unforgivable sin of a son's conversion to Christianity. Given that Iraq, Palestine, and Israel share many cultural traits common to the wider Middle East, I suspect that the Muslim family's reaction as they dealt with the public shame brought on by their son's conversion (as described graphically in the book) is probably not so different from the *kezazah* ceremony described by Bailey.

Even in our own times we occasionally hear of families that experience this kind of tragic and heartbreaking rupture of unity. Divorce, of course, is one of the ways that it happens, but occasionally one hears of divisions and "excommunications" within families for other reasons, as well. Have we not all heard heart-wrenching stories of a son or daughter being cut off from the family for becoming or marrying a Muslim or a Jew, for declaring himself or herself an atheist, or for coming out as gay or a lesbian? Though the *kezazah* ceremony described by Bailey is unique to first-century Judaism, the shame caused by breaking with the sacred rules of the clan is tragic in all times and in all cultures.

The Bible frequently recounts stories about people tearing their garments as a sign of public disgust or shame. For example, "Jacob tore his garments and put on sackcloth" after receiving the news of his son Joseph's apparent death (Gen 37:34). One can imagine the people in Jesus' day "tearing their garments" in utter disgust after hearing the story of the prodigal son's disgraceful departure and shameful squandering of his inheritance. They would have been unable to believe that a son could willingly bring such shame upon his family. They would also have found it hard to believe that the boy's father would have acquiesced to his son's request, handing over his share of the inheritance with no questions asked.

From the very beginning of the parable, then, we are given a powerful hint: this *Abba* is different from the others; he does not play by the established rules. His presence in the parable is clearly unconventional, even a bit dangerous. He breaks with deeply ingrained cultural rules here, and it does not seem that he does so haphazardly. If we miss this detail, we may miss the parable's power to surprise us into conversion. We will see this unusual behavior again at the end of the parable, when we stumble upon the *Abba* as he waits anxiously, even lovingly, for his wayward son's return (Lk 15:20).

One gets the sense that Jesus frames the parable in this way to shake us up a bit; it will not be the only time. Kenneth Bailey suggests that, "The image of *father* [in this parable] is transformed from that of a tribal chief into a metaphor that can be used for God."[27] It is a portrait of a father who acts with the tender compassion of a mother.[28] Theologian Sandra Schneiders agrees wholeheartedly:

> Jesus' parable about the father actually constitutes a radical challenge to patriarchy. The divine father who has been understood as the ultimate justification of human patriarchy is revealed as the one who refuses to own us, demand our submission or punish our rebellion. Rather, God is the one who respects our freedom, mourns our alienation, waits patiently for our return and accepts our love as pure gift.[29]

In the parable, when the younger son sets out on his journey he is exhilarated, perhaps a little frightened, and eager to discover what he can learn. Little does he know that his journey will bring him untold suffering. He will return tattered, hungry, feeling like a failure. He will have experienced what it means to be totally lost.

The beloved Son knows—and has known from all eternity—that he is loved. He knows that everything that his *Abba* has is his, for he and his *Abba* are one (Jn 10:30).[30] This *knowing* is the greatest inheritance of all.[31] The Son has no need to search for his freedom, because his *Abba*'s love *is* freedom. The Beloved Son knows that he is free to leave the protection and safety of his *Abba*'s home and travel into the distant country, a country of suffering and sin. He longs to seek out and find those who have lost their way, like sheep that stray from the shepherd's watch.

The Beloved Son does not break his relationship with his *Abba*. In fact he wants wants nothing more than to follow the example of his *Abba*, to go *out of himself*, to live for others, to *empty himself* through love. He sets off with a piece of his *Abba*'s heart so that he can help build a world free of fear and small-mindedness, where people *trust* life and *live it* rather than measuring it. He wants to share his *Abba*'s inheritance with the friends that he hopes to meet in the distant country. He wants to get to know the tax collectors and the prostitutes, the Gentiles and the lepers, listen to their stories, understand their worldviews, and share their experiences. He wants to engage with the rabbis and the philosophers and learn from the simple faith of the poor and the outcast. He wants to find those who are lost, to heal those who are broken, to feed those who are starving.

The journey of Jesus is the Church's journey. Says Pope Francis:

> I prefer a Church which is bruised, hurting and dirty because it has been out on the streets, rather than a Church which is unhealthy from being confined and from clinging to its own security...If something should rightly disturb us and trouble our consciences, it is the fact that so many of our brothers and sisters are living without the strength, light and consolation born of friendship with Jesus Christ, without a community of faith to support them, without meaning and a goal in life. More than by fear of going astray, my hope is that we will be moved by the fear of remaining shut up within structures which give us a false sense of security, within rules which make us harsh judges, within habits which make us feel safe, while at our door people are starving and Jesus does not tire of saying to us: "Give them something to eat" [Mk 6:37].[32]

Coming down the mountain: The journey of Jesus

> During those days Jesus went out to the mountain to pray; and he spent the night in prayer to God. And when day came, he called his disciples and chose twelve of them, whom he also named apostles...He came down [from the mountain] with

them and stood on a level place, with a great crowd of his disciples and a great multitude of people from all Judea, Jerusalem,
and the coast of Tyre and Sidon. They had come to hear him
and to be healed of their diseases; and those who were troubled
with unclean spirits were cured. And all in the crowd were trying to touch him, for power came out from him and healed all
of them. Then he looked up at his disciples and said:

> Blessed are you who are poor, for yours is the Reign of
> God.
> Blessed are you who are hungry now, for you will be
> filled.
> Blessed are you who weep now, for you will laugh.
> Blessed are you when people hate you, and when they
> exclude you,
> revile you, and defame you on account of the Son of
> Man.
> Rejoice in that day and leap for joy, for surely your
> reward is great in heaven;
> for that is what their ancestors did to the prophets.
>   (Lk 6:12–13, 17–23)

With that one sermon Jesus announces the essence of his entire mission, revealing clearly who he is—a river of compassion and *blessing*,
flowing out into the world from the Wellspring of his *Abba*'s heart.

In the midst of this key gospel text, in which Jesus gives us one of
his greatest treasures—the Beatitudes—we discover two very powerful
and *symbolic actions* that form the background and the movement of
Jesus' entire life. The first is the movement *upward*. He goes up the
mountain, alone, to spend the night in prayer and intimacy with God
(Lk 6:12). This is the time when Jesus can sink into the great Source,
the heart of his *Abba,* and listen. As in the case of Moses and Elijah,
Jesus' mountaintop prayer is an essential preface to any mission or
proclamation of God's good news. He cannot announce what he has
not first received. His entire mission, in fact, flows from his prayer,
rooting him in the underground river of his *Abba*'s love. Says Maria
Boulding:

His [*Abba*], to whom he escaped at times for long stretches of
prayer, was immensity and space to breathe, to breathe the
Spirit of their mutual love through his human prayer. He must
have needed the space, the silence, the call to stretch beyond the
narrowness of day-to-day ministry, but for all that, it was
within the narrow confines that he knew the Father and listened

to his word. By creatively accepting the limitations he invested them with Easter significance, and thereby empowered us to do the same.[33]

The second symbolic action in this text from Luke is Jesus' *movement of compassion*, which is a *downward movement*. The text says that after his night of prayer, Jesus *came down* from the mountain with his disciples and apostles, *looked up at them* and proclaimed the Beatitudes: "Blessed are you who are poor..." (Lk 6:20). Jesus, the man of deep prayer, does not speak *at* the crowd from a lofty pulpit of power, but *comes down* to be with the people. He looks into their eyes and speaks to them as friends. On that day, standing on level ground, eye-to-eye with his disciples and with people who are suffering from diseases and unclean spirits (Lk 6:18), Jesus reveals his mission. He wants the whole world to experience the words that he heard that day at the river: "You are my beloved."

Jesus' *downward movement* into the midst of the people of God is the movement of the incarnation, the movement of love. As we have mentioned above, by taking on human flesh, the eternal and creative Word of God *flows out like a river of love* into the human condition, into the human heart—the heart of sinner and saint alike. In the gospel of John, Jesus makes reference to this dynamic movement by referring to himself as "the bread of God... which *comes down from heaven* and gives life to the world" (Jn 6:33). Pope Francis refers to the need for the Church to follow Jesus in this self-giving movement of love: "The ministers of the Gospel must be people... who know how to dialogue and to *descend* themselves into their people's night."[34]

Kenneth Bailey comments on the Hebrew verb *shub,* which is usually translated as repentance, return, or restoration. In the New Testament this same verb is translated into Greek as *metane,* or *metanoia:* conversion of mind and heart. The Hebrew understanding of this verb, notes Bailey, is that repentance is possible only if the sinner *returns* (*shub*) to God. "Great is repentance, for it reaches up to the Throne of glory...If a [person] commits a sin...it is said: Take with you words, and return to the Lord."[35]

In other words, until Jesus' day it is the sinner who must *return* to God. The lost sheep has to find its own way back home. Jesus adds a new dimension to this ancient parable of life. Says Bailey, "Jesus tells the story of the shepherd who rescues his lost sheep. Supported by the theology of Isaiah 55:10–11 ("For as the rain and the snow *come down from heaven*...so shall my word be that goes out from my mouth"), Jesus emphasizes the need for *God to come to us*...Repentance is not possible if the shepherd is unwilling to pay the high price required to carry the lost sheep back to the village ... He must find the sheep, pick it up and carry it back to safety in order to save its life."[36]

This *downward movement* of God toward humanity is made real and tangible for us in the incarnation of Jesus. Jesus' journey sets the example for the rest of us, for as he comes "down the mountain" and into the heart of humanity, bringing God's healing love to our broken, sinful and suffering world, he looks back at us and says, "Come, follow me" (Mt 19:21). This incarnational *descent* into the heart of the world is beautifully prefigured in a text from the book of Wisdom, proclaimed each year during the Christmas season:

> For while gentle silence enveloped all things,
> and night in its swift course was now half gone,
> your all-powerful word *leaped from heaven*, from the
>   royal throne,
> into the midst of the land that was doomed.
>   (Wis 18:14–15)

Jesus, the incarnate Word of God, in response to his *Abba*'s overflowing love, freely chooses to risk everything, *leaping down* from the heavenly heights to share his life with us here on earth.

> The Son of God "went out" of his divine condition and came to encounter us ... No one is excluded from the hope of life, from the love of God. The Church is sent to reawaken this hope everywhere, especially where it is suffocated by difficult existential conditions, at times inhuman, where hope does not breathe but is suffocated. There is need of the oxygen of the Gospel, of the breath of the Spirit of the Risen Christ, to rekindle it in hearts. *The Church is the house whose doors are always open* not only so that everyone can find welcome and breathe love and hope, but also because ... the Holy Spirit drives us to go out ... to the fringes of humanity.[37]

2

Amazing Grace
A Contemporary Parable

The "parable" that follows did not appear in Jesus' original reper-toire. In fact, it did not appear in any of the first drafts of this book. It had never occurred to me to include this particular piece of my own story in these pages, until a Jesuit priest said to me, about halfway through the writing of the book, "Why not, Brian? You know, it would give a human face to your writing."

It is never very easy, as many of you know, to be vulnerable and share one's own story in public. I believe, though, that preaching re-quires that the preacher take risks, empowering the Word of God to take on a human face *here and now*. In this way, the Word of God be-comes *flesh* anew. Having said that, I must honestly add that I would be happier if someone else were to do the "incarnating" this time around! But I *will* try to be obedient, as I trust that this is of the Spirit.

As I mentioned at the beginning of this book, this preaching was born fifteen years ago in Honduras, when the parable of the Prodigal Son sent a seismic shock through my entire being. I knew that day that not only was this parable speaking *about Jesus*, but it was speaking *to me!* Now, in the writing of the book, I have come to realize that this preaching began much earlier, at least during my high school years, and probably even before that. This grace-filled journey into the 'distant country' is real; I know it from the inside out. It is a piece of the life that God has given to me, and I share it as precisely that.

When I was eighteen years old, about a month before setting off to begin my university studies, I went through what today I would de-scribe as an existential dark night. Of course, I did not even know what the phrase "dark night" meant back then, but when I look back now I think that is precisely what it was. To my knowledge, no one else was aware of the deep darkness that had enveloped me. All I can say is that I felt like I was in hell.

Looking back, I think it all began subtly the year before, when I was seventeen, just a few days before I was sent as a foreign exchange student to a mountainous town in the Andes in Peru. I had never thought that I would travel to a foreign country, and so the upcoming trip filled me with incredible excitement. Two days before flying to Peru, I participated in an orientation program in Miami, with seventy or eighty young people, all of whom were, like me, heading to Latin America as exchange students. At one point during the program there was a pool party held at a large, Olympic-size swimming pool. I can still remember that it was a beautiful evening. I was walking toward the diving board when suddenly I noticed a body at the bottom of the deep end of the pool. I shouted for help, and then, without even thinking, instinctively dove into the pool to bring the body to the surface. A young woman with whom I had become friends during those days also dove in and helped me pull the young man out of the water. Immediately, almost as if it had all been rehearsed, I began to give this young man, whom I did not know, mouth-to-mouth resuscitation. The young woman and I alternated doing CPR for about twenty minutes, until an ambulance arrived and the medics took over. Two or three hours later we got the news that the young student had died. The doctor said that he had probably died even before we got him out of the water.

Two days after that, still shaken by the experience at the pool, I was on a plane to Peru. The year was 1977, and the country was under a military government that had decided to crush the student uprisings in our town. Having grown up in a small city in Texas, I had never witnessed any act of horrendous violence. I realize today that to have grown up in such a safe environment is rare in our world. During my first month in Peru, I repeatedly woke up in the middle of the night, gasping for breath, reliving the tragedy at the swimming pool. And if that were not enough to keep me on edge, the town where I was staying had just been put under a military curfew. When the exchange program organizers notified us about the curfew, they used the Spanish term *toque de queda*, which, of course, none of us understood. Realizing that we had not understood this phrase, they gave us a very succinct definition: "If you walk outside of your house between 6 PM and 6 AM the army will kill you!" We learned the term very quickly. It was becoming clear to me that this whole experience was going to change my life.

During the next month or two I saw violence that I never dreamed existed in our world. I had no categories for understanding what was happening. Given that we lived across the street from the university, we saw the worst of both the rioting and the repression. One morning that I will never forget, my host family and I were awakened with gunfire ricocheting all around our house. School that day was out of the question, of course; we spent most of the morning on the living room floor, for protection, listening to the gunfire and the sound of tanks rumbling through the streets. At one point a group of about two hundred students poured out of the university. Through a sliding glass door that opened onto the field behind our house we could see them as they ran past our house and disappeared into the distance. I presumed that the soldiers had stormed the campus, thus causing the sudden exodus. This was followed by about twenty minutes of an eerie kind of calm.

Suddenly a lone student ran past our house, following the path of the other students. Behind him came an army truck filled with soldiers, who lifted their guns and began firing at the unarmed student. He fell once, got up and tried to run, and then, after more gunfire, fell a second time. Ten or so of the soldiers got out of the truck, and with the butts of their rifles, beat the body of this young student into a pile of flesh and bones. They then picked up his lifeless body and heaved it like garbage into the back of the army truck. I cannot remember if I cried or gasped or vomited, but I do know that I had absolutely no way to understand what I had just seen. The image of the violence and the young man's dead body was seared somewhere in my consciousness, festering like an open wound. In a period of a few weeks I had seen two young men die. Until then, I had never even seen a dead body. Why did they die? Why am I alive? Until then, such questions had never entered my mind.

For the next months my mind and my heart struggled to find some meaning to all this death and violence. What had happened? Was this what life is all about? Does it all just end in a moment of meaningless violence? My Peruvian friends were fond of partying, so without really paying much attention I began to soothe my confusion and my many unanswered questions by drinking more Pisco sours than I should have been drinking! Though my time in Peru was marvelous and changed the course of my life radically, I had also looked into the face of death and of horrendous evil.

I returned to the United States for my final year of high school. It was a busy year, enriched by my involvement in the local AFS foreign exchange student group. I enjoyed my last year of advanced Spanish with crazy and wonderful Mrs. Holland, and she, of course, was shocked that I had finally learned to conjugate verbs. Much of that year was focused on preparing for college.

I had been raised in a loving family and was blessed with very good friends. Even so, something was not right. The run-in with horrible, unexplainable violence and the death of those two young men had shaken my very foundation. Big existential questions began to plague me. Why are we here on this earth, if it all ends in the blink of an eye? Life itself began to feel *unjust*, void of any ultimate meaning. A kind of existential darkness settled deep inside me, like an inner violence. It felt like the insides of my being were dying. Why are people poor? Why do people die?

Besides the faces of the two young men who had died violently—images that I could not shake from my memory—there was also the face of an indigenous woman that kept coming back to me, as well, after returning to the United States. My Peruvian host family and I had made an unforgettable trip through some of the small rural towns and villages along the beautiful Urubamba River Valley, the *Valle Sagrado*. At one point, as we were driving on a bumpy dirt road through a small, very poor Quechua village, we had to stop the car, probably to let some donkeys or llamas cross in front of us. At that moment a poor, barefoot indigenous woman appeared at the car window next to where I was sitting. She stood there looking at me with a pitifully sad face, her outstretched, empty hand begging for a coin. Her face was even emptier than her hand. The car suddenly lunged forward and we continued our comfortable trip, surrounded by the worst poverty and some of the most spectacular natural beauty that I had ever seen in my life.

As with the violent deaths of the two young men, I was at a loss as to how to process this overwhelming poverty. The indigenous woman's face, with the large, sad eyes, haunted me for a long time. Today, though, I give thanks to God for that vision that is etched into my memory. My one great regret is that I did not at least reach out to touch her hand, to assure her that I had seen her. Still, something happened inside me that day—not on a conscious level, but at some deep existential level. Though I felt completely overwhelmed by her wretched condition, I knew (without "knowing") that one day I would return to those beautiful and broken lands and find a way to share my love with the people. This "knowing" is difficult for me to put into words. Though I was sickened by what I had seen and overwhelmed by my inability to *do* anything, I knew that something like a seed had fallen onto my dry, broken heart. How that seed survived I do not know, but it took root. Sometimes, when I look back at my life, I think that my call to be a Dominican friar "happened" that day. On the surface I was overwhelmed, sick to my stomach, but deep in my being God was tilling the ground. Thanks to God, I have seen that face and reached out to touch that hand many, many times. Today her face is a face of courage and dignity for me. Today I see her face as the face of God.

It is clear to me today that, though my experience as a foreign exchange student is undoubtedly one of the most important periods of my life, it took time for that clarity to come. I arrived in Peru unprepared for all that I was to witness, and my return home left me overwhelmed with unanswered questions that began to eat at me from the inside, making me question whether life—mine or anyone else's—had any real meaning to it. Though on one level I *knew* the love of family and friends, it was *life itself* that I was questioning: Is it worth it? Can I *believe* in it anymore? I was drinking and partying more than usual—probably as a coping mechanism—and that, of course, along with a good dose of Catholic guilt, only made the existential darkness worse. I began to feel isolated. I had a story inside me that was choking me. The world seemed filled with violence all of a sudden, and that violence had somehow found its way into my own heart. The suffocating darkness got darker and darker. If I could not understand what was happening, how or to whom could I go and ask for help?

Looking back, it was as if the drowning of the student and all the violence that I had seen in Peru, combined with this sudden avalanche of inner violence and darkness, were teaming up to destroy me. I had graduated from high school and was a few weeks away from leaving home for college, and suddenly everything seemed dead. I am, of course, reading this situation almost forty years later, but this is how I remember it. I truly felt like I was dead.

What happened next is wrapped in a kind of mental fog. Finding myself in this tunnel of darkness, I saw no way out. Looking back today, I think I felt something like that young university student in Peru, running for his life, while knowing that he would never make it to freedom. It did not matter how fast I ran, life was unfair, and the world would eventually destroy me. On one of those suffocatingly dark days, I found myself locked in the bathroom, with a bottle of pills in my hand, trying to muster up the courage to swallow them.

I cannot describe with much detail what happened next. I do not remember setting the pills down, but I did (or *somebody* did). The next thing I remember is paging through a telephone book, looking for the phone number of a priest whose name I was unsure of. I remembered him from years before, when my family had attended Mass for some months at a different parish. After flipping frantically through the phone book, for what seemed like an eternity, I made a telephone call, not even sure I was calling the right number. The priest himself answered the telephone. I asked him if I could speak with him, and he responded, "I am free; you can come right now." He gave me directions to the parish rectory, which I had never visited, and within about thirty minutes I was sitting face-to-face with a priest whom I had seen no more than ten times when I was eleven or twelve years old. I had never spoken to him before that day.

I sat down and wept for more than an hour, as he sat quietly in a chair, facing me. I could not breathe; the darkness was choking me. I will never forget the patient compassion of this priest. I had the feeling that he would have waited for all eternity for me to "come home," to speak a word. When I did finally break the silence and begin to try to talk a bit, telling him about the pills and my feeling of falling into a dark hole, he responded, offering some kind, soothing words. I do not remember the words that he spoke, but I do remember what happened after that. Father 'J' stood up and motioned for me to follow him. We walked over to a mirror on the wall, and he said, "Brian, look into the mirror and say to the person that you see there: *I love you.*" I took a deep breath and did what he said. I did not *feel* the words the first time, but I said them. He asked me to repeat it two or three more times. Little by little, through some extraordinary grace of God, the fog began to lift. We spoke for a while and set an appointment for a follow-up visit, and then I thanked him and returned home. Though it took several days to recover from the tension and stress, I began to experience, little by little, that I was being raised from the dead. I have never experienced that kind of existential darkness again. Never.

> *Oh guiding night!*
> *O night more lovely than the dawn!*
> (St. John of the Cross)[1]

After leaving the priest's house, I stopped by the church before returning home. Inside the front door I saw a Bible sitting on a table. It shames me to say (though today it makes me chuckle) that, until that day, I had never opened a Bible. It opened to a psalm, which I read. Some years later I found it again:

> I waited patiently for the LORD, who inclined to me and
>   heard my cry.
> The LORD drew me up from the desolate pit, out of the
>   miry bog,
> and set my feet upon a rock, making my steps secure.
> The LORD put a new song in my mouth, a song of praise to
>   our God.
> Many will see and fear, and put their trust in the LORD.
>   (Ps 40:1–3)

Today, whenever one of those very fervent, "out to save the world" Christians approaches me and asks, "Are you saved?" I always respond "Yes." I am never quite sure if *their* question and *my* answer are necessarily pointing to the same reality, but the truth is, from that day on, I have known without a doubt that God has saved me. "The LORD inclined to me and heard my cry that day...and set my feet upon a rock." I was rescued from a deep and "desolate pit." How I found and dialed the phone number of a priest whose name I did not know is still a mystery to me, and always will be. And that this priest answered the phone and said, "You can come right now," continues to seem unbelievable. In theological words, what I experienced that day is called *grace*.

God bent down and drew me out of the teeth of death that fateful day. I know this as surely as I know that the sun rises every morning in the east. It is called "Amazing Grace." I was lost and sinking into the miry bog, and God reached down and said, "I am not finished with you yet, Brian!" I am not speaking here of "salvation" only in a religious or Christian sense, though the two are intimately related. My life was saved, because God is good and wanted me to keep living.

Amazing Grace[2]

Amazing Grace, how sweet the sound,
That saved a wretch like me.
I once was lost but now am found,
Was blind but now I see.

'Twas grace that taught my heart to fear,
And grace, my fears relieved.
How precious did that grace appear
The hour I first believed.

Through many dangers, toils and snares,
I have already come;
'Tis grace that brought me safe thus far
And grace will lead me home.

The Lord has promised good to me.
His word my hope secures.
He will my shield and portion be,
As long as life endures.

When we've been there ten thousand years,
Bright shining as the sun.
We've no less days to sing God's praise
Than when we first begun.

3

Who Is This Man?

Café Capernaum

It is a lovely, sunny afternoon, and Jesus is relaxed, just being himself, chatting with two tax collectors, new acquaintances that he has just met on the outdoor patio at Café Capernaum. They have invited him to sit with them, an invitation he has graciously accepted. He knows that the two tax collectors are probably involved in some less-than-honest dealings, but God's mercy is patient, and he knows that, too. Though he certainly does not expect radical conversions to take place over lunch, he looks forward to the dialogue, trusting in the grace of his *Abba*. Changing a heart attached to money, after all, is no easy task. Jesus is in no hurry, though. "One step at a time," he reminds himself. "One human heart at a time."

He has not been at the café for long when a scribe and a Pharisee, both of whom "just happened to be in the vicinity," stroll by. They post themselves "inconspicuously" next to the big Boulder, a huge stone that serves as a kind of meeting place in the town square. They have heard about the recent ruckus in Nazareth, involving a so-called "Jesus," and have been on the watch for the new wandering preacher ever since. Their detective work has paid off, and today their antennae will be extended as high as possible, ready to pick up any suspicious signals.

The scribe and the Pharisee watch Jesus' every move while "holding court," so to speak, next to the big Boulder, talking in loud stage voices so that Jesus knows they are nearby. Though he thinks that this is the first time that he has been spied on, he is sure that it will not be the last. He will proceed prudently, but he also knows that the moment is ripe to speak a word of good news. "It's worth the risk," he reminds himself. After all, there is always someone hungry to hear the good news.

Once he has finished his lunch, he excuses himself, stands up beneath a large palm tree in the middle of the café patio, looks around at the people present, and begins to narrate some folk parables. He directs his words to anyone who wants to stay around and listen, beginning each of the stories by setting the stage in a simple way:

> Which one of you, having a hundred sheep and losing one of them, does not leave the ninety-nine in the wilderness and go after the one that is lost until he find it . . . ? (Lk 15:4)

> What woman having ten silver coins, if she loses one of them, does not light a lamp, sweep the house, and search carefully until she finds it . . . ? (Lk 15:8)

The silence in and around the café is palpable as Jesus narrates his parables. Passersby stop to listen. Even the two tax collectors, with whom Jesus is sharing lunch, seem fully engaged. Many people at the café, in fact, are smiling, nodding in agreement as Jesus makes his points. Of course, a few of the already uncomfortable patrons become even more uncomfortable. In fact, two of them get up and leave. The people clearly have never heard teachings like this. The Pharisee over at the Boulder, pretending to be indifferent, watches Jesus' every move out of the corner of his eye. His face, red with anger, gives him away. The scribe, on the other hand, is busily jotting notes onto a piece of papyrus, his sunburned face shining with glee.

Jesus then tells the third parable:

> There was a man who had two sons. The younger of them said to his father, "Father, give me the share of the property that will belong to me." So he divided his property between them. A few days later the younger son gathered all he had and traveled to a distant country, and there he squandered his property in dissolute living. When he had spent everything, a severe famine took place throughout that country, and he began to be in need. So he went and hired himself out to one of the citizens of that country, who sent him to his fields to feed the pigs. He would gladly have filled himself with the pods that the pigs were eating; and no one gave him anything. But when he came to himself he said, "How many of my father's hired hands have bread enough and to spare, but here I am dying of hunger! I will get up and go to my father, and I will say to him, 'Father, I have sinned against heaven and before you; I am no longer worthy to be called your son; treat me like one of your hired hands.'" So he set off and went to his father. But while he was still far off, his father saw him and was filled with compassion; he ran and

put his arms around him and kissed him. Then the son said to him, "Father, I have sinned against heaven and before you; I am no longer worthy to be called your son." But the father said to his slaves, "Quickly, bring out a robe—the best one—and put it on him; put a ring on his finger and sandals on his feet. And get the fatted calf and kill it, and let us eat and celebrate; for this son of mine was dead and is alive again; he was lost and is found!" And they began to celebrate. (Lk 15:11–24)

Jesus pauses a moment, looking around at those who are listening, and continues:

"Now his elder son was in the field; and when he came and approached the house, he heard music and dancing. He called one of the slaves and asked what was going on. He replied, "Your brother has come, and your father has killed the fatted calf, because he has got him back safe and sound." Then he became angry and refused to go in. His father came out and began to plead with him. But he answered his father, "Listen! For all these years I have been working like a slave for you, and I have never disobeyed your command; yet you have never given me even a young goat so that I might celebrate with my friends. But when this son of yours came back, who has devoured your property with prostitutes, you killed the fatted calf for him!" Then the father said to him, "Son, you are always with me, and all that is mine is yours. But we had to celebrate and rejoice, because this brother of yours was dead and has come to life; he was lost and has been found." (Lk 15:25–32)

Kenneth Bailey, who has lived for sixty years in the Middle East, growing up there as a child, and later teaching scripture,[1] has written extensively on the parable of the Prodigal Son. He reminds us that when the Pharisees speak about "the man who receives sinners," they mean *Jesus*, who replies:

You accuse me of eating with sinners. You are absolutely right. That is precisely what I do. But as a matter of fact I not only sit down and eat with sinners, I rush down the road, shower them with kisses and drag them in that I might eat with them. It is much worse than you imagined! Let me tell you a story to explain how this happens."[2]

In his epic poem, "The Portal of the Mystery of Hope," Charles Péguy (1873–1914) captures the transforming power of "hope" in Jesus' trilogy of parables.

> All three of them are parables of hope . . .
> All three sisters like three very young children . . .
> Equally dear . . . equally loved . . .
>> But among them all; among the three of them the third
>> parable advances.
> And this one, my child, this third parable of hope . . .
> Unless one had a heart of stone, my child, who could hear
>> it with out crying . . .
>> It's as if it were the first time . . .
> *A man had two sons.* It's beautiful in Luke . . .
> It's beautiful on earth and in heaven. It's beautiful
>> everywhere.
> Just by thinking about it, a sob rises in your throat.
> It's the word of Jesus that has . . . found the deepest
>> resonance in the world . . .
> in the believing heart, in the unbelieving heart.[3]

While most of the folks at Café Capernaum are paying attention to Jesus' every word, the Pharisee and the scribe try to give the impression that they are not interested. It is enough for them to hear that the "lost have been welcomed home with parties and celebrations" to shift into their autopilot mode. Though they themselves did not *invent* the words "shall" and "shall not," they love the sound of them, and employ them frequently in their tidy black-and-white world. There is very little "gray middle ground" in their clean and tidy universe.

The unconventional rabbi

Several times in the gospels we find people who, having met Jesus or watched him from a distance, ask the question: "Who is this?" People are truly mystified. Though he shows great love and compassion—like a true man of God—he also seems to break some pretty sacrosanct rules. A few of his actions, in fact, are outright scandalous. Some have begun to call him "Rabbi," but he isn't your everyday rabbi either. Some applaud his actions, while others label him a heretic. Who is this man who heals sick people, embraces lepers, befriends sinners, and does it all without being overly concerned with the details of the Law? Who is this storytelling rabbi who dares to speak of a father who welcomes home a good-for-nothing loser of a son? Who is this man who is turning the world upside-down with parables?

Of course, most everything they say about him is true. He clearly does not act like the other rabbis of his day. He has no need to shame and condemn sinners in public in order to prove his orthodox credentials. On the other hand, he has a unique capacity to *see* and *hear* what other religious leaders are either oblivious to or simply too callous and self-centered to be concerned about. His heart is expansive and welcoming in an almost shocking way. He hears the cry of the poor. He touches wounded humanity with a compassion that, though somewhat unorthodox, is full of healing power. Surely he knows that if he keeps responding with this kind of unbridled compassion he will be harshly judged. It does not seem to bother him, though. When he sees someone suffering, his first response is not to think about laws and protocol but to freely pour out his love and healing compassion.

> One day, while Jesus was teaching ... some men came, carrying a paralyzed man on a bed. They were trying to bring him in and lay him before Jesus; but finding no way to bring him in because of the crowd, they went up on the roof and let him down ... into the middle of the crowd in front of Jesus. When he saw their faith, he said, "Friend, your sins are forgiven you." Then the scribes and the Pharisees began to question, "Who is this who is speaking blasphemies? Who can forgive sins but God alone?" When Jesus perceived their questionings, he answered them, "Why do you raise such questions in your hearts? Which is easier, to say, 'Your sins are forgiven you,' or to say, 'Stand up and walk'? But so that you may know that the Son of Man has authority on earth to forgive sins"—he said to the one who was paralyzed—"I say to you, stand up and take your bed and go to your home." Immediately he stood up ... and went to his home, glorifying God. Amazement seized all of them, and they glorified God. (Lk 5:17–26)

How could anyone be opposed to an act of such gentle mercy? Unfortunately, it doesn't take long for some of Jesus' words and actions to reach the ears of the Jewish hierarchs, which wins him the privilege of now having his name inscribed on their list of dangerous rebel-rousers. No sooner do the scribes and Pharisees see Jesus in town than suddenly their adrenalin begins to boil, as if they are just itching for a juicy confrontation. Sadly, legalism has deadened their hearts, making it impossible for them to grasp the deeper meaning of Jesus' loving concern for the poor. St. Cyril of Alexandria, writing around the year 440 asks, "Tell me, O Pharisee, why do you grumble because Christ did not scorn to be with publicans and sinners, but purposely provided for them this means of salvation? To save people, he yielded himself to emptiness, became like us, and clothed himself in human poverty."[4]

Gregory Boyle is a Jesuit priest who lives and works in a Catholic parish in the heart of one of Los Angeles' most gang and crime-ridden neighborhoods. The parish has become a home—or perhaps one might say a "mother"—to hundreds of young people who are caught in a never-ending spiral of drugs and gang violence. Every night street people sleep in the church, because it is one of the few safe places in the neighborhood. Boyle, reflecting on the gospel story of Jesus' healing of the paralyzed man who was lowered down through the roof by his friends, says:

> Compassion isn't just about feeling the pain of others; it's about bringing them in toward yourself. If we love what God loves, then, in compassion, margins get erased...Jesus is in a house so packed that no one can come through the door anymore. So the people open the roof and lower this paralytic down through it, so Jesus can heal him. The focus of the story is, understandably, the healing of the paralytic. But there is something more significant than that happening here. They're ripping the roof off the place and *those outside are being let in*.[5]

Boyle goes on to tell the story of Memo, a young gang member who starts coming by the parish, trying to take some steps toward turning his life around. He is one of God's little ones who, though he finds himself *outside* the fullness of life, longs to find a way *in*. Boyle decides to invite Memo and another gang member to accompany him on a speaking tour to Alabama. While there, Memo, who has lived his entire life in the gang-ridden streets of Los Angeles, sees for the first time the extreme poverty of rural America. Boyle himself admits that it was the worst poverty he had ever seen. Later that day Memo goes to look for Boyle.

> I look up, and Memo is standing in my doorway, crying...I ask him what's happening..."That visit...I don't know, it got to me. It got inside of me. I mean [and he's crying a great deal here] how do we let people live like this?" He pauses, and then says, "I don't know what's happening to me, but it's big. It's

like, for the first time in my life, I feel, I don't know, what's the word . . . I feel compassion for what other people suffer."

"Memo," notes Boyle, "finds his core wound and joins it to [the town's] core wound . . . The deepest place in Memo finds solidarity in the starkest wound of others. Compassion is God . . . A beloved community of equals has been fostered and forged there, and *the roofs just keep getting ripped off*. Soon enough, there won't be anyone left outside."[6]

Jesus, the Good Shepherd, wants nothing more than to be sure that none of the sheep are lost, that nobody is left outside of the house of his *Abba*. That is why, when the friends remove the tiles to let the paralyzed man down, Jesus' heart leaps for joy. He smiles because he realizes that these friends "get it"; they have understood his message of unconditional love. He smiles not only because the roof of Israel is being ripped off so that now more people can come in, but also because the local people are taking the matter into their own hands. They have understood what it means to tap into the dynamic power of God's liberating love, and in this way, free themselves from oppressive religious laws that suck life from the poor and oppressed.

Unfortunately, the joyful leap inside Jesus' heart is cut short when the scribes and Pharisees oppose his show of mercy in defense of the "holy Law." Yet in spite of seeing religious laws being used to shackle the boundless love of his *Abba*, his hope actually grows stronger. The friends of the paralyzed man have crossed a threshold that will change them forever. They have discovered God's Spirit, and once that power is released, nobody will be able to stuff it back into the bottle of religious repression.

Blessed Oscar Romero, the martyred archbishop of El Salvador,[7] shortly after returning from the Latin American Bishops' Conference in Puebla, Mexico, made use of the same gospel text of the healing of the paralytic to speak about faith and hope in the midst of El Salvador's difficult social and political situations:

I have often been asked here in El Salvador: What can we do? . . . I, filled with hope and faith, not only divine faith, but human faith, say: There is a solution . . . God urges us on. Just like in the healing of the paralytic there was a need for others to get him to the roof in order to lower him before Christ, so too . . . God wants people to help pick up the paralytic—called the nation or society—so that with human hands, human solutions, human ideas, we can set him before Christ, who is the only one who can say, "I have seen your faith. Get up and walk." I believe that our people *will* get up and *will* walk.[8]

And that is precisely what happened. Just as Jesus witnessed the paralyzed man leave the house on his own two feet, so too did Archbishop Romero, who lived through one of the darkest periods of his country's history, witness the miracle of an entire nation being healed of subservient passivity and centuries of oppression, learning to stand up and journey as the people of God toward self-respect and liberation.

Seeing and hearing our neighbor

Jesus shows his spontaneous mercy and love again when he raises from the dead the son of the widow of Nain. Luke, the evangelist, tells us that when Jesus "*saw her* he had compassion for her and said to her, 'Do not weep.' Then he came forward and touched the bier, and the bearers stood still. And he said, 'Young man, I say to you, rise.' The dead man sat up and began to speak, and Jesus gave him to his mother" (Lk 7:11–15).

It is very important to notice what at first seems like a rather insignificant detail in this story. As Jesus walks into the crowd that has gathered for the funeral, his attention is *not* focused primarily on the deceased son, as one would expect. Luke reminds us that he looks instead at the widowed mother. *She* is the poorest and most vulnerable person in this moment. *She* is the *anawim*, the one who soon will be abandoned by society, now that her son is dead. The moment Jesus *sees her*, his heart is moved with compassion, and he responds by returning the dead son to life. In other words, Jesus raises the son out of compassion *for the mother*. Could it be that he sees his *own* mother in her poor suffering face, wondering what will happen to her the day that he dies? The people in the funeral procession are deeply moved by this gesture of compassion for the widowed mother, so much so that John the Baptist, after hearing of the miracle, sends two of his disciples to Jesus to ask, "Are you the one who is to come, or are we to wait for another" (Lk 7:20)? In other words: "Who is this man?"

A few verses later Jesus again crosses the boundaries of proper religious etiquette, this time responding with incredible gentleness toward a woman who bathes, anoints, and kisses his feet during a meal at the house of a leading Pharisee. Luke carefully points out that, in the midst of such a high-powered meal, Jesus clearly breaks the rules of "political correctness" by disengaging from the *official* conversation and focusing on the woman. Why not? She is, after all, the most important person in Jesus' field of vision. Turning and *looking directly at her*, Jesus asks his host, "Simon, do you *see* this woman" (Lk 7:44)? In other words, "Simon, have you taken the time to *notice* her? Do you even *recognize* the fact that she exists?" Jesus continues:

"I entered your house; you gave me no water for my feet, but
she has bathed my feet with her tears and dried them with her
hair. You gave me no kiss, but from the time I came in she has
not stopped kissing my feet. You did not anoint my head with
oil, but she has anointed my feet with ointment. Therefore, I
tell you: *Her sins, which were many, have been forgiven; hence
she has shown great love.*[9] But the one to whom little is forgiven, loves little." Then he said to her, "Your sins are forgiven." (Lk 7:44–48)[9]

Scripture scholars rightly note that the sinful woman's *great love* flows
precisely from her having experienced *great forgiveness*. Says Edward
Schillebeeckx, "Everything is forgiven...therefore the greatest sinner
has the greatest love."[10]

For Simon and his friends, the woman who anoints Jesus' feet is a
"nobody," a nuisance. By labeling her "a sinner" they can dispense with
her. She ceases to exist in their eyes, relegated to the "distant country"
of social invisibility where so much of humanity lives. How easy it is to
judge a person without ever truly seeing him or her. "Do you *see* this
woman?" is the penetrating question that Jesus asks, a question born
from his contemplative heart. Have you taken the time to *see* the hunger
for healing in her face? Do you not *see* that she is a child of God, like
you, made in God's image? How can you judge her if you do not look
into her eyes and see the reflection of God? Several of the invited guests,
clearly shaken by Jesus' words and actions, ask, "*Who is this* who even
forgives sin" (Lk 7:49)?

Jesus is undoubtedly ruffling a few feathers as he journeys from
town to town. He is not afraid to confront the spiritual blindness and
deafness that possess many of those who consider themselves righteous
followers of Torah. He is discovering this new path step by step, meeting the challenges as they come. For Jesus, the Reign of God is now or
never, right here before our very eyes.

As Jesus and his disciples and a large crowd were leaving Jericho, Bartimaeus, son of Timaeus, a blind beggar, was sitting by
the roadside. When he heard that it was Jesus of Nazareth, he
began to shout out and say, "Jesus, Son of David, have mercy
on me." Many sternly ordered him to be quiet, but he cried out
even more loudly, "Son of David, have mercy on me." *Jesus
stood still* and said, "Call him here." And they called the blind
man, saying to him, "Take heart; get up, he is calling you." So
throwing off his cloak, he sprang up and came to Jesus. Then
Jesus said to him, "What do you want me to do for you?" The

blind man said to him, "My teacher, let me see again." Jesus said to him, "Go; your faith has made you well." Immediately he regained his sight and followed him on the way. (Mk 10:46–52; cf. Lk 18:35–43)

"Jesus stood still." Do we sense how powerful and prophetic this gesture is? In the midst of all the "important noise" and "busy-ness" of the world that grab the daily headlines and muffle the cries of the poor, *Jesus stands still.* He refuses to be swept up into the hectic pace of a world that ignores the poor and most vulnerable. He is always looking beyond the official border, into the *distant country.* How can we ever hear the gospel or hear the cry of the poor if we do not cultivate some form of inner silence and *stillness* in our lives?

When Bartimaeus cries out, "Jesus, Son of David, have mercy on me," the religious authorities respond by attempting to silence him. Only Jesus is *still enough, rooted enough* to hear his desperate cry and respond with compassion. How many years had he cried out from that same spot on the road? As the world ignores Bartimaeus, Jesus hears him and heals him. That is not all, though. He returns to Bartimaeus the very human dignity that he has been denied since birth, and, per-haps more importantly, he welcomes him into his band of disciples, as Mark the evangelist tells us: "He regained his sight and followed him on the way" (10:52).

Jesus does not allow himself to fall victim to the plague of social in-difference. He purposely moves toward the *other,* toward the *distant country* of alienation, so that he can hear the cry that rises up from the edge of the road. His contemplative heart allows him to *see* the human face that others ignore, to *hear* the cry that the world's busy-ness at-tempts to silence. When the Church stands up for the human rights of prisoners or for the protection of immigrants, when it opposes the death penalty or rejects abortion as a form of birth control, the Church is doing nothing more than reminding the world that there are voices and faces that we cannot turn our back on. Has it ever occurred to us that *indifference* is a mortal sin precisely because it leads to the death of real people? If we walk mindlessly past Bartimaeus because we are in a hurry to go to church or to buy the latest iPhone, we are just one more pawn in the anonymous crowd of modern society, drunk on ourselves. Only a heart rooted in stillness and mindfulness can *see and hear* what our busy world often walks past with sinful indifference, as if it were rubbish on the side of the road.

We find this same *contemplative stillness* again in the midst of a storm that catches Jesus and the disciples by surprise one day on the Sea of Galilee. Mark (4:35–41) tells us that Jesus is with the disciples in the boat. As the waves beat against the boat, Jesus is asleep—on a cushion, of all things! This is when the wise student of scripture must hit the "pause button" and pay close attention, because something *very strange* is going on here. The disciples are watching their lives pass before their eyes, while Jesus is *still and quiet*, sleeping (meditating?) on a cushion in the midst of a storm. The disciples start crying out, "Teacher, do you not care that we are perishing?" Mark continues, "*Jesus woke up and rebuked the wind, and said to the sea, "Peace. Be still."* Then the wind ceased, and there was a dead calm" (Mk 4:39).

To what or to whom is Jesus speaking the words, *"Peace. Be still"*—to the wind and the sea? Could it be that he is directing these words to his disciples and to us? The wind and the sea are just doing what they know to do. The disciples, on the other hand, are in a tizzy—doing everything *but* being peaceful and still. It is obvious that Mark is not too terribly concerned with maritime navigation in this text. It does seem, though, that he is saying something about contemplative stillness and trust in God. Let's hope that the disciples eventually got the point. Have we gotten it?

Sin, society, and survival—a serious business

As we make our way with Jesus through small-town Galilee, it is important to be mindful of the fact that sin and all the socio-religious legalities connected to it are serious business in his day. The more observant Jews, in an attempt to maintain a sense of national and religious coherence and identity, simply do not hang out with anyone who might stain their clean world: not sinners, or Gentiles, or the socially marginalized. The fact that Jesus has clearly broken open that mold has certainly not won him any points with the religious officials of the day.

It is helpful for us to remember that by the time Jesus begins his preaching and healing ministry, the people of Israel have been under Roman occupation for approximately ninety years (since 63 BCE). They are fed up with being a colony of Rome. Their world feels a lot like a repeat of a bad movie that they have already seen, entitled "Slavery in Egypt—Part II" or "Babylonia: The Sequel." Having already lived through horrendous periods of oppression in their long history, they have had it. Enough is enough. They are *tired* of being slaves in an empire that purposely tries to erode their unity by undermining the sacred foundations of their religious faith and identity. Unfortunately, they have no choice but to carry on with a delicate mixture of hope and caution. They know that they must not upset the status quo, for the fear of being completely annihilated by the Romans is never far from their minds.

One need not be a sociologist of religion to realize that, given the menacing presence of the empire, many Jews see no other option than to go along quietly with their unfortunate reality, obeying the rules of the empire (paying taxes, etc.), while creating their own "safe and secure" world at home, within the confines of their religion. They compensate for the loss of socio-political freedom by placing greater emphasis on their religious practices, always aware that their entire religious heritage could be demolished in an instant if Rome suspected that a revolt were in the works. Apart from the Zealots and a few other splinter groups, most Jews know that revolution is simply out the question. David may have defeated Goliath once, but one must not tempt God. So, the Jews in Jesus' day opt for keeping the *inside* of the house (and the *outside* of the cup—Lk 11:39) extra clean. This at least provides them with the feeling that they have some control over their lives. Unfortunately, as is often the case, the attempt to create a perfect and pure religion easily becomes the breeding ground for religious fundamentalism. This context is no different.

Few contemporary scripture scholars have delved into the topic of Jesus' treatment of sin and social exclusion with as much clarity as José Antonio Pagola, whose book, *Jesus: An Historical Approximation*, is undoubtedly one of the best international compendia of Christology to come out in years. Pagola, who has a marvelous capacity to synthesize huge swaths of writings into clear and concise summaries, makes Jesus' dealings with sinners come alive. Says Pagola:

> It is his friendship with sinners that brings down scandal and hostility on Jesus. Nothing like this has ever happened in the history of Israel. Never has a prophet approached sinners with such respect, friendship and sympathy. What Jesus does is unheard of. People remember the Baptist very differently. His main concern was to eradicate the sin that was contaminating ... and endangering the covenant with God ... The Baptist's approach didn't scandalize anyone. It was what they expected of a prophet, a defender of the people's Covenant with God. But Jesus' approach is surprising. He doesn't speak of sin as causing God's wrath. On the contrary, there is room in God's Reign for sinners and prostitutes too ... [But] how can he associate with publicans and sinners? ... How can a man of God accept them as friends? How dare he eat with them? This behavior is certainly Jesus' most provocative trait. Prophets don't act like that.[11]

Of course, some of the sinners in Jesus' day have clearly earned the title. The *tel nai*, or tax collectors, also called *publicans*, are especially hated. In charge of collecting tolls, imposts, taxes, customs, and tariffs, they are known to be notoriously greedy and corrupt. Some of them have also become quite wealthy. They frequently resort to extortion and violence to make a profit. This, more than the fact that they collaborate with the Roman Empire, is the reason they are so hated.[12]

> The "publicans" in the gospels are the collectors of taxes on merchandise and transit rights through major highways, bridges, or ports of some cities. There are also "chief tax collectors," such as, for example, Zacchaeus, who have gained control of these transit fees and customs duties in a given region and work through their slaves and other subordinates who sit in the collection booths.
>
> Tax collectors have no better way to make a living. Their activity, like that of thieves and other dishonest people, is so shameful that it is sometimes assigned to slaves. It is these tax collectors that Jesus meets in his travels. They are . . . discredited sinners, much like "prostitutes" . . . [who] are also slaves, sometimes sold by their own fathers. The prostitutes who circulate in the villages are almost always repudiated wives or widows without a male protector, who look for clients at parties and banquets. Apparently these are the prostitutes who come to meals organized in Jesus' circles.[13]

The good news, though, is that in the midst of this complicated social situation, "Jesus [shows] sympathy and understanding for these [tax collectors] who, like the prostitutes, always get the blame . . . He dares to stand up and say that the prostitutes and tax collectors will be entering God's new world ahead of the religious leaders (Mt 21:31)."[14]

Others groups of vulnerable people are grouped into the category of "sinners" as well, for the simple fact that they work in trades that render them unclean or are considered despicable. Among such people are tanners, donkey-drivers, dung collectors, shepherds, beggars, launderers, barbers, weavers, and peddlers. Many of them are just ordinary folks with little or no power over their plight, forced to find less-than-honorable ways to survive. Then there are the truly innocent victims of social exclusion, the people who in all cultures and all times are silently pushed to the fringes of society because they suffer from physical or mental handicaps, disabilities, poverty, widowhood, and so forth.

The process of globalization, notes South African theologian Albert Nolan, radically transforms both the daily life and the practice of faith on the part of the poor and vulnerable in the time of Jesus. While the powerful and wealthy live in luxury and decadence, the poor and the uneducated people are punished for not being able to follow all the minor details of the law. Says Nolan, "The laws and customs...are so complicated that the uneducated are quite incapable of understanding what is expected of them. Education...is a matter of knowing the...law and all its ramifications [which means that] the illiterate and uneducated are immoral," socially *invisible*; they simply count for nothing.[15]

Though the religious leaders and the elite of Jesus' day have become quite adept at erecting all kinds of exclusive barriers, Jesus' main "transgression," according to the strict legalists, has to do not so much with issues of purity or impurity, as was once thought,[16] but instead with his association with *sinners*. In fact, the most serious offense, according to Edward Schillebeeckx, has to do with Jesus' claim to *forgive* them:

> In Judaism God alone can forgive sins...Even in the Jewish tradition of messianic expectation, while the "latter day" messiah may intercede with God on the sinner's behalf, he cannot forgive any sins. To ascribe that authority to a human being is blasphemous (cf. Lk 5:21)...This acknowledgment of Jesus' power to forgive sins is obvious most of all from [the] account of a dinner party for tax collectors, attended by Jesus, at the house of Levi (Lk 5:29–32)...[It attests to] his role as the "eschatological messenger" of God, that is, as the one who proclaims...to tax collectors...the invitation to the great eschatological feast of fellowship with God...What Jesus means is to *include* those who are *excluded* by the Pharisees ...From the viewpoint of official Judaic piety Jesus has "declassed" himself by eating with tax collectors. His self-defense is that...the sinners must be invited to God's table...The sheep that is lost and isolated from the flock must be searched out.[17]

Schillebeeckx highlights something quite important here, namely, that Jesus takes a huge risk by accepting the invitation to Levi's party. He does so, it seems, precisely because he wants to communicate to the tax collectors that his *Abba* is calling them, too, waiting for them with his arms of mercy wide-open, around the table of an even *bigger banquet*, that of the Reign of God. Jesus clearly understands that, in his dealings with sinners, he is the incarnation of his *Abba*'s mercy. "The Christian community, therefore, has in no way distorted its picture of [Jesus'] life on earth when it explicitly ascribes 'the authority to forgive sins' to the earthly Jesus."[18] Joachim Jeremias adds a final note, reminding us that not only was Jesus' practice of extending mercy to sinners a bit shocking, but the fact that he chose to do so *within the context of table fellowship* would have been seen as truly scandalous:

> Judaism knew that God was merciful and could forgive...
> Even the sinner could be saved...The message that God wants
> to have dealings with sinners and...that God's love extends to
> them is without parallel at the time...[and] finds its most strik-
> ing expression in the mocking description of Jesus as a "glutton
> and a drunkard, a friend of publicans and sinners"...[If] the of-
> fense *after* Easter was Jesus' accursed death on the cross—his
> table fellowship with sinners was the pre-Easter scandal.[19]

Today salvation has come to this house!

No one denies that Jesus promises the *fullness* of the Reign of God in the end-times (cf. Lk 21:31). One of the novelties of his preaching, however, is that God's Reign is breaking into the world and into time *here and now* (Lk 10:11; 17:21; 21:31). In other words, we can already see and touch the Reign of God in our world today. The Lord's Prayer, taught to the disciples by Jesus himself, does not say that our daily bread and God's forgiveness are gifts that we have to wait for until some distant, eschatological end-time. A final fullness will be manifest then—yes—but it is already happening *today*! It is as real as fresh bread baking in the oven right now. "*Abba, give us today our daily bread.*"

Jesus is praying one day, and when he finishes, one of his disciples says to him, "Lord, teach us to pray, as John taught his disciples." He answers them, saying,

> When you pray, say:
> Father, hallowed be your name.
> Your kingdom come.
> Give us each day our daily bread.
> And forgive us our sins,
> for we ourselves forgive everyone indebted to us.
> And do not bring us to the time of trial. (Lk 11:2–4)

This marvelous fulfillment *in the here and now* is portrayed beauti- fully and powerfully in Jesus' grace-filled encounter with Zacchaeus, who is not only a tax collector, but the *chief* tax collector (i.e., the "head honcho," the most despised one of all). It all begins when Jesus sees Zacchaeus up in a sycamore tree. "Zacchaeus, hurry and come down; for I must stay at your house *today*" (Lk 19:5). Barbara Reid points to Zacchaeus as an example of how Jesus "turns the tables" on the call to discipleship: "The novelty and offense of Jesus's message was his affirmation that sinners who heeded him would be included in the reign of God...To the Pharisees and scribes who complained...Jesus replies, 'I have not come to call the righteous to repentance but sinners' (Lk 5:32)."[20]

Zacchaeus, realizing that this grace-filled visit of Jesus has provided him with the light that he has been waiting for to turn his life of thievery and injustice around, stands before Jesus and says, "Half of my possessions, Lord, I will give to the poor; and if I have defrauded anyone of anything, I will pay back four times as much." Jesus, lifting his goblet of wine, looks at Zacchaeus and at his wife, both of whom are beaming with joy, and says, "*Today* salvation has come to this house" (Lk 19:8–9). Let us not forget that no law-abiding Jew would ever think that salvation could *squeeze through* the door of a wicked chief tax collector's house. Jesus not only squeezes through the door, but he anoints both Zacchaeus and his family with the oil of his abundant and scandalous mercy.

Dismantling the Walls

Jesus is clearly demolishing—with words and gestures—the walls that have been erected to separate the "sinners" from "the just." The building of separation walls of any kind, whether they be physical or psychological, cultural, political, or spiritual, is a cry to heaven and a sign that the Reign of God is still waiting to be realized in our world. Whether the walls separate clean and unclean, healthy and sick, strong and weak, Jew and Gentile, sinner and just, learned and illiterate, Muslim and Jew, Catholic and Protestant, gay and straight, married and divorced, rich and poor—they are *all* the result of sin. *Difference* and *diversity* are part of God's plan. Red-breasted robins and loud, squawking blue jays happily sing from the same tree. God does *not* erect walls; sinful human beings do.

In his Angelus greeting on the feast of the Dedication of the Lateran Basilica in Rome in 2014, Pope Francis seized the opportunity to make reference to an important European anniversary: the twenty-fifth anniversary of the fall of the Berlin Wall. Pope Francis commented that the wall, a symbol of the ideological divisions that existed (and exist?) in Europe and the world, fell thanks to those who resisted, fought, and prayed, among whom was his predecessor, St. John Paul II, who, noted Pope Francis, had a leading role in its fall. The pope pointed out that our world is "capable of bringing down all the walls that still divide the world [so that] no longer will innocent people be persecuted and even killed on account of their belief and their religion." The Holy Father ended with this powerful and striking statement: "Where there is a wall there is a closed heart. We need bridges, not walls!"[21] Given that he spoke these words on the feast of the Dedication of the Lateran Basilica, one can only imagine that the pope dreams of more bridges and fewer walls within and between the churches, as well.

Unfortunately in the first-century world, once society has assigned you to the side of the wall reserved for "sinners," there are not very many doors or bridges that can help you find your way back home. Even if you *long* to experience God's love and lead a godly life, you are rarely given a chance. A leper is always a leper and a widow is always a widow, and both live far from God's mercy (unless the leper is miraculously healed). Entire categories of poor, broken people, sick people who have no one to care for them, are simply pushed aside, abandoned, and labeled "sinners." Religious leaders' interpretations of the "Law" have, in many instances, supplanted the presence of the living God. Jesus, however, begins to ask different questions and propose *new ways* of living together: How is it possible to consider "just" a law that abandons a widow, punishes a child who is born blind, or marginalizes a woman who, for one reason or another, is unable to bear children? What kind of God would institute such laws?

Shortly after teaching the disciples the "Our Father," Jesus is invited to dine at the house of a Pharisee, an invitation that Jesus readily accepts. Noticing that Jesus skips the ritual washing, the Pharisee registers a look of shock. Jesus, noticing the surprised look, finishes his soup and then says:

> "You Pharisees clean the outside of the cup and of the dish, but inside you are full of greed and wickedness. You fools! Did not the one who made the outside make the inside also? ... Woe to you Pharisees! You love to have the seat of honor in the synagogues and to be greeted with respect in the marketplaces" ... One of the lawyers [says], "Teacher, when you say these things, you insult us, too." Jesus [says], "Woe also to you scribes! For you load people with burdens hard to bear, and you yourselves do not lift a finger to ease them ... You have taken away the key of knowledge; you did not enter yourselves, and you hindered those who were entering." (Lk 11:39–40, 43, 45–46, 52)

Before long, word begins to spread around town that this prophet, Jesus, sees things differently. Sinners who want to learn the way of discipleship are welcomed—no background checks required. Rather than focus on what it is that makes people sinners, Jesus looks at them and wonders what might be needed to make them saints. Jesus sees their potential, not their mistakes. He knows that the human condition is fragile, and that is why he wants nothing more than to initiate a dialogue, extend a welcoming hand, speak a word of compassion, so that the wound of sin and exclusion can be healed. It is not that he is indifferent toward sin; he simply is more committed to loving, healing, and welcoming the sinner back home. Says theologian Donald Goergen:

> Those who were attracted to Jesus, who longed to hear him, who chose to follow him as their prophet and teacher were not one homogeneous group. Yet what emerges is how popular Jesus was, how sought after by the poor or the common and ordinary people, the religiously marginal people ... by those without status from economic, social, or religious points of view. They loved him. He made them laugh. He respected their tears. He knew their pain. He associated with them, respected them, enjoyed their company. They listened to him, learned from him, believed in him, had hope because of him, and he lived for them. He taught them, spoke of the nearness of God to them, made them feel holy and righteous. He reached out to them, compassionately, generously, faithfully, humbly, joyfully. He healed their sick. He made them feel human again. He preached an impending social reversal. They were his people, and he was their teacher.[22]

Jesus is always ready to tell the poor and sinners about the boundless compassion of his loving *Abba*. It is *that voice*—the voice of unconditional love—that never ceases to echo in the depths of his being. It is a very different voice from that of the religious authorities who use the Law to punish sinners and the vulnerable, so that they can accumulate power and control. The one sin that Jesus clearly does *not* tolerate is the sin of excluding the sinner from the mercy of God. Pope Francis echoes this same primacy of mercy when he says, "The confessional is not a torture chamber, but the place in which the Lord's mercy motivates us to do better."[23] Pagola sums it up this way:

> Compassionate love is behind all Jesus' activity, inspiring and shaping his whole life. For him compassion is not just another virtue, another attitude. His life is entwined with mercy: he aches with the people's suffering, makes it his, and turns it into the central principle of his activity. He is the first to live like the "father" in the parable who, "filled with compassion" (in his

deepest bowels), embraces the son who comes back defeated by hunger and humiliation; or like the "Samaritan" who, "moved by pity," went to the aid of the man fallen by the wayside.[24]

Today, thankfully, in most parts of the world we do not categorize a blind person as a sinner, or ostracize and abandon a person who has a contagious skin disease.[25] This certainly does not mean that the social exclusion of people based on mental, psychological, racial, sexual, religious and cultural prejudices does not still exist today. We know that the scourge of exclusion is still very real. A visit to most prisons, mental hospitals, refugee camps, orphanages or residences for the elderly—in both poor and more developed countries—surely reveals how far we still have to go to break down the walls of exclusion and restore the human family back to its original beauty, created in the image of God.

Religious zeal or fearful fundamentalism?

While Jesus' words and actions instill hope among the poor and those whose hearts are not hardened, his unsettling questions and his ever-growing group of "questionable" friends never cease to create tension with the religious authorities. Mark, the evangelist, describes a rather tense, though fairly typical, encounter between Jesus and religious leaders tied to legalistic practices:

> Now when the Pharisees and some of the scribes who had come from Jerusalem gathered around Jesus, they noticed that some of his disciples were eating with defiled hands, that is, without washing them. (For the Pharisees, and all Jews, do not eat unless they thoroughly wash their hands...) So the Pharisees and the scribes asked him, "Why do your disciples not live according to the tradition of the elders but eat with defiled hands?" Jesus said to them, "Isaiah prophesied rightly about you hypocrites, as it is written:
> 'This people honors me with their lips,
>   but their hearts are far from me;
> in vain do they worship me,
>   teaching human precepts as doctrines.'
> You abandon the commandment of God and hold to human tradition..."
>   Then he called the crowd again and said to them, "Listen to me, all of you, and understand: there is nothing outside a

person that by going in can defile, but the things that come out are what defile." (Mk 7:1–3, 5–8, 14–15)

From our vantage point two thousand years later, it is important to pause and try to understand the situation. We begin with a simple question: What is it that drives some of the scribes and Pharisees into a deadly legalism that focuses on *punishing* sinners rather than shepherding them to freedom? Why does Saul (a Pharisee prior to his becoming a disciple of Jesus) nod in approval as a mob of crazed fanatics stone innocent Stephen to death, simply for being a disciple of Jesus (Acts 8:1)? Does a mother not applaud and praise her child's first wobbly steps? If the child who is learning to walk is scolded for every fall, he or she will never learn.

> The scribes and Pharisees are very religious people, concerned to observe the law of God to the last detail. Since God is a God of infinite holiness, they believe that strict avoidance of all that is unholy is required of all those whom he has called. This includes the complete avoidance of sinners... Little wonder that they take offense at the behavior of Jesus, who not only mixes with sinners, but claims to be doing so in the name of God! ...They who serve God so faithfully resent the idea that God does not confine his love to them, but extends it in equal measure to outcasts and sinners.[26]

It is tragic to see that something as noble and lofty as *holiness* has a shadow side to it as well. Albert Nolan underlines the fact that Jesus really does try to reach out to the scribes and Pharisees. He truly wants them to understand the essential relationship between God's holiness and God's mercy.

> It could be plausibly argued that the vehemence of Jesus' attack upon the Pharisees was exaggerated by the gospel-writers because of the hostility between the early church and the party of the Pharisees; but this would not answer our question. Did Jesus love the Pharisees or not? ...If Jesus had refused to argue, discuss and mix socially with the Pharisees, then, and then only, could one accuse him of excluding them and treating them as outsiders. The Gospels abound in examples of his conversations and meals with them and of his persistent attempts to persuade them. In the end it was they who excluded him; at no stage did he exclude them.[27]

The root of the word "Pharisee" comes from the Greek word *pharisaioi*, meaning "to separate."[28] It seems to have been derived from the Pharisees' obsession with *separating* the weak, impure and "sinful" elements of society from the righteous ones. Along with their partners, the scribes, the Pharisees are clearly a force to be reckoned with in Jesus' day. They work together as a kind of "clean team," dedicated to purifying and strengthening the Jewish nation through the strict enforcement of religious laws. They oppose Jewish teachers, like Jesus, who do not follow the rules, seeing such lax practice as caving into the destructive values of the Roman Empire. The Pharisees' obsession with measuring righteousness by strict adherence to the letter of the Law provides them with a sense of security in the face of the Roman occupation. Since they cannot overthrow the Romans, they control what they can, that is, the situation "inside their own house."

To be fair, we must not forget that the scribes and Pharisees are authentically pious people who love their faith. No one questions that. The problem, unfortunately, is that they see every move of Jesus and his disciples not through the lens of faith, but in light of the letter of the Law. Whenever a particular legal problem pops up (Jesus having lunch with tax collectors and sinners, for example), the clean team shows up almost miraculously. They seem to have a rare gift for picking up the scent of a juicy legal "situation." They argue their case impeccably, every word, of course, backed up by texts from the sacred scriptures. Sometimes they lay out their argument without even looking at the "sinner" whom they are judging. "Why look at the sinner?" they ask. "It's all right here in the book!" They *really* love the book. Imagine a scribe clarifying a particular situation regarding a person with leprosy. Chapter 13 of Leviticus alone has fifty-nine detailed prescriptions for handling the case of a leper, and that is only one of the many chapters with legislation on leprosy. Who would not be impressed with such "well-rehearsed wisdom"?

The ability of the Pharisees and scribes to give quick answers to legal questions does, in a way, have a kind of stabilizing effect on Jewish society, giving them at least a feeling of security and self-determination. Their absolute certainty in the realm of legal matters instills a sense of protection and safety as they try to live from day to day under the oppressive, watchful eye of Rome. Of course, that is precisely why the entire situation is both comical and tragic. While entire nations and provinces struggle to survive under Roman occupation, with its scourge of taxation, the Jewish religious leaders are excommunicating people who have not washed their hands correctly before eating.

As we know, St. Paul himself, before becoming a disciple of Jesus, had been a staunch member of the Pharisee party, probably of the more militant, separatist wing. In fact, he even testifies to his radical views at his trial: "All the Jews know my way of life from my youth...They have known for a long time, if they are willing to testify, that I have belonged to the strictest sect of our religion and lived as a Pharisee...I not only locked up many of the saints[29] in prison, but I also cast my vote against them when they were being condemned to death" (Acts 26:4–5). Paul gives the impression that in his "Saul days" he had more merit badges pinned to his tunic than anyone else in all of Israel!

The problem, of course, is not the Law itself. The ancient scriptures, born from an experience of communal wisdom and in-*spired* by God's Spirit, have always been intended to be a living testament to God's Wisdom—a guide to living the covenant. Is this not precisely what St. Paul finally discovers on the road to Damascus? The very Law that had turned him into a religious fanatic suddenly takes on a human face—a *communal* face—becoming a source of inspiration and transformation for him. What has changed is not the Law, but *Saul himself.* His encounter with the Risen Christ gifts him with new eyes and a new heart—in fact, a whole new life.

The same happens in a lesser degree to two other prominent Pharisees, namely Nicodemus and Gamaliel. Like Saul, their eyes are opened to see the true face of Jesus, recognizing his loving, universal heart. Both, in fact, are remembered honorably in the Christian scriptures. While Gamaliel cautions the high priest and the Council against making too rash a judgment against the followers of Jesus (Acts 5:33ff), Nicodemus shows a profound nobility of spirit when he and Joseph of Arimathea, a secret disciple of Jesus, brave the horrible violence in order to bury the tortured and crucified body of Jesus, whom they clearly recognize as a man of God (Jn 19:38–42).

If there is one thing for which Jesus clearly has very little tolerance, it is the mixing together of religious laws, money, and power. His overturning of the tables of the moneychangers and his harsh criticisms against the temple being turned into a marketplace (a text found in all four gospels—Mt 21:12–17; Mk 11:15–19; Lk 19:45–48; Jn 2:13–20), are among his most forceful attacks on the abuse of religion. Of course, the Jewish leaders and the strict defenders of the Law quickly interpret Jesus' actions as blasphemous. To them, such actions seem almost treasonous. As far as they are concerned, any public critique that appears even *remotely* like a lack of respect for the institutions of holy Israel clearly suggests some kind of collaboration with Roman imperialism, and that sin is always unforgivable.

Though Jesus loves both the Law and the temple he does not back down. "His protest against the desecration of the temple was neither an attempted political uprising nor an attack on institutional religion. It was a way of affirming the real nature and pure purpose of religion."[30] Jesus knows very well that if they continue to profane the temple and, with it, Israel's true faith, then the temple will be destroyed. While the Jewish authorities are principally preoccupied with protecting their religious autonomy and power, Jesus is concerned with the gradual deterioration of true worship. The temple is turning into a corrupt business that manipulates religiously vulnerable people. In Jesus' mind *that*, more than the Roman Empire, will eventually bring down the Jewish nation.

We glimpse these tensions in the aftermath of the raising of Lazarus from the dead. While Martha, Mary, and Lazarus's friends are weeping with joy, "Some [people] went to the Pharisees and told them what Jesus had done. So the chief priests and the Pharisees convened the Sanhedrin and said, "What are we going to do? ... If we leave [Jesus] alone, all will believe in him, and the Romans will come and take away both our land and our nation" (Jn 11:46–48). Some of the Jewish leaders are so afraid of losing their power that they cannot celebrate the good news that has just been made manifest before their very eyes. Protecting the temple made of stone (i.e., their temporal power) has become more important for them than worshiping the *living God*. They are unable to celebrate God's miraculous raising of a dead man back to life, because to do so might force them to rethink just *who* this Jesus is, and they have already decided that he is far too dangerous for their self-serving worldview. Sadly, they have turned themselves into prisoners of their own fear.

Jesus' temple criticism, of course, has nothing to do with siding with the abusive power of the Roman authorities, who are beginning to be a bit suspicious of this rather unorthodox, wandering rabbi who makes occasional references to a "kingdom" not of this world (cf. Jn 18:36). Jesus' hope is to encourage God's beloved people to put an end to all forms of adulterated temple worship and abuse of religious power so that, worshiping in Spirit and truth (Jn 4:23), they can save their nation from another catastrophe. Unfortunately, the events that unfold forty years later, leading to the temple's destruction, only confirm that few paid attention to Jesus' prophetic words.

The seed of the gospel is sown among the Gentiles

It is important to be mindful of the gospel's historical context when speaking of certain tensions, as in the case of Jesus' frequent confrontations with the Jewish religious leaders of his day. As the gospel is preached in the Gentile world, the religious, cultural, and political realities change quite radically. Most scripture scholars agree that Luke writes his gospel in and around Antioch (the political and cultural capital of Syria, part of the Roman Empire and today a city in Turkey, near the Syrian border). This means that the tension between the strict Pharisaic/scribal group and everyday Jews is no longer a hot issue. Luke's community, after all, does not live in a predominantly Jewish world. In Antioch the Jews are a small minority. The big challenge there is to translate the teachings of Jesus and navigate Christian discipleship within a Gentile milieu, where few people would have ever heard of *Pharisees and scribes*. Why then, one might ask, does Luke so frequently emphasize the tension between Jesus and the scribes and Pharisees if he is writing in a predominantly non-Jewish environment?

Scripture scholar Eugene LaVerdiere suggests that a kind of "neo-Pharisee" tendency had very likely begun to cause friction among the disciples in Antioch. Luke apparently sees the need to remind the Gentile converts of "the Way" that love and mercy take precedence over legalistic purity and perfection. Evidently, some of the new converts are acting like Pharisees and scribes, being judgmental and creating legalistic tensions in the young community. Says LaVerdiere, "Many elements in Luke's narrative are incomprehensible unless we view the Pharisees as Christians,"[31] specifically "as symbols for neo-Pharisees in the gentile communities addressed by Luke."[31] To grasp the situation at hand, we might imagine one of the elder members standing up in a community celebration in Antioch to address the divisive tensions caused by legalism:

> Brothers and sisters, why is there so much harsh and judgmental infighting? Have we forgotten that God mercifully rescued our spiritual ancestors from slavery in Egypt? Why then are some members of our community unable to embrace the *new Exodus* that Jesus has inaugurated, welcoming us into the freedom of the children of God? If we heap upon our new converts here in Antioch heavy legalistic burdens, are we not just sending them back to slavery in Egypt? Has Jesus freed us only to become slaves again?

Says author Christopher Hayden, "While obvious sinners hear the parable [of the Prodigal Son] gladly, as an invitation to turn to God and trust in his love ... the parable of the prodigal son tells the scribes and Pharisees that they have things wrong: God is not an exclusive God, waiting to condemn sinners and those who live outside of the covenant. God is a loving Father, waiting for the sinner to return, and rejoicing in the sinner's repentance . . . The scribes and Pharisees, who cannot accept God's generosity, run the risk of a self-imposed exclusion . . . just like the older brother in the parable."[32]

Jesus longs for all of God's people to come home to the universal heart of a loving God. He will spend the three years of his public ministry saying time and time again, "The Reign of God is like . . ." Sometimes he will speak of a woman who kneads yeast into the dough, and at other times he will tell of a sower who goes out to sow seed (Lk 13:21; 8:4–7). Always, though, he will insist that his heart is open to all: "Let *anyone* with ears to hear listen!" (Lk 8:8).

Jesus' recounting of the three parables in Luke 15 is not the first time that he has ruffled a few feathers. His visits to the towns and villages around Galilee have begun to elicit a fair bit of local gossip. While many express admiration for the young, wandering preacher from Nazareth, his mixing and mingling with just about anyone who wants to sit down and chat is not winning him many friends among the local religious authorities. The civil authorities do not seem too terribly concerned. After all, it is not against Roman law for a Jew to sit down and share a meal of dried fish and lentil soup with a tax collector or reach out in compassion to a widow or an orphan. It is the religious authorities who are getting upset. Notes N. T. Wright: "Jesus is making a habit of having celebration parties with all the 'wrong' people."[33]

Though for Jesus it is a source of great joy to know that "All the tax collectors and sinners [are] coming near to listen to him" (Lk 15:1), such news is judged dangerous among the religious elite of his day. Jesus does not alter his game plan, though. The fact that his presence and words are communicating to people who are normally kept at a distance from God's love that it is all right to come near, to listen and to begin anew brings nothing but great joy to his *Abba*, who longs to draw near to the world and to those who suffer. It is the Good Shepherd, after all, who always takes the first step, setting off to seek out the lost and bring them home. The good news does not get much better than that.

4

Jesus the Prodigal Son

When he had spent everything, a severe famine took place throughout that country, and he began to be in need. So he went and hired himself out to one of the citizens of that country, who sent him to his fields to feed the pigs. He would gladly have filled himself with the pods that the pigs were eating; and no one gave him anything. But when he came to himself he said, "How many of my father's hired hands have bread enough and to spare, but here I am *dying of hunger*." (Lk 15:14–17)

As I write these pages, "the distant country" is filled with news of ethnic cleansing and interreligious violence, racism and nuclear stockpiles, economic inequality and war. While some of the world's poor try to escape from the spiraling violence of demonic drug wars, others are drowning in the Mediterranean, victims of the illegal trafficking of immigrants and refugees fleeing from war and poverty. As always it is the poor whose lives are expendable. How many mothers will bury their children before this crucifixion of the innocent comes to an end? How much greed, indifference, and violence can our world withstand before it simply implodes? How much destruction of the environment will occur before we remember that this planet is our mother? Of course, I am not so naïve to think that my own country is not a major actor in feeding this great machine of sin, greed, and violence.

There is hope, though, for here in the midst of the suffering and violence, here in the heart of the distant country, we discover that the prodigal Son, the one who left the safety of his *Abba*'s house, has come to be with us, to live in our midst. His name is *Emmanuel*, "God is with us" (Mt 1:23). His presence strengthens our faith. He is a poor man living among the poor, a refugee among refugees (Mt 2:13–15). He comforts those who have lost loved ones to sickness and brings us a promise of new life that fills us with hope. Jesus is the prodigal Son

51

who has chosen to journey into our world and experience the struggles of life *with us*, even to the point of "dying of hunger" *with us* (cf. Lk 15:17). That is not all, though. He also shares with us the joy and hope of the gospel. He teaches us to practice peace and reconciliation by reaching out in love to our neighbor—even in the midst of the violence. Why, we ask, would someone *want* to come into this world and share in our suffering? How are we to comprehend such steadfast love, so contrary to the ways of the world? Says Maria Boulding:

> The early Christian writers delighted to repeat, "What has not been assumed [by the incarnate Son] has not been healed." There is nothing in our human experience that he has not been through from the inside; the idea of Jesus traveling through life with some kind of divine immunization against failure, ignorance, passion and laughter is intolerable. The only experience he did not share was sin, and that was no disadvantage, since it makes us less human; in any case he felt the full impact of evil to a degree of intensity the rest of us can scarcely conceive. All the tedium, weariness, pain, joy and exhilaration, all the effort to understand and grow, all the love given and received that make human life, he knew... The ambiguities, the gaps between what should be and what is, he accepted and lived from the inside, making of the whole dislocated human condition the place of response to that Love which stood beyond the barrier, asking.[1]

The great German Protestant theologian, Karl Barth, who was dismissed from his teaching position in Bonn and deported to Switzerland for refusing to sign an oath to Hitler, dedicates an ample section of his *Church Dogmatics* to the incarnation, seen through the lens of the journey of the prodigal son. Barth, in fact, makes as clear an association between Christ and the prodigal son as any prominent theologian that I have stumbled upon. He pulls this off masterfully, prefacing the entire effort by assuring us that the prodigal son's journey, "is certainly not *in any direct sense* the way of the Son of God who is obedient to the Father."[2] Yet as soon as Barth announces that the prodigal son is *not* to be associated "*in any direct sense* with the Son of God," he then dedicates several pages making the case for that very association. Let us listen to his argument:

> In the parable the son comes with his greedy and arbitrary demand, takes his inheritance from the hands of his father, [and] makes his way into a far country... This is the way of human-

ity in its breaking of the covenant with God—the way of lost Israel, of the lost "publicans and sinners," ... It is certainly not in any direct sense the way of the Son of God ... *And yet it cannot be denied that the way of the latter [Jesus, the Son of God] is in fact the way into the far country of a lost human existence*—the way in which He accepts identity and solidarity with this lost son, *unreservedly taking his place*, taking to himself his sin and shame, his transgression, as though He himself had committed it, making [the prodigal's] misery his own as though He himself had deserved it.[3]

Barth holds nothing back, stating clearly and boldly that Christ *unreservedly takes to himself the prodigal son's sin and shame*. He then follows up the affirmation with St. Paul's insightful words from the second letter to the Corinthians: "For you know the gracious act of our Lord Jesus Christ, that *for your sake he became poor* although he was rich, so that by his poverty you might become rich" (2 Cor 8:9). Christ makes an option for the poor *by becoming poor himself*. He shares in humanity's prodigal journey and misery "as though He himself had deserved it." Barth continues, "The frightfulness of this far country, the evil of the human situation, is revealed in its full depths only as it becomes His situation, that of the holy and righteous Son of God."[4]

We are the recipients of this "gracious act," that is, of Christ's loving and gratuitous solidarity, his complete "taking on" of our human situation. This is the meaning of his pilgrimage of incarnation and love into the heart of our world. It is truly unbelievable. The prodigal Christ purposely chooses to *not* remain in the safety of the heavenly realm, in the comfort of the *Abba*'s house. He does *not* want to be separated from humanity's sufferings. On the contrary, he begs from his *Abba* the right to set off on this terrible journey of love, "taking to himself [the world's] sin and shame." His deep longing is to break his life like bread and share it with alienated humanity. Put simply, he has come in search of us and to pour himself out so completely that by his poverty we might become rich.

Can we grasp the freedom of Christ's passion and love for humanity? Albert Nolan tells us that, "When we are radically free or on the way to radical freedom, divine energy can flow through us unhindered. This divine energy, which is also called the Holy Spirit, is infinitely powerful, creative, and healing. We see it at work in the prophets, the mystics, and the saints, but above all in Jesus. The Holy Spirit is Jesus' spirit."[5] The good news is that Jesus wants to give us that very same Spirit. Do we believe this? Henri Nouwen, one of contemporary Christianity's great teachers, confesses that it took him a long time to finally surrender to this most wondrous truth.

For most of my life I have struggled to find God, to know God, to love God...Now I wonder whether God has been trying to find me, to know me, and to love me. The question is not "How am I to find God?" but "How am I to let myself be found by God?"..."How am I to let myself be loved by God?" God is looking into the distance for me, trying to find me, and longing to bring me home...It might seem strange, but God wants to find me as much as, if not more than, I want to find God...I am beginning now to see how radically the character of my spiritual journey will change when I no longer think of God as hiding out and making it as difficult as possible for me to find him...Wouldn't it be good to increase God's joy by letting God find me and carry me home?[6]

Barth responds to Nouwen's question with an unequivocal "Yes." Is that not what this love story is all about? Barth is trying to break into our hard shell and convince us that Jesus takes on the prodigal son's misery precisely because of love, "as though He himself had deserved it." Does Christ's unbelievable solidarity with our human sojourn on earth not overwhelm us with awe and gratitude beyond all telling? The prodigal Christ leaves the bliss of heaven and willfully journeys into our world, accepting to be wounded by sin and injustice so that he can pour upon us his unconditional love and breathe into us the contagious freedom of his Spirit.

What is even more startling is that the good and gentle *Abba* goes so far as to "send" him on this wretched mission, without putting up a single obstacle. (In the parable, it is precisely this—the *Abba*'s attitude, the *Abba*'s love—that causes such a violent reaction in the elder son.) Is the *Abba* out of his mind or does he know something that we do not know? As the apostle John says: "God's love was revealed among us in this way: God *sent* his only Son into the world so that we might live through him. In this is love, not that we loved God but that God loved us..." (1 Jn 4:9–10). How, though, does one speak of a love that is willing to sacrifice literally *everything*, even one's own son, in order to find and bring home those who are lost?

Come follow me

Jesus does not just tell us the parable of the Prodigal Son and then set off on his merry way. As he tells the story he looks directly at us with his piercing gaze and says, "Come, follow me."[7] In other words, he does not set off into the "distant country" alone. He calls us to be his disciples, to join him on the Way. Though we are called to be servants, we are more than servants. Jesus calls us his sisters and brothers (Rom 8:29). He calls us his friends (Jn 15:15), and he invites us to announce the Reign of God with him.

> As they were going along the road, someone said to him, "I will follow you wherever you go." Jesus said to him, "Foxes have holes, and birds of the air have nests; but the Son of Man has nowhere to lay his head." To another he said, "Follow me." But he said, "Lord, first let me go and bury my father." But Jesus said to him, "Let the dead bury their own dead; but as for you, go and proclaim the kingdom of God." (Lk 9:57–60)

Jesus' call to discipleship is radical and urgent; it is not something we do "next week." It is now or never, all or nothing. *Today* we are invited to be his companions (the word "companion" is derived from two Latin words: *cum* and *panis*, meaning "with bread"). In other words, *today* we are being invited to share in Jesus' breaking of the bread, following him into the distant country in order to embrace sinners, heal the sick, and preach the good news of salvation.

Sister Thea Bowman, an African American Franciscan who died of cancer in the prime of her life and ministry, challenged the Church to truly become a *universal* community of disciples. "Go into a room," says Sr. Thea, "and look around and see who's missing, and *send some of your folks out to call them in* so that the Church can be what she claims to be, truly Catholic...I travel all over the country, and I see it: black people within the church...who are invisible...Decisions are made that affect the black community...and they're made in rooms by white people behind closed doors...How can people still have a voice and a role in the work of the Church? Isn't that what the Church is calling us all to?"[8]

As the community of disciples grows and diversifies, we gradually learn that no two disciples are cut from the same cloth. Jesus emphasizes the universal call to discipleship in a parable about a group of people who are invited to a wedding feast. The "respectable folks" are much too busy to attend, so the master says to his servant: "Go out into the roads and lanes [sometimes called "the highways and the byways"], and compel people to come in, so that my house may be filled. For I tell you, none of those who were invited will taste my dinner" (cf. Lk 14:23–24). Sr. Thea reminds us that if we truly follow Jesus we will eventually find ourselves on the outskirts of the world, what Pope Francis calls the "periphery." And if we are *not* on the periphery, we need to get there—soon.

"Send some of your folks out," insists Sister Thea. This project called the Reign of God is looking for people who are prepared to cross boundaries, people on fire for justice. This urgency to "get out into the world, to the periphery" is what Jesus' incarnation is all about; it is his passion. If we are not out in the world, smelling like sheep, says Pope Francis, then something is wrong.

> A Church that limits itself to the administrative, that only watches over its small flock, is a Church that, in the long term, becomes sick. The shepherd who locks himself in is not a true pastor for [the] sheep, but just a "hairdresser" for sheep, putting in their curlers, instead of going out to seek others... The act of getting out there to meet people also means getting out of ourselves a bit, getting away from the enclosure of our own opinions to see if they might also be... closing the door to God.[9]

Unfortunately, there are still some followers of Jesus playing with curlers, far removed from the path of true discipleship. They have misunderstood the gospel's call to selfless service, seeking instead to climb to secure a place of honor at the heavenly banquet. The older brother in the gospel parable complains about his brother's frivolous journey into the land of sin and debauchery, but he never risks a single step in the direction of those who suffer. Is that not the greatest tragedy?

As we saw earlier, when Jesus says, "Come, follow me," he is not talking about climbing a ladder to heaven. Jesus is heading *downward*, into the world of the poor, the oppressed, and those who have lost their way in life, and it is along that road that he invites us to journey with him. The people in the distant country hunger for a word of peace and a healing gesture of love. Before we get too obsessed with heaven, we are first called to be com-*pan*-ions to those who hunger for justice and mercy here on earth. "Now is the acceptable time," says St. Paul; "see, now is the day of salvation!" (2 Cor 6:2).

Our final destination is not a "destination" at all; it is a way of life, a way of being; it is what Jesus calls the "Reign of God." To be a disciple of Jesus is to set off into the world as bearers of Christ's marvelous gift of merciful love, announced in his Sermon on the Mount (Mt 5–7; cf. Lk 6:17–49). It is a radical path of obedience that leads us into the heart of humanity.

> We can say without hesitation that from [the beginning of his ministry] Jesus devoted his time, his energy, and his whole life to what he called "the reign of God." That was certainly the

core of his preaching, his deepest conviction, the passion that inspired all his activity. Everything he said and did was in the service of God's reign. That reality gave everything its coherence, true meaning, and passionate force... All the sources agree on this: Jesus in Galilee was not teaching a religious doctrine for his listeners to learn and follow. He was proclaiming an event... His goal was not to perfect the Jewish religion, but to hasten the coming of the long-awaited reign of God, which meant life, justice and peace... Jesus never said exactly what [the reign of God] was. Somehow the people guessed what he was talking about... [it] was the hope that sustained them.[10]

Christianity does, of course, speak of the promise of eternal life, but there is a lot of terrain to cover between baptism and heaven, between our first, "Here I am, Lord" and our final, "Into your hands I commend my spirit." What happens in the in-between time is what we call "discipleship," and though there are thousands of ways to live Jesus' call to discipleship, they all have one thing in common: they eventually lead us into the distant country of sin and suffering, of violence and injustice. This is the great and unavoidable mystery, the liberating path that will eventually lead us into the heart of God.

Most of the religious leaders of Jesus' day are convinced that one is supposed to avoid contact with sin and sinners at all cost, which is why Jesus' healing embrace of our fallen world is so scandalous to them. Few understand the prodigal Son's disregard for proper religious protocol and his urgency to set off on his mission of healing and freedom. Only the *Abba* gets it, which is why he smiles with a deep and loving joy. The Son's journey of radical love will eventually get him (and us) into trouble, but not even that is too terribly worrisome. After all, we believe in the resurrection.

We are there because of Jesus

In 1996, three months after seven Trappist monks from the monastery of Tibherine, Algeria, were brutally beheaded,[11] the latest victims in the long and complicated history of colonial and interreligious violence that has plagued Algeria for decades, our Dominican brother, Pierre Claverie, the bishop of the diocese of Oran, Algeria, was also assassinated, along with his Muslim friend of many years, Muhammad. A few weeks before their tragic deaths, Bishop Claverie, preaching to a community of Dominican nuns in the south of France, responded to the concerns of some of his friends and colleagues who were asking why someone would stay in Algeria, risking so much, in the midst of such violence. Bishop Claverie spoke from the heart:

> Through the dramatic events in Algeria, I have often been asked: "What are you doing there? Why do you stay? Shake off the dust from your sandals. Come back home."
>
> Home...Where are we at home?...We are there for the sake of the crucified Messiah. We're not there for any other reason, or for any other person. We have no interests to protect, no influence to maintain...We have no power, but are there as at the bedside of a friend, of a sick brother, silently holding his hand or wiping his brow. We are there for the sake of Jesus, because he is the one suffering there amid violence that spares no one, crucified again and again in the flesh of thousands of innocents...Isn't it essential for Christians to be present in desolate and abandoned places?[12]

Pierre Claverie, like the Trappist monks of Algeria, knew what it meant to go into the heart of the "distant country" and run the risk of life and death alongside those who live that reality day in and day out. These modern disciples of Jesus show us that to be faithful one must be willing to follow the footsteps of the Master all the way to the end. Jesus sets off into this broken world of sin and violence to open up a path of love, and as he walks he beckons us to follow him in radical faith. An incarnate faith is not possible without the willingness to risk. In the words of Japanese Dominican friar Shigeto Oshida, "Faith... issues forth from the reality of the unbreakable clasp of God's hand with ours—in all nakedness and mercy. This grasp is unbreakable because even when a sinner is still a sinner, God is constantly reaching out with everlasting mercy."[13]

Claverie and Oshida remind us of two essential truths: First, God is always faithful. And second, one cannot be a true Christian and live risk-free, loving his or her neighbor from "a prudent distance." Love requires *proximity*, as Pope Francis often says, and proximity requires the willingness to risk all for God. Jesus risked everything when he set off for the distant country. Incarnation is not supposed to be pretty. It is about entering into the messy world of brokenness and sin: "The Word became flesh and lived among us..." (Jn 1:14). The Incarnate Word is a fire that both heals us and burns us; it is all or nothing. "Jesus brings us with him into the heart of chaos through the cross," Claverie says, while, "the Spirit keeps open the wound of love that nothing can heal or assuage."[14]

Perhaps the question that each of us has to eventually ask is: Am I willing to be wounded by love? The prodigal son's pilgrimage into the land of poverty and exile ends with a cry, not so unlike the cry of the crucified Jesus: "Here I am dying of hunger" (Lk 15:17). Jesus is doing nothing more than putting into practice his words from the Sermon on the Mount, "Blessed are those who hunger and thirst for righteousness" (Mt 5:6). Are we willing to enter into that burning hunger and thirst for a more just world, even to the point of "dying" for it?

Jerome A. Miller, writing about the need to find a way out of the unending cycle of violence and revenge that plagues our world, addresses Christ directly: "The Incarnation [testifies to] your will to 'descend' into the world, [as] the flow of love out of yourself and into human history... When You pour your love into history You hold nothing back... You become the violated [person] with whom you identify... Your response to the wound that cries out to heaven would be to divinize it—to pour your love into it so that it becomes You."[15]

Jesus, as he draws near and fully embraces our world, invites us to walk this path with him, making his loving embrace our own: "I do not call you servants any longer, because the servant does not know what the master is doing; but I have called you *friends*, because I have made known to you everything that I have heard from my Father" (Jn 15:15). He calls us to follow him into the heart of the world, to share in the same risks that the world faces. "No one has greater love than this, to lay down one's life for one's friends" (Jn 15:13). He lives with us here in the "distant country," begging and wandering with us from village to village, announcing good news to the poor, proclaiming release to captives and recovery of sight to the blind, letting the oppressed go free (cf. Lk 4:18–19). He does this because we are his friends. He shares our tears and our laughter, our joys and our hopes. It is a dangerous path, one that he embraces with love.

One time when he was asked why he had convened the Second Vatican Council, Pope John XXIII did not respond with lofty theological words. He told the world that he simply wanted to do what Jesus had done: make the human journey on earth a little less sad. We are sent into the world to embrace the world:

> By the tender mercy of our God,
>   the dawn from on high will break upon us,
> to give light to those who sit in darkness and in the shadow of death,
>   to guide our feet into the way of peace.
>   (Lk 1:78–79)

What does it mean to follow Jesus "into the heart of chaos," to use Bishop Claverie's phrase, knowing that our discipleship, if lived faithfully, will plunge us into the world's chaos, leaving us wounded by love? The prodigal Christ finds himself wounded and dying of hunger, precisely because he accepts being the *Abba*'s incarnation of love in the midst of a broken and sinful world. He embraces suffering not as a good in itself, but as a consequence of his mission to love unconditionally. It will ultimately lead to his being deserted by some of his disciples and left to die, his side pierced with a soldier's spear (Jn 19:34). What person in his or her right mind is willing to be wounded so as to be faithful to the commandment of love? Don't the self-help books say that we should do everything possible to protect ourselves from suffering?

God made Jesus to be sin

Saul of Tarsus, who first appears in the New Testament as the tragic enemy of the good news of Christ, dedicated to destroying the beautiful garden of love that Jesus has sown among his followers, becomes the "new man" *par excellence* after his unforgettable encounter with the Risen Christ on the road to Damascus (Acts 9:1–20). Yes, Saul—the the card-carrying enemy of Jesus and his friends—finally stumbles upon the mystery of God's eternal and unconditional love made manifest in Christ Jesus. He who was once lost in the darkest realm of the distant country is, through the sheer grace of God, sought out by the prodigal Christ and carried home to God's infinite mercy on the shoulders of the crucified Shepherd of Israel. Saved by the blood of the Lamb and given a new name, St. Paul finally rises from the realm of those who are dead because of sin and hatred to announce the good news of God's radical and inclusive love to the whole world:

> There is no longer Jew or Greek, there is no longer slave or
>   free, there is no longer
> male and female; for *all* of you are one in Christ Jesus."
>   (Gal 3:28)

Paul's conversion breaks him open, allowing him to finally understand that Jesus chooses to descend into the heart of sinful humanity, into the hell that is sin, for no other reason than to incarnate here, among us, God's universal heart of love. Descending into this holy mess is the mysterious path that God takes to search us out and bring us home. The light of Christ finally heals Paul's blindness: "My grace is sufficient for you, for power is made perfect in weakness" (2 Cor 12:9).

In his letter to the Galatians, Paul recalls a line from scripture that once directed his life of bigotry and violence, hidden beneath a veil of religious legalism: "Cursed is everyone who does not observe and obey all the things written in the book of the law" (Gal 3:10). The old Saul was, of course, just trying to be a good Jew, following obediently the book of Deuteronomy's stern warning: "'Cursed be anyone who fails to fulfill any of the provisions of this law.' And all the people shall answer, 'Amen!'" (Deut 27:26). Before his conversion, Saul truly believed that those who did not follow every letter of the Law were cursed. That was, of course, before God's "amazing grace" finally tracked him down, turning his neat and tidy world upside-down so that the old Saul could be born anew.

> Now it is evident that no one is justified before God by the law...Christ redeemed us from the curse of the law by *becoming a curse for us*, for it is written, "Cursed is everyone who hangs on a tree"—in order that in Christ Jesus...we might receive the promise of the Spirit through faith. (Gal 3:11–14)

God bless our brother, Paul. We have to admit that he does a lot of holy wandering and struggles with an army of inner demons before he finally stumbles upon the truth. His admission of blindness is an act of great humility and courage. He never gives up. He never stops listening to God's voice and seeking the truth. Even in the midst of all the contradictions, Saul keeps believing, keeps saying his prayers, until God finally breaks through. The same hardheaded Saul who mercilessly judged those who did not follow the law perfectly finally understands that "Jesus *becomes a curse* so that we can be saved from the curse" (Gal 3:13). And again, to the disciples in Corinth, he writes: "For our sake *God made him to be sin who knew no sin*, so that in him we might become the righteousness of God" (2 Cor 5:21). "Welcome home, brother Paul! Let the Church say, 'Amen!'"

Seeing the picture more clearly

The two texts from St. Paul mentioned above, namely Galatians 3:13 and 2 Corinthians 5:21, finally brought to a happy conclusion my long treasure hunt for the truth. At last I had received an answer to the curious question that I had posed to my brother, Alberto, many years earlier. As mentioned in the introduction to this book, it was the earth-shattering experience of hearing the father of the prodigal son say, "This son of mine was dead and is alive again" (Lk 15:24) that sent me scurrying to ask Alberto if the prodigal son could possibly be a symbol of Jesus, risen from the dead. "Impossible!" he said emphatically: "The prodigal son is a sinner and Jesus is not." Alberto was right, of course: Jesus clearly is *not a sinner*. But Alberto was not *completely* right either.

Thanks to St. Paul, we are able to see the picture more clearly. Though it is true that Christ never *sinned*, it is also true that "God made Jesus *to be sin* who knew no sin" (2 Cor 5:21). In other words, though Jesus is not a sinner in an *essential* way, we can say with utter conviction that he so completely and compassionately embraces us, taking on our sin in a singular act of solidarity, that he is finally judged a reprobate and crucified as a sinner (Gal 3:13). The Roman and Jewish hierarchs, working in tandem, execute Jesus publicly to humiliate him, portraying him as a sinner and a criminal.

Of course, in some ways Jesus' enemies *are* telling the truth. The prodigal Christ, desiring nothing more than to search for us, the lost sheep of his beloved flock, *does* cross the picket line. In other words he immerses himself so fully into our sinful world that he ends up looking a lot like one of us, a sinner amongst sinners. Because of this unbelievable compassion and solidarity, Jesus is finally accused, condemned, cursed, and nailed to the tree of the cross—as a sinner. He ends his life in the most distant of countries—the cursed realm of one who "is hung on a tree" (Deut 21:23). That curse, strangely enough, is our greatest hope; it is our saving grace. The prodigal Christ, the cursed one who hangs on a tree, is finally revealed to us as the Savior of the world. It is a mystery that has confused humanity for two thousand years, a paradox that we profess each year at the beginning of the Easter Vigil celebration: "O *felix culpa*. Oh truly necessary sin of Adam, destroyed completely by the death of Christ. Oh happy fault that earned so great, so glorious a Redeemer..."[16]

Paul is not the only one who has to struggle with this very strange good news. Peter has *his* battle with inner demons, as well. One day, while praying on the roof of his house (probably a nice, cool place to pray) Peter has a vision, which at first seems more like a nightmare. He sees all kinds of unclean animals: four-footed creatures, reptiles and birds, and worse yet, he hears a voice telling him:

> "Get up, Peter; kill and eat." But Peter said, "By no means, Lord; for I have never eaten anything that is profane or unclean." The voice said to him again, a second time, "What God has made clean, you must not call profane." (Acts 10:13–15)

At about the same time that Peter is having his dream/revelation some folks from Joppa knock on his door to tell him that Cornelius, a Gentile, is expecting a visit from Peter in the town of Joppa. Peter is sure that all of these strange hallucinations are the devil's trickery, because good Jews do not hang out with Gentiles, no matter how nice they are. Again the voice speaks to him: "Now get up, go down, and go with them without hesitation; for I have sent them" (Acts 10:20). Peter finally gets the message and sets off to visit Cornelius and his family. While at the house of Cornelius they share a meal together—something unheard of for any law-abiding Jew. At the end of the meal Peter stands up, clears his throat and speaks, "I truly understand that God shows no partiality, but in every nation anyone who fears him and does what is right is acceptable to him" (Acts 10:34–35). Peter's legalistic faith crumbles before his very eyes, revealing to him the God of infinite mercy. Without knowing exactly how, he realizes that he has crossed the border into the "distant country" called *grace*. What once seemed evil and untouchable becomes the very place where he hears God's good news.

Breaking the bread of life in the distant country

During the decade of the 1990s, while living in Latin America, the brothers of my Dominican community and I volunteered several days a week at a hospice for homeless men and women, most of whom were street people, all suffering and most dying as a result of HIV/AIDS. On some days our brother Kevin would spend the morning at the hospice bathing, shaving, and giving haircuts to the men. They loved "Hermano Kevin," whose Irish humor could make a wooden chair laugh. Our brother Jim and I alternated on different days, spending time with the patients, listening to their stories—most of which were terribly tragic—and celebrating the Eucharist for the sisters, the staff, and the patients of the hospice.

There is a day that I will never forget. As I was moving from bed to bed, visiting with the patients, I noticed a very tall, elderly black man, who had just arrived the day before. He was very thin and walked with great difficulty. We chatted a bit, and he told me that he had lived for many years on the streets. Seeing that he was still quite exhausted with the transition to his "new home," and noticing that it was about time to get ready for Mass, I mentioned to him that there was a celebration of the Eucharist each day in the small chapel. I pointed out the chapel door and told him that if he ever wanted to attend Mass, he was certainly welcome.

I visited a few more people and then left to prepare for Mass. About halfway through the scripture readings, I saw the tall, elderly black man enter through the chapel door, walking slowly with a cane. He sat down in the last pew in the chapel. I remember the moment well, given that he was a head taller than everyone else. Even though he was quite sick, he was very attentive during Mass. Communion time came, which was always something of a three-ring circus at the hospice. There were patients with canes and others with walkers. Most shuffled with difficulty to communion, and frequently those who could walk pushed another person's wheelchair. Many years later I still remember those Masses as a marvelous image of broken humanity hearing the voice of God and walking together, helping one another on the journey toward the Reign of God.

As people began coming up the aisle for communion, I happened to notice that the new patient, the elderly black man, had stood up and was slowly shuffling down the aisle. He was the very last one in line. I can still see his face as he made his way toward the altar. Though he looked tired, the expression on his face was filled with a luminous hope, as if crying out with joy, "I am home. Thank you, Lord Jesus. At last I am home." Suddenly—almost violently—one of the hospice workers jumped up and yanked the elderly man out of the communion line, forcefully sitting him down. Needless to say, I was aghast. Rather than interrupt communion, though, I waited to talk to the worker after Mass. When I asked her about the incident, she replied in a very matter-of-fact way, "He isn't prepared to receive communion." That was all. She spoke with a certainty that shocked me, as if she could see into the innermost recesses of this man's soul and make a judgment as to his ability to receive God's mercy and unconditional love. I was utterly speechless. I could not erase from my mind the image of the man's luminous face crying out, "I am home. I am home. Finally, I have come home." Two days later, after receiving communion, he died.

The experience in the hospice that day shook me to my roots. Thanks to God, it ended beautifully. He received communion and died in peace. As a follower of Jesus and as a person who has seen much suffering in our world, I never want to forget this incident, but neither do I want to ever see it repeated. I did eventually speak with the hospice worker, a person very committed to the poor, and tried to help her understand the implications of what she had done. I remember asking her, "Did you by chance look at his face? Did you see his eyes as he was coming, with great difficulty, to receive communion? Did you take into consideration the fact that he is a human being, loved by God, before you judged him unworthy to receive the Body of Christ? Can anyone know the spiritual state of another person's soul?" Her response seemed almost rehearsed: "He has been living in the streets. We know our people."

How easily we can fall into the temptation to approach the heart of another human being as if it were some *thing* we can discuss and make a judgment about, like one might do when discussing the day's movement in the stock market. Behind every human heart there is a person, a story—and above all, the presence of God. When, through the mouth of the prophet Ezekiel, the Lord asked the shepherds of Israel, "Where are the sheep that I left in your care?" they had no answer. The sheep were a *thing* to them; they did not know where they were, because the sheep were not important to them. It had never occurred to them to go and search for the lost sheep; it was "none of their business." Then God spoke:

> Thus says the Lord God: "Ah, you shepherds of Israel who have been feeding yourselves. Should not shepherds feed the sheep? You eat the fat, you clothe yourselves with the wool, you slaughter the fatlings; but you do not feed the sheep. You have not strengthened the weak, you have not healed the sick ...you have not sought the lost, but with force and harshness you have ruled them. So they were scattered, because there was no shepherd...they became food for all the wild animals... My sheep were scattered over all the face of the earth, with no one to search or seek for them." (Ez 34:2–6)

Are we not all trying to see and follow Jesus, the same Jesus whom the elderly man at Mass hungered to be with after many years of wandering, lost in a world of rejection and suffering? Tired and sick, he wanted nothing more than to *be found*, to *come home*. Had Jesus not set off to search for him at Mass that day, like the Good Shepherd who seeks out the one lost sheep, in order to welcome him home and feed him at the table of God's mercy (cf. Lk 15:3–7; Jn 10:11–18)? What did Jesus experience that day when he discovered that a wall had been erected around the eucharistic table of love, keeping this very sick man from reaching the bread of life? Why would anyone interrupt the spiritual homecoming of a wounded human heart? Does God not long for *all of us* to come home? Does the Good Shepherd not go out to search the hills and valleys, refusing to rest, even if it is for just *one* lost sheep? Pope Francis sums up his dream for the Church with these words:

> I dream of a church that is a mother and shepherdess. The church's ministers must be merciful, take responsibility for the people and accompany them like the Good Samaritan, who washes, cleans and raises up his neighbor. This is pure Gospel. God is greater than sin. The structural and organizational reforms are secondary—that is, they come afterward. The first reform must be the attitude. The ministers of the Gospel must be people who can warm the hearts of the people, who walk

through the dark night with them, who know how to dialogue and to descend themselves into their people's night, into the darkness, but without getting lost. The people of God want shepherds, not clergy acting like bureaucrats or government officials.[17]

These pages are an attempt to grapple with what it means to follow Jesus today in an imperfect, complicated, and beautiful world. Jesus, as we know, was no stranger to imperfect worlds and messy politics. He tells the parable of the Prodigal Son precisely in response to people who are complaining about the growing group of rather suspicious friends with whom Jesus is sharing table fellowship. Jesus, the prodigal Son of God, is not afraid to cross borders and boundaries. He *begs* his *Abba* to let him go into the heart of our broken world to search for us, the lost sheep, carrying with him the bread of life, the bread of his unconditional love and compassion. His greatest joy is to share that bread with all— the poor, the outcasts, prostitutes, tax collectors, prisoners, sex offenders, sinners, saints, you and me and everybody in between. In his *Abba*'s house there is bread enough for all. That is why he can say with utter confidence, "I am the bread of life. Whoever comes to me will never be hungry, and whoever believes in me will never be thirsty" (Jn 6:35).

5

Becoming a Neighbor

Jesus went about all the cities and villages, teaching in their synagogues, and proclaiming the good news of the kingdom, and curing every disease and every sickness. When he saw the crowds, he had compassion for them, because they were harassed and helpless, like sheep without a shepherd. (Mt 9:35–36)

"When he *saw* the crowds..." The prodigal Christ's journeys through the many towns and villages offer him abundant opportunities to be a neighbor to those whom he meets along the way. Each compassionate response, each helping hand, each healing touch and shared piece of bread is Jesus' way of responding in love, while also serving as a teaching for the disciples who accompany him. Once again we are invited to learn from Jesus' open-eyed mission of compassion. Recally the gospel incident in which, having turned toward the woman who is anointing his feet with her tears, Jesus asks Simon, the Pharisee, "Simon, do you *see* this woman" (Lk 7:44)? Jesus sees and hears what the world, lost in its busy-ness and tragic indifference, frequently ignores.

Jesus does nothing less than incarnate the same attentive love that his *Abba* has shown from the beginning of history, as manifested in the encounter at the foot of Mt. Horeb in the desert between Moses and God in a burning bush:

The Lord said, "I have observed the misery of my people who are in Egypt; I have heard their cry on account of their taskmasters. Indeed, I know their sufferings, and I have come down to deliver them from the Egyptians, and to bring them up out of that land to a good and broad land, a land flowing with milk and honey..." (Ex 3:7–8)

Israel knows that God is with them, that God is aware of their suffering and their hardships, their oppression and their cry for freedom. A sign of the ongoing importance of this story of God's liberating and healing love for the people of Israel, all the way up to the time of Jesus, is that it forms part of the long discourse that Stephen preaches to the high priest and the Sanhedrin in the final minutes of his life, as he prepares for martyrdom:

> Listen to me... an angel appeared to Moses in the wilderness of Mount Sinai... The Lord said to him, "Take off the sandals from your feet, for the place where you are standing is holy ground. I have surely *seen* the mistreatment of my people who are in Egypt and have *heard* their groaning, and I have come down to rescue them... You stiff-necked people, uncircumcised in heart and ears, you are forever opposing the Holy Spirit, just as your ancestors used to do. Which of the prophets did your ancestors not persecute?" (Acts 7:2, 30, 33–34, 51–52)

God saw Israel's suffering and heard their cry for freedom. We will never be able to respond to our neighbor if we do not see him or her. If we do not hear the cry of the poor, rising up from the desperate and neglected corners of the distant country, how will we answer that cry with a word of hope, a piece of bread, a healing embrace? This is the crucial issue in the final judgment scenario found toward the end of the gospel of Matthew.

> "Lord, when was it that we saw you hungry and gave you food, or thirsty and gave you something to drink? And when was it that we saw you a stranger and welcomed you, or naked and gave you clothing? And when was it that we saw you sick or in prison and visited you?" And the king will answer them, "Truly I tell you, just as you did it to one of the least of these who are members of my family, you did it to me." (Mt 25:37–40)

The Church cannot offer good news to the world if it is blind and deaf to the faces and voices that call to us from the edge of the world. In the first letter of John we see how crucial was this link between attentiveness to the plight of the poor and the preaching of the good news: "We declare to you what was from the beginning, what we have heard, what we have seen with our eyes, what we have looked at and touched with our hands, concerning the word of life—this life was revealed, and we have seen it and testify to it..." (1 Jn 1:1–2). When we see and hear and touch our neighbor, we see and hear and touch Christ, the incarnate Word of God.

A number of years ago, while living in Peru, I attended a series of events at the Catholic University in Lima, celebrating the fiftieth anniversary of the Universal Declaration of Human Rights. On one of the days I attended a photo exhibit of Peruvian children who had suffered during Peru's twenty years of war and internal violence that left nearly seventy thousand people dead. The exhibit consisted of dozens of panels, each with thirty of forty large black-and-white photographs, some of which were accompanied by quotes from the child in the photograph. I spent several hours contemplating these faces filled with suffering. I was particularly captivated by one powerful photograph; it was of a young boy who was clearly malnourished and poor. Beneath his photo the small card read:

> "*Saben que yo existo, pero nadie me ve.*"
> "They know I exist, but no one sees me."
> —Gabriel, eight years of age

Almost more than the picture itself, Gabriel's words pierced my heart. They were so true. Like numberless children throughout the world, he knew he was invisible, not important enough to be noticed by the structures of power. It took the contemplative eyes of a photographer to *see* little Gabriel and to take the time to ask his name and speak with him, to remind him that he was a human being. So many people like Gabriel appear on the flow charts of sociology textbooks and in the registers of national and international statistics, but do we *see* them? They are numbers, but are they human beings?

Invisibility is one of the greatest tragedies of our times. Huge swaths of humanity appear on no one's radar screen, because they are not important, because they do not produce anything that interests the market. Is indifference not the greatest blindness of all? St. Catherine of Siena once cried out to God in one of her prayers, "Give my eyes a fountain of tears with which to draw down your mercy over all the world,"[1] to which God responded, "Bring, then, your tears and sweat, you and my other servants. Draw them from the fountain of my divine love and use them to wash the face of my bride."[2] We will never be able to wash the wounded face of our world if we do not first *see* our neighbor who suffers. Maybe what we need most of all is to pray for the gift of tears, to be healed first of our own spiritual blindness so that we can reach out in compassion to the wounded Christ in our neighbor.

God is helplessly in love with us

The prodigal Christ travels to the distant country of poverty and brokenness first of all because he knows it exists. The world of the "other" is not absent from his radar screen. He is sent by his *Abba* as the incarnate Word of God, to be present in their midst, in their world. He is aware that there are real people who live there, people who are like sheep without a shepherd, people who suffer. He wants to get to know them and befriend them. It is not enough for him to just know that they exist as anonymous human beings in a world plagued by indifference. There is urgency in his request; he must go. "*Abba*, I want to go to the people in the distant country." His mission is born from his awareness, his attentiveness, his longing to love these people who experience this painful distance from God. He travels to the faraway land out of love, to be with them, speak with them, love them, break bread with them. He knows that it is a dangerous thing to do, and he risks suffering greatly, but it is worth that risk.

God, who always wants to be with us, contemplates us like a mother who watches with great joy as her children build sand castles on the beach. This is our tenderhearted God who "sends" the beloved Son into the world so that the *Abba*'s own heart can be close to us. Do we dare let ourselves be overwhelmed by this unfathomable, liberating love—offered to us unconditionally? In his book, *Faith within Reason*, Herbert McCabe suggests that God's love is not so complicated after all:

> God, the real God, is just helplessly and hopelessly in love with us...His love doesn't depend on what we do or what we are like. He doesn't care whether we are sinners or not. He is just waiting to welcome us with joy and love. Sin doesn't alter God's attitude to us; it alters our attitude to [God]...We change him from the God who is simply love and nothing else, into this punitive ogre, this Satan...[3]

Could it be that this entire venture is much simpler than we ever imagined? Maybe the prodigal Christ has come searching for us in the distant country not to *explain* some great and complicated mystery to us, but simply to surprise us with love. "I came so that they might have life and have it more abundantly" (Jn 10:10 NAB).

What a great tragedy to not be able to understand love for love's sake. The older brother in the parable of the Prodigal Son has spent his entire life *earning* his *Abba*'s love by hard work, and now—suddenly—

his world has been turned upside-down. How dare his younger brother treat life so lightly, so irresponsibly!

True love, of course, is always a free gift, a scandalously gratuitous gift. We cannot possibly *earn* God's love, any more than we can *earn* the rays of morning sun that warm us on a cold day. We just soak in the gift with gratitude. Can we ever make sense of God's gratuitous love?

As McCabe says, God "is just helplessly and hopelessly in love with us." Is this not what Jonah finally discovered when he found himself confounded by God's mercy and love, sitting under a wilted gourd plant that God used to trick him into conversion (Jon 4:6–8)? God's plan to convert Nineveh made no sense whatsoever to Jonah. "What did you say, Lord? Did you say the Ninevites? Are you crazy?" In Jonah's mind it was a waste of time and energy, a lost cause from the very beginning. You cannot love people who are lost in sin. Is God out of his mind?

God pursued poor Jonah relentlessly, though, until he had no other option but to surrender to God's crazy plan of love. Jonah eventually becomes an instrument of God's grace in spite of himself. He finally realizes that he cannot understand the mind of God, and *that* is what sets him free for God. The illusion that we can *possess* the truth and know all the answers leads to a kind of fundamentalism that deafens us to hearing the voice of the living God. Once truth is possessed, it no longer is a vehicle of grace; it can no longer set us free. Timothy Radcliffe reminds us that:

> Truth is both revealed and yet beyond us. We cannot master it, or simply take possession of it. Thomas Aquinas stated—and this is the very heart of his theology—"What God is, we cannot say." Words cannot enclose God; they can only let us approach the edge of the mystery... Augustine said, "God is always more."[4]

So, though it seems like God keeps making the same mistakes, calling the same weak people to do this really important divine work of salvation, what is happening in the background of this story is the slow and gentle work of grace. Grace, as was noted in an earlier chapter, is like a river that "streams forth as ineffable love"[5] without calling a lot of attention to itself. Grace is God's shy side, quietly teaching the world to trust the flow of *love*.

Learning to walk in the direction of grace

While the older brother in the parable is preoccupied by what he and his brother *should* and *should not* do, the younger brother is already on his way to the distant country. He is not afraid to set off into the unknown, to take risks, to make mistakes. Could it be that he somehow intuits that love walks ahead of him?

Our journey, thankfully, is not along an uncharted path, and that is a great consolation. The one who is the *way, the truth and the life* (Jn 14:6) walks both ahead of us and with us. It does not matter if we are heading to Nineveh or to some other "distant land" of struggle and hope, we walk confident that Jesus' amazing grace is with us. That is his promise: "I am with you always" (Mt 28:20). Thanks to the prodigal Jesus, the path to the distant country has already been trod. Our task is to follow.

God is simply love and nothing else. That is our good news, our daily bread. When Jesus looks out at those who are responding to his call, all he sees are children of God, loved by God—each and every one a unique mixture of clay and divine breath, of sin and grace. There are not *pure* people and *impure* people, just *people* made in God's image. Jesus calls *everyone* to discipleship. That is the radical novelty of his movement. Jesus' new school is called "the Way" (Acts 9:2) precisely because discipleship is a verb for Jesus—not a *thing*. There is no "discipleship diploma" to hang on the wall; you just *do* it, step by step.

Jesus' call, then, is rather simple: he invites us to set off walking toward grace, and if we take a couple of steps in the direction of sin, we simply laugh at our awkward selves, tell one of the other disciples along the way that we have stumbled, then *turn around* (conversion, *metanoia*) and keep walking. In this school, who is the sinner? Who is the saint? There are only people learning day by day what it means to be a disciple. That is, of course, bad news for the scribes and Pharisees, because they suddenly begin to realize that with that kind of religious worldview they may soon be unemployed!

For Jesus, this school of discipleship takes place not exclusively in the desert, as some thought, but in the sacrament of daily life (cf. Acts 2:42–47). "The coming of the kingdom of God cannot be observed," says Jesus, "and no one will announce, 'Look, here it is,' or, 'There it is' ... The kingdom of God is among you" (Lk 17:20–21). Jesus teaches us that God is not a goal that we hope someday to reach. God is the world where we "live and move and have our being" (Acts 17:28). God is here and now, present in each and every breath.

Conversion, then, is about sharpening our spiritual senses so that we can *see* the path of grace and walk in it. It seems that the principal rite of initiation that Jesus leaves in place consists basically of two words: "Follow me" (Lk 5:27, 9:23, 9:59, 18:22, etc.). The rest unfolds naturally, organically—along the way—with his words "I am with you always" tucked into our travel bag (Mt 28:20). And if, at this point, you are beginning to think that this *might not be very easy,* you are probably right.

Washing feet along the way

Pope Francis gives us some encouragement as we set off on our "prodigal journey" by reminding us to not be afraid to wander out toward the many "peripheries" of humanity, and to be ready to set off with Jesus on "the Way." Through his humble faith and Christ-like gestures he spells out his vision of a Church dedicated to the radical practice of mercy, compassion, and unconditional love.

In the first two years of his pontificate, to mention only one of dozens of examples, he has chosen to celebrate the ceremonial Holy Thursday washing of the feet among the poor, recalling Jesus' humble gesture of washing the feet of his disciples the day before he was crucified. Is he not reminding these poor women and men that they, too, are disciples with a mission in the world, and that their feet are being washed and anointed for service to their neighbor? For millions of Christians around the world, the image of a pope on his knees, washing the feet of juvenile offenders, the disabled, immigrants, and the elderly is very powerful, very Christ-like. We usually associate being on our knees with prayer, which it surely is. True prayer leads to a true living out of the gospel. Pope Francis offers us an icon of the paschal Christ who prayerfully pours out his life in loving service. In fact, he goes on to say that, "Only those who have first allowed Jesus to wash their own feet can offer this service to others."[6]

On his second Holy Thursday in Rome (2014), the Vatican communicated that the Holy Father had washed the feet of nine Italians, an Ethiopian woman, a Muslim from Libya, and a young man from Cape Verde, all of whom suffer from different illnesses. Preaching during the Mass, the pope spoke of Jesus as a servant, saying, "He has made this road for love; you also ought to love . . . and be servants of one another. This is the legacy that Jesus leaves us." The Holy Father went on to remind those present that in washing the disciples' feet, Jesus was taking on the role of a slave.[7]

"He has made this road for love; you also ought to love . . ." Pope Francis is reminding us that we are called to imitate Jesus' self-emptying love and his descent into the world of the poor and sinners, so that we can embrace Christ in the distressing disguise of the poor, to use a phrase dear to Mother Teresa of Calcutta. His drawing near to embrace the outcasts of our world today—men and women, Christians and non-Christians, young and old, sinner and saint—is a prophetic sign in a Church called to give witness to the mercy and compassion of Christ.

Pope John Paul II evoked a similar image when, in 1983, he visited the prison cell of Mehmet Ali Agca, the Turkish man who had attempted to assassinate him two years earlier. His visit and the pardon of his would-be assassin reflect Christ's own humility and mercy. Are not such images of tenderness and compassion needed in our Church and world today, as violence and revenge increasingly become routine?

Several years ago, I read an article about a woman whose husband was one of hundreds (perhaps thousands) of political prisoners imprisoned, tortured, and held indefinitely during the brutal years of the Somoza dictatorship in Nicaragua, with no access to a legal process or to lawyers. The woman faithfully visited her husband and other prisoners for years, taking them food and clothing, and most of all gifting them with her gentle presence and conversation. The Sandinista revolution finally ousted General Somoza, and the country's political prisoners were set free.

Unfortunately, history repeats itself in ugly and tragic ways. Not long after the triumph of the revolution, the prison cells filled again with political prisoners from the other side of the political divide—those who had formed part of the Somoza dictatorship. The wife of the now-freed Sandinista fighter was overjoyed to have her husband back home again but, as a wife and mother whose faith in the God of unconditional love knew no divisions, she could not rest, knowing that those same prison cells were filled again with a new batch of political prisoners. Even though she knew that her decision would be severely criticized, she continued to visit the prison, taking food and clothing to the new prisoners, some of whom may very likely have been responsible for her husband's suffering and torture. She did not let "political correctness" get in her way; she shared the mercy of Jesus with prisoners from both sides of the political divide. She was sure of "the one thing" that really mattered: the voices that spoke to her from those dark, godforsaken cells were the same voice that she had heard proclaimed in the gospel: "I was in prison and you visited me" (Mt 25:36).

Words like grace, mercy, and unconditional love are not easily understood in a world where revenge is revered almost as a "human right." I have no doubt that Pope John Paul II was criticized by some in the Church for his show of what some probably labeled "cheap mercy" toward the man who had tried to kill him. After all, it could appear that the Church is being "soft" on sin. There have been criticisms of Pope Francis's Holy Thursday gestures of tenderness and mercy as well. I wonder if there were outcries of "political and liturgical incorrectness" when Jesus forgave the repentant thief who pleaded from the cross: "Jesus, remember me when you come into your kingdom" (Lk 23:42)?

Are we who follow Jesus willing to risk our reputation and our very lives by practicing radical mercy, even when it is not popular? I wept with joy some years ago when I read about the solidarity shown toward a young girl in grade school who lost all of her hair after undergoing several rounds of chemotherapy. When she returned to school, she was shocked to discover that all of her classmates had shaved their heads too! Now that is truly creative compassion.

It is important to remember that Jesus tells the parables of Luke 15 in response to criticisms regarding his friendliness with sinners, which in his day was not only a serious religious offense, but politically suspicious, too. If you hang out with sinners you probably are one. That people are scandalized in the year 2014 because a pope washes the feet of a Muslim woman on Holy Thursday clearly suggests that we have not yet heard the gospel in its fullest sense. Jesus shocks his fellow Jews in a similar way one day when he criticizes their lukewarm faith while *praising* the faith of the poor and outcast:

> I thank you, *Abba*, Lord of heaven and earth, because you have hidden these things from the wise and the intelligent and have revealed them to infants; yes, *Abba*, for such was your gracious will...Come to me, all you that are weary and are carrying heavy burdens, and I will give you rest. (Mt 11:25–26, 28).

Jesus invites *anybody* who is weary and burdened to come to him. His heart is universal, and when he invites "all you that are weary and are carrying heavy burdens" he means everybody. The word "all" *does* mean "all" after all. Jesus befriends sinners, stands with a woman condemned to death, breaks his bread with foreigners, touches lepers, shares the *living water* of his love with a Samaritan woman, heals on the Sabbath, calls a tax collector to be an apostle, and the list goes on and on. And we are upset because the pope washes the feet of a Muslim woman? Should we not be dancing with joy? The Jesuit Gregory Boyle says:

> Jesus' strategy is a simple one: he eats with [sinners and outcasts]...He goes where love has not yet arrived...Jesus didn't seek the rights of lepers. He *touched* the leper even before he got around to curing him. He didn't champion the cause of the outcast. He *was* the outcast. He didn't fight for improved conditions for the prisoner. He simply said, "I was in prison."[8]

Mercy, mercy, mercy

Once, while preaching a retreat to priests, Archbishop Fulton Sheen was asked to focus one of his retreat conferences on the theme of reconciliation. Sheen, a world-renowned preacher, stood up in the pulpit and gave a conference that probably lasted less than thirty seconds. This is what he preached: "Mercy... Mercy... Mercy." When he finished saying those three words, he sat down. I suspect that it was one of the most powerful conferences given during the entire retreat. Archbishop Sheen had understood the heart of Christ. "The Church is called to be the house... with doors *always* wide open,"[9] says Pope Francis. Is this not just another way of saying, "Mercy... Mercy... Mercy"?

Cardinal Walter Kasper, in a recent reflection on mercy and the parable of the Good Samaritan, reminds us that the Church must always move from the *theology* of mercy to its *praxis* in everyday life.

> The customary perspective in theology starts from above... Mercy leads us to... start not from above but from below ... When Jesus was asked, "Who is my neighbor?" he did not give an abstract answer. He told a concrete story, the story of the good and merciful Samaritan (Lk 10:30–37)... This is exactly how God... deals with us. *God bends down in order to raise us up*; to comfort us and to heal our wounds; and to give us a new chance... Mercy is the call to be a real Christian, who... meets Christ in his or her suffering brothers and sisters.[10]

Kasper is reminding us that if theology is to lead us in the way of love and mercy it must engage our hands, our feet, our mind, and our heart. As Pope Benedict XVI said in his 2013 Lenten message, "The Christian life consists in continuously scaling the mountain to meet God and then coming back down, bearing the love and strength drawn from him, so as to serve our brothers and sisters with God's own love."[11] To profess faith in Christ without doing our best to accompany it with love is not true discipleship. When the man with AIDS was denied the opportunity to receive communion in the hospice chapel, the person who made the decision forgot to "bend down in order to raise up the neighbor in need." Mercy, as Cardinal Kasper suggests, requires a different starting place.

In the mid-1980s I participated in a religious delegation to El Salvador, along with another Catholic priest, a Protestant minister, and Catholic Bishop, Thomas Gumbleton, from Detroit. Our task was to

travel from the capital city of San Salvador to a small village in the De-
partment of Chalatenango that had been bombed and completely destroyed by the Salvadoran Armed Forces a couple of years earlier. All of
the survivors of that bombing had fled to a refugee camp in Honduras,
where they had been living ever since their experience of living hell.

As our small group was heading north to the bombed and burned-
out village, the survivors were heading south, in a large caravan, "coming home" from the Honduran refugee camp, accompanied by faith
communities and representatives of the United Nations. Their one
dream was to be repatriated to their beloved country and to rebuild
their destroyed village. El Salvador was highly militarized during those
years, and the trip of our small religious delegation, heading north, was
a bit risky, to say the least. We were stopped and searched several times
along the way. Because it was known that this would be the case, we
had all been told to wear our clerical garb, with the hope that this
would help us get through the more difficult roadblocks. At one of the
roadblocks, which we reached at about dusk, we were pulled out of the
Jeep and very forcefully frisked. Since it was getting dark, I remember
feeling very nervous. The soldiers clearly knew where we were going,
and they wanted to let us know who was in control of the situation.
The language being used by the commanding officer was, no doubt, intended to intimidate us.

A young soldier, probably no more than seventeen years old, was
assigned to frisk me, supposedly to see if I was carrying any weapons to
the revolutionaries. As he set about doing his "job," I was aware that
he was being much gentler with me than the other soldiers were being
with my companions. Pretending, though, to look rough and menacing,
at one point he leaned toward my ear and whispered, *"Padre, no nos
dejan ir a misa*... They do not let us go to Mass." Careful not to ex-
pose the fact that he had spoken to me, I glanced into his pleading eyes,
trying to communicate in silence that I had heard him and that God
was with him and loved him. I could say nothing for fear that I would
put him—and the rest of us—in jeopardy. His few words were clearly a
confession, but more than that. It was a plea for mercy, for freedom
from the hell he was living through. I knew by the look on his face that,
in the midst of a very tense situation, he was trying to say, "I am sorry.
I do not want to be doing this. Please forgive me." I knew that it was as
painful for him to *not* be able to ask for forgiveness as it was for me to
not be able to say clearly to him that God forgave him and was with
him. All I could do was to return a glance of compassion, hoping and
praying that he would understand my silent words.

I learned two very powerful lessons in those few seconds. First of
all, I had to rethink my entire image of the Salvadoran army (which

simultaneously meant rethinking my image of the world). That young kid had no more desire to be part of that diabolical enterprise than I did. How easily I had begun to feel hatred for these soldiers, aware of the unbelievable atrocities committed by them. And yet, how many of those young soldiers had been forced to commit crimes that they did not want to commit, massacres that will plague them for the rest of their lives.

Second, I was aware perhaps more than any at other time in my life that as a Christian I must always be ready to share God's unconditional mercy, setting aside my political agenda, and just *do* what God *does*. How I would have longed to be able to speak a healing word to that young man, assuring him that God had heard his cry and forgiven him. I will never know if my eyes were able to express what my heart wanted to say with full force, but as I remember that young soldier today, I pray that he may know God's unconditional love and mercy. I pray that he is alive—and free at last from the slavery of war. He may never know how important was the lesson that he taught me.

By calling to mind again this story, I am reminded that there can be no distance between the gospel preferential option for the poor and the Church's mandate to be a wellspring of mercy and compassion for all. The Nicaraguan woman who visited political prisoners of both sides of the political divide understood that very well. If we call ourselves followers of Jesus and hesitate to embrace a broken sinner whom we meet along the way—even if he or she is our enemy—woe to us!

I am as guilty of judging others as any, and perhaps the reason that the parable of the Prodigal Son exploded in my heart some years ago was because God wanted to open my eyes to the supremacy of mercy over judgment. For many years I have looked at the soldiers in Central America with disdain, and yet how many of them cry out for mercy, begging to be relieved of their diabolical service to "Caesar," obligated to kill their own brothers and sisters? In words spoken the day before he shed his blood for his people, Archbishop Romero cried out for a conversion of heart:

> I would like to appeal in a special way to the men of the Army, and in particular to the troops of the National Guard...Brothers, you belong to our own people. You kill your own brother and sister peasants; and in the face of an order to kill that is given by a man, the law of God should prevail that says: "Do not kill!" No soldier is obliged to obey an order counter to the law of God. No one has to comply with an immoral law. It is time now that you recover your conscience and obey its dictates, rather than the command of sin...Therefore, in the

name of God, and in the name of this long-suffering people, whose laments rise to heaven every day more tumultuous, I beseech you, I beg you, I command you in the name of God: "Stop the repression!"[12]

The welcome sign

How easy it is to judge and condemn. Do we Christians not commit serious sin by standing with our "pious arms" crossed while passing judgment on "those sinners"? How many prodigal sons and daughters would love to return home but cannot, having been told that there is no room for them (at home or at the local church, synagogue, or mosque)? Even if we do not post the "entrance requirements" on the front door of our churches or our homes, we all know that the *"If you are a sinner you are not welcome"* sign is just as easily communicated through words and gestures. If Jesus were to suddenly appear in one of our churches today with a couple of transvestites and a member of the communist party, with a Hare Krishna disciple and a prominent politician caught in adultery, would we welcome them with a warm embrace or turn and walk in the other direction? Until my silent encounter with the Salvadoran soldier, it had never occurred to me that the armies that commit heinous crimes against humanity are made up of young, mostly innocent teenagers, who would much prefer to be studying in a university than murdering poor peasants.

The Old South Church has this sign on its front door:

> *Skeptic. Certain. Confident. Fearful. Gay. Straight. Bisexual. Jesus didn't turn people away. Married. Divorced. Single. Looking. Partnered. Female. Male. Trans. Saint. Sinner. A little of both. Immigrant. Native. Strong. Weak. Got-it-together. Lifelong screw-up. Longtime member. Just walked in the door. Parent. Child. Housed. Homeless. Believer. Questioner. Questioning believer. Doubter. Sports junkie. Tree hugger. Geek. Cool kid. Loner. Rich. Poor. Just barely making it . . . Confident. Fearful. Beloved. Jesus didn't turn people away. Neither do we.*

Would Jesus feel at home in such a church? Would we? I am not suggesting that every church, synagogue, and mosque hang a sign like this one on the front door. Jesus did not walk around town with a big sign hanging on his chest. The tax collectors and sinners did not need to see a sign to understand who he was. The ten lepers who approached

Jesus on the outskirts of a village between Samaria and Galilee (Lk 17:12–14) knew just by looking into his eyes that they could approach him. The expression on his face was enough for them. Jesus' mercy and compassion poured forth from every cell of his body, which of course is precisely what caused problems with the religious authorities. This torrential outpouring of Christ's mercy is what the Polish visionary, Sister Faustina, experienced in 1931. She heard Jesus say, "I am offering people ...a fountain of mercy...I first open wide the doors of my mercy. Whoever refuses to pass through the doors of my mercy must pass through the doors of my judgment."[13] Is the Church not called to follow in the footsteps of Christ, opening its doors of mercy first, before ever passing judgment?

Preaching to a group of twenty newly appointed cardinals, Pope Francis weaves together three separate gospel stories into a coherent tapestry of pastoral ministry, inspired by what he calls the *logic* of Jesus' mercy: the parables of the Prodigal Son (Lk 15) and of the laborers in the vineyard (Mt 20) and Jesus' courageous and compassionate reaching out to touch and heal a leper (Mk 1:40–45):

> In healing the leper, Jesus does not harm the healthy. Rather, he frees them from fear. He does not endanger them, but gives them a brother...Indeed, Jesus frees the healthy from the temptation of the "older brother" (cf. Lk 15:11–32), the burden of envy and the grumbling of the laborers who bore "the burden of the day and the heat" (cf. Mt 20:1–16). In a word: charity cannot be neutral, indifferent, lukewarm or impartial. Charity is infectious, it excites, it risks and it engages. For true charity is always unmerited, unconditional and gratuitous. (cf. 1 Cor 13)...Contact is the true language of communication, the same endearing language which brought healing to the leper...[who] once cured, became a messenger of God's love. The Gospel tells us that, "he went out and began to proclaim it freely and to spread the word" (cf. Mk 1:45).
>
> Dear new Cardinals, this is the "logic," the mind of Jesus, and this is the way of the Church. Not only to welcome and reinstate with evangelical courage all those who knock at our door, but to go out and to seek, fearlessly and without prejudice, those who are distant, freely sharing what we ourselves freely received.[14]

Is it not important, then, to constantly ask ourselves this question: At what table is Jesus seated today? Maybe he is breaking bread with school counselors and law enforcement officers who meet once a month to talk about juvenile crime. Maybe he is sharing a cup of coffee with a group of sex-offenders and alcoholics who meet every Monday after their group therapy session in the basement of the church; or with business students who meet regularly with gambling addicts to help them find ways out of the maze of addiction and debt; or with young Israeli soldiers and a group of high school students from Gaza who are learning what the phrase "Love your neighbor" might mean today.

Do they not all hunger for the same *bread of life* that you and I hunger for, even if they might use different words? Do we not all long to be understood, loved, welcomed, and forgiven by another human being's healing embrace? Did Jesus not say, "Come to me, all you that are weary and are carrying heavy burdens, and I will give you rest" (Mt 11:28)?

Jesus' heart is universal, all-embracing, which in no way suggests that he and his disciples simply skip through Galilee blessing sin since, "In the end it's all the same anyway." Jesus is not interested in winning a popularity contest; nor is he out to "harm the healthy," as Pope Francis reminds us. By welcoming into his circle those who are pushed to the margin of life, Jesus is in no way mocking those who truly strive to live a life of gospel holiness. He *is* reminding all of us, though, of the essential goal of his ministry: "I have come to call not the righteous but sinners to repentance" (Lk 5:32). He longs to share God's mercy and love with the whole world and, because of that, he never misses the opportunity to reach out with preferential love to a person with a broken heart or a burdened soul. "Contact is the true language of communication...the logic of Jesus," emphasizes Pope Francis, and contact requires nearness, proximity. The very same arms that embraced the world from a cross on the outskirts of Jerusalem two thousand years ago continue to reach out in a healing embrace today, longing to set humanity free from the shackles of sin and exclusion.

> Jesus was teaching in a synagogue on the Sabbath. And a woman was there who for eighteen years had been crippled ...she was bent over, completely incapable of standing erect. When Jesus saw her, he called to her and said, "Woman, you are set free of your infirmity." He laid his hands on her, and she at once stood up straight and glorified God. But the leader of the synagogue, indignant that Jesus had cured on the Sabbath, said to the crowd in reply, "There are six days when work should be done. Come on those days to be cured, not on the Sabbath day." The Lord said to him in reply, "Hypocrites!

...This daughter of Abraham, whom Satan has bound for eighteen years now, ought she not to have been set free on the Sabbath day from this bondage?" When he said this, all his adversaries were humiliated; and the whole crowd rejoiced. (Lk 13:10–17)

Jesus does more than offer physical healing to the bent-over woman; he frees her from *exile*, from the public scourge of living as one who is less than human. He also deals with the synagogue leader, pointing out his blatant hypocrisy. Jesus does not need to look at the calendar to see if healing is permitted on a particular day; his love is as powerful on the Sabbath as on a Tuesday afternoon! Since when does Love take a day off?

The sinner is my neighbor

For a number of years in Latin America I visited and accompanied pastorally a group of political prisoners, men in their thirties or forties who were facing long prison sentences for their involvement in illegal political and revolutionary activity. It was not a ministry that I sat down one day and decided to get involved in. Two of these young men were brothers, the sons of a dear friend of mine. I got involved as a friend of the family, never expecting those first, friendly visits to grow into something bigger.

After the initial visits to the prison, I was approached by a group of about ten inmates who asked if I would accompany them in studying the Bible and theology as part of a distance learning program offered by a local Catholic diocese. It had never occurred to me that a group of fairly radical Marxist revolutionaries would make a request like that, but it filled me with joy and, in a couple of weeks, we began to study the exciting world of theology and scripture. It turned out to be a very rich and enlightening experience for me. I only wish that "the world" could have heard these men talk about God and their hope that one day the Reign of God would become a reality in our world. Their insights and dreams for a more just world moved me deeply on more than one occasion.

During the few years that I accompanied them, some of the men appeared before parole boards, seeking clemency or shorter prison terms. Ninety-nine percent of those requests were denied. One of the hardest parts of that ministry was to sit with one of these men after he had heard another emphatic, "Denied. Try again in two years."

I soon discovered that one of the most painful aspects of the process of incarceration begins very soon after prisoners are set free, and this is the point that I am most interested in for our present dialogue. The exuberant joy of their release from prison usually lasts only a few days. It does not take long for them to realize that no one wants to hire a thirty-year-old who, in a country that has been through years of violent revolution, has had no work history for the previous fifteen years. These men are marked for the rest of their lives, stigmatized, never truly forgiven, and rarely given a chance to start completely anew.

In my work with them, I have witnessed the tragedy that comes with being marked for life as a "sinner." I have written letters of recommendation, attempting to help these men get jobs after being released from years behind bars. The dreaded moment is when they are asked to produce their *curriculum vitae*. Once they do, they have no choice but to brace themselves for the obvious question: "Excuse me, sir, I see that there is a fifteen-year span with no employment references. Could you tell me why?" The interviewer asking the question usually already knows the answer, and sometimes I wonder if the question isn't asked just to humiliate the applicant even more.

A young person who chooses to fight for social change by taking up arms has to accept the consequences of that decision. An adult who has sex with a minor or a person who is charged with murder due to drunk driving must be held accountable for his or her actions. These people do not stop being human beings, though. We believe that the wounds of both victim and victimizer can be healed. This is our radical faith in the resurrection of Christ. Life can be born from death. "He once was lost but now is found, was blind but now he sees."[15]

Being welcomed back into society after a political, moral, or legal mishap is not easy. Twelve-step groups are "anonymous" partly because to be a recovering alcoholic, drug addict, sex addict, gambling addict or any other expression of addiction still relegates one to the category of "outcast" in many societies today. As people of faith, though, we believe that healing and conversion are possible.

As Christians, we need to look at issues like these with honesty. Can we call ourselves "Christians" and concede only partial or conditional mercy to another person? Does Jesus ever forgive only partially in the gospels? Does he ever say, "Sorry, my friend, but you've sinned one time too many and now I can't trust you?" No. Jesus forgives unconditionally—clean slate. From the cross, he cries, "*Abba*, forgive them; for they do not know what they are doing" (Lk 23:34). "Take heart...your sins are forgiven" (Mt 9:2). Is he covering over sin? Is he protecting the sinner? Or could it be that Jesus *truly* believes in his *Abba*'s capacity to make all things new (cf. Rev 21:5)? Do we?

This challenging topic has reappeared in public debates in the last years around the tragedy of sexual abuse, made even more complicated due to institutional dysfunction and, worse yet, attempts to cover up the abuse. A Marxist revolutionary who has just been released from prison probably has a better chance at getting employment in our world today than a publicly known sex offender. There are few groups in society that are more stigmatized and ostracized than sex offenders. Whether the offender be an uncle or a neighbor, a member of the clergy or a school teacher, to be labeled as a sex offender is to be an eternal pariah. Even in prisons sex offenders are often brutalized. It is, of course, a huge and very complicated topic, and I do not propose to confront the multi-leveled issues at stake in these few lines. I know some people who, as children, were abused sexually by adults and I also know people who have been accused of sexual abuse of minors. It is a tragic, heart-wrenching reality no matter how one looks at it or tries to talk about it. I try to have compassion for both.

No matter how serious a human being's sin may be, I do not think that a person who is unwilling to try to forgive can call himself or herself a Christian. I am not saying that we will not frequently have to struggle with forgiving someone and sometimes for a very long time. That is normal; it is important to allow people the time needed to go through the process of forgiving. What I speak of is the person's *willful* decision to *not* forgive. We cannot pretend to follow Christ and say at the same time, "I will never forgive that person." The last twenty-four hours of Jesus' life plunged him into a terrible dark night of struggle with the betrayal of some of his closest friends. He has taught us how to cross to the other side of the road and embrace our enemy, the one who has betrayed us.

Some years ago a convicted sex offender, known only by his initials JH, wrote a book called, *These Were My Realities: The Prison Journal of an Incarcerated Sex Offender*. The author came to understand holiness in a very unique way, telling his story through a character who freely "takes on" the broken, shame-filled reality of a social outcast:

> He withdrew from the realm of the respectable. He became a wanderer once again, a vagabond, a man without a home in his own land or any other. He became mentally ill and spent time in state hospitals. He became retarded and spent time in institutions for people who could not tie their shoes. He became a criminal and spent time in prisons. He became a bag

lady and an illegal alien and a beggar. He lived the lives of different sex perverts, and he suffered their condemnations. He stepped outside the circle of acceptable humanity, and he went to live with the riffraff, the outcasts, the slime-balls, the ignorant, the deformed, and the demented. He vowed that he would never step back into the circle of respectable humanity again until every last broken and despicable pariah was welcomed back with him.[16]

Jesus *becomes the sinner* in his trial and crucifixion, giving away his very life in solidarity with the poor, the condemned and with sinners of all ages. As followers of Jesus, are we willing to follow in his footsteps, struggling with the reality of sin, our own and that of our neighbor? If the pointed finger does not occasionally point to our own fragile human heart, reminding us that we too are sinners, then something is wrong. Being conscious of this humble truth opens us up to the healing gift of solidarity with other sinners. This is what Jesus teaches St. Paul, whose hands are covered with the blood of Stephen, stoned to death under the approving eye of Saul. When Ananias finally embraces Saul in Damascus, saying, "Brother Saul, the Lord Jesus has sent me [here]," God sets aside the past and helps Saul take a step toward mercy, toward the resurrection (Acts 9:10–19). Saul, now healed, becomes an apostle of mercy. This story reminds us that between indifference and hateful punishment there is a middle ground called *compassion.* It is a call to practice resurrection here and now.

Jesus, the prodigal Son, journeys to the distant country of brokenness and sin precisely to rescue and bring home both victims and victimizers. He does not wait for the sinner to make the long trip back home to God. He is the Good Shepherd who leaves behind the ninety-nine and sets off to bring home the one lost sheep. His is a love that sets us free.

Gestures of love

Donald Goergen, reflecting on the letter to the Hebrews, asks an important question: "How can the heavenly priest, Jesus, sitting in the presence of God, be interested in our trials and sorrows?" It is an important question, one that challenges us to try to articulate our image of God. Goergen responds: "Because he has experienced them himself ...he himself has suffered and been tempted...[and his] life is full of compassion."[17] The letter to the Hebrews says, "We do not have a high priest who is unable to sympathize with our weaknesses, but we have one who in every respect has been tested as we are, yet without sin. Let us therefore approach the throne of grace with boldness, so that we may receive mercy and find grace" (Heb 4:14–16).

Jesus does not love *from a distance*; he is not afraid to come down from the mountain and be human with us, to "sympathize with our weaknesses." He has lived the human condition fully and has been tested in many of the same ways that we are tested. He is God's eternal love made flesh, a love that is human and vulnerable—just like us. He draws near to us not to judge us, but so that he can walk with us in the midst of daily life. Benedictine monk Laurence Freeman writes:

> Mortality is our human gift to God, enabling God to fulfill the hunger of love... dying not just *for* us but *with* us. Unity between God and creation is only possible if God knows what it is like not to be God. This is the unimaginable kenosis, the self-emptying of the incarnation... Jesus died loving. Therefore he died whole. He died humanly.[18]

Jesus died loving. Is this not our greatest joy, our blessed hope? He dies *with* us and *for us*, not just once, but many times, long before he gives his life away on the cross. Each time that he pours his love out fully and freely, Jesus dies, giving his life to the world. Each verbal attack that he suffers with patience, misunderstood for the mercy shown toward sinners and the poor, is one more way that he *comes down* as God's incarnate presence here in our midst. "No one has greater love than this..." (Jn 15:13). With tremendous conviction, N. T. Wright says, "Jesus shares the pollution of sickness and death, but the power of his own love—and it is love, above all, that shines through these [gospel] stories—turns that pollution into wholeness and hope."[19]

Whether breaking bread or washing feet, Jesus discovers early on that his gestures of compassion and mercy are his most powerful pulpit:

> *Gestures.* Jesus sees human faces and hears human cries. His outstretched hand erases distances and heals a leper: beautiful, dangerous, illegal mercy.

> *Gestures.* He anoints blind eyes with mud and spittle, immersing the man in a pool of new life. Earth, water, word: "Behold, I make all things new" (Rev 21:5).

> *Gestures.* Jesus breaks bread with sinners and heals on the Sabbath. Good news becomes flesh. Every day is a holy day.

Gestures. Finding her guilty, the angry crowd bends down to pick up stones. Jesus also *bends down*, to pick up his cross. There is no greater love (cf. Jn 15:13).

Gestures. Jesus drives from the temple those who use God's house to make money. Their decision is unanimous: Money must live. He must die.

Gestures. Jesus rides a poor colt into holy Jerusalem. "Hosanna in the highest!" (Mk 11:10). The barefoot king soon to mount his throne made of wood.

Gestures. Wrapped in a towel (or is it a shroud?), he washes their feet with motherly mercy: "Do you see what I have done? Do this in memory of me" (cf. Jn 13:12–15).

Gestures. A disciple strikes the high priest's servant. Jesus stretches out his healing hand: "I say to you: love your enemies" (Mt 5:44).

Gestures. Bread is broken; wine is poured out. "This is my body...This is my blood" (cf. Lk 22:19–20). River of love. "All you who are thirsty come to the water" (Is 55:1 NAB).

Gestures. "Jesus, Remember me when you come into your kingdom." Mercy and humility embrace: "Today you will be with me in Paradise" (cf. Lk 23:42–43).

Gestures. Absent, yet present—dead, though alive. "It is I. Have you anything here to eat?" (cf. Lk 24:39–41). Breath. Breathing. Spirit. "Go and be my disciples!"

Simple *human* gestures: Touching, washing, anointing, bending down, feeding, eating, healing, loving, dying, rising...He breaks bread, pours wine, reaches out, washes feet, announces good news, embraces lepers, forgives sins, anoints with mud, empties himself, laughs, cries and hands over his Spirit—each gesture an expression of his *kenosis*, his utter and total *out-pouring* in love, "taking the form of a slave..." (Phil 2:7). "No one has greater love than this, to lay down one's life for one's friends" (Jn 15:13).

Putting on the mind of Christ

Jesus' *preferential option for poor and broken humanity* is the driving force that sets into motion his *kenosis*, the total giving of himself that reaches its tragic fulfillment on the cross. As Barth has said, "It cannot be denied that the way of . . . [the Son of God] is in fact the way into the far country of a lost human existence."[20] St. Paul transmits this mystery to us most profoundly through the ancient hymn of the early Christians of Philippi:

> Let the same mind be in you that was in Christ Jesus,
> who, though he was in the form of God,
> did not regard equality with God as something to be exploited,
> but emptied himself, *taking the form of a slave*, being born in
>   human likeness.
> And being found in human form, he humbled himself
> and became obedient to the point of death—even death on a
>   cross.
>
> Therefore God also highly exalted him
> and gave him the name that is above every name,
> so that at the name of Jesus every knee should bend,
> in heaven and on earth and under the earth,
> and every tongue should confess that Jesus Christ is Lord,
> to the glory of God the Father. (Phil 2:5–11)

The scandal of the incarnation continues to baffle and confound humanity. Could God have made a mistake? The prophets never said that the coming of the Messiah would be this messy. Not only does the prodigal Jesus *descend* into the heart of our world, into the *distant country*, standing in solidarity with the poor, sinners, and the oppressed, but he does so *as one of us—with* us, while we are still sinners. He embraces our reality completely, with all its contradictions, for no other reason than love. Etienne Charpentier, by way of an important biblical contrast, reminds us that, while Adam (the "elder son"), wants to "snatch at equality with God," by *climbing up the ladder to be like God* (Gen 3:5), Jesus, by way of the incarnation, *lowers himself* into our limited human condition, *letting go of his equality with God* to be in solidarity with human beings who are lost and cannot find the way home (Phil 2:6–11).[21]

This mystery, namely God's free choice to love from within the limited confines of a single human life, is the channel by which Jesus reveals the face of God to us. The limitations of the Law are healed from inside the human condition, thanks to the eternal Wellspring of love that flows out, through Jesus, into our limited world. This is what many of the religious leaders cannot comprehend. They *have* the Law and the Word of God, but they have become disconnected from the Source. It may be water, but it is not the *living water* that flows from the Source, through the Word-made-flesh, invigorating the people of God's practice of a *living* faith. The living Truth is deeper than the Law; it is the Source of the Law. It gushes forth from God, through the heart of Jesus, and out into the world. This is the *Truth* that has the capacity to set us free (Jn 8:32).

He opened the rock, and water gushed out. (Ps 105:41)

I will pour water on the thirsty land...
I will pour my spirit upon your descendants... (Is 44:3)

Everyone who thirsts, come to the waters. (Is 55:1)

The water that I will give will become in them
a spring of water gushing up to eternal life. (Jn 4:14)

Jesus calls us to draw near to the living waters, to the river of divine love that flows through him from God's heart. It is very likely that Jesus does not yet know that one day that river of living water will flow through his own pierced and crucified heart. On that day the world will be set free (Jn 19:34):

Then the angel showed me the river of life-giving water, sparkling like crystal, flowing from the throne of God *and of the Lamb*. (Rev 22:1)

Becoming a neighbor

A lawyer stood up to test Jesus. "Teacher," he said, "what must I do to inherit eternal life?" Jesus said to him... "You shall love the Lord your God with all your heart, and with all your soul, and with all your strength, and with all your mind; and your neighbor as yourself..."

But wanting to justify himself, he asked Jesus, "And who is my neighbor?" Jesus replied, "A man was going down from Jerusalem to Jericho, and fell into the hands of robbers, who stripped him, beat him, and went away, leaving him half dead. Now by chance a priest was going down that road; and when he saw him, he passed by on the other side. So likewise a Levite... passed by on the other side. But a Samaritan while traveling came near him; and when he saw him, he was moved with pity. He went to him and bandaged his wounds... Then he put him on his own animal, brought him to an inn, and took care of him. The next day he took out two denarii, gave them to the innkeeper, and said, "Take care of him; and when I come back, I will repay you whatever more you spend." Which of these three, do you think, was a neighbor to the man who fell into the hands of the robbers?" He said, "The one who showed him mercy." Jesus said to him, "Go and do likewise." (Lk 10:25–36)

Having been born in the contemplative heart of Jesus, the parables of the Good Samaritan and the Prodigal Son both call us to "put on the mind of Christ" (1 Cor 2:16). Both invite us into the freedom and the joy of giving ourselves away in love. To discover this blessed gift can be dangerous, though. Jesus is eventually crucified for extending the wide embrace of his compassionate love beyond the accepted limits. Though it is risky to love those who live on the margins of society, Jesus did not shy away from that risk. Is that not what leads him to the cross, which he embraces with love?

Peruvian theologian Gustavo Gutiérrez has delved deeply into the parable of the Good Samaritan, challenging us to live the gospel with radical compassion:

> The well-known parable of the Good Samaritan (Lk 10:25–37), which has left a deep impression in Christian memory, empha-sizes the primacy of the other, one of the principal points of the message of Jesus. The question, "Who is *my* neighbor?" places the one asking the question in the center... Jesus turns it upside down and responds with another question: "Who was the neighbor to the *wounded person* left along the side of the road?... We now find ourselves on another stage: at center stage is the one who was assaulted and left on the side of the road...
>
> Our "neighbor" is not, then, the person we happen to bump into along the way... but instead the one whom we go in search of... It is about "becoming a neighbor" to the one who is far away, the one who is not necessarily part of my world. In a way, we could say that we don't "have" neighbors, but that we "create" neighbors through our initiatives, gestures and commitments... Towards the end of the story, Jesus asks: "Which of these three acted like a neighbor?" (v. 36)[22]...
>
> The respected priest and Levite... neither leave their path, nor do they draw near to the situation of the man wounded by criminals. In fact, they actually distance themselves... The

other man, on the other hand, the despised Samaritan . . . takes
the initiative to leave behind his path and to draw near to the
wounded man . . . What motivates his action is compassion—in
the sense of sharing the suffering of "the other." Luke chooses
a strong [Greek] verb to point this out: *splankhnízomai*: "to be
moved in the depths of one's guts." This is a love that has become flesh—literally speaking—not remaining on some ab-
stract, neutral level.[23]

Gutiérrez, by going to the heart of this challenging parable, purposely makes us feel a bit uncomfortable. One gets the sense that he is
inviting us to a new version of the traditional "examination of conscience." This time, though, we are invited to look at the soles of our
shoes to see if they are sufficiently worn down. In other words, Jesus is
asking us an important question: "Have you crossed over to the other
side of the road enough to wear the soles of your shoes down or do
they still look *as good as new*?" Are we getting accustomed to shifting
our path, re-routing our journey, changing our plans so that we can attend to the needs of our wounded neighbor? Have we gotten close
enough to see in our neighbor's face the face of Christ?

Celebrating the Eucharist on the edge of the road

Jesus, the prodigal Son, having left behind the security of home and
clan, moves in love toward the *other*, toward the excluded one, toward
those living in the distant country. The good Samaritan follows a similar path. Both remind us that love requires *movement*. There is no imi-
tating Jesus' love without movement and risk, without following in his
footsteps. Says Pope Francis:

Following Jesus means learning to come out of ourselves . . . to
go to the outskirts of existence, ourselves taking the first step
towards our brothers and sisters, especially those farthest
away, those who are forgotten, those most in need of understanding, consolation, help . . . He has placed his tent among us
to bring us God's mercy that saves and gives hope. We, too, if
we want to follow Him and stay with Him, must not be con-
tent with staying in the enclosure of the ninety-nine sheep, we
must "come out," to seek out with Him the lost sheep.[24]

Though he is hated and despised by the Jews, it is precisely the
Samaritan in the parable who freely crosses over to the *other side* of the

road, the *other side* of a world divided into "us and them," "saint and sinner" "Jew and Gentile. " He does so for no other reason than to serve his neighbor through unconditional love. By moving *toward* the one whom others ignore, he discovers the presence of God in his neighbor. As he touches and washes the wounds of the man left half dead on the side of the road, he touches the body of Christ, transforming his gesture of charity into Eucharist.

During the decade of the 1990s I served pastorally among rural *campesino*[25] villagers in the mountains of northern Honduras. For several years we celebrated Holy Week by moving each day from one village to another, walking several hours in procession while singing hymns as the children played and the women carried beans and corn *tortillas* to be shared with all at the end of the day's celebration. Beginning on Palm Sunday and ending on Easter Sunday we celebrated each holy day in a different village. None of this would have been possible without the dedicated work of the men and women catechists and Delegates of the Word who still today sustain the bulk of the rural pastoral work in Honduras.

An elderly man, named Don Miguel, almost always accompanied me on my pastoral visits. I would get off the bus at the foot of the majestic Merendón mountain range, and there would be Don Miguel, with his *bordón*, or walking stick, in hand and a big smile on his face. After a joyful greeting, we'd begin our climb. Though these visits included several-hour hikes, frequently in monsoon rains, Don Miguel never missed the chance to accompany "*el Padrecito*"[26] for the busy Holy Week circuit. He was a lovely man, an elderly, illiterate farmer, and the father, grandfather, and great-grandfather of what seemed like "many nations"! Don Miguel was a man of incredible humility and deep faith.

Every year for the Holy Thursday celebration, at which there were usually about eighty to a hundred people present, all gathered outside under towering coconut palm trees, the Delegates of the Word and I, each with a plastic *palangana*, or small wash basin, to celebrate the ceremonial washing of the feet with the community. *Everyone* had his or her feet washed, including the newborn babies. Each year we explained the procedure, asking that each person come forward one-by-one, remove their shoe or sandal (which frequently was not necessary, given that many, especially the children, rarely wore shoes), and place one of their feet into the *palangana* for the ritual washing. The Delegates of the Word and I, crouched down, with a towel draped over our knees, would reverently reenact Jesus' humble gesture of servant love in preparation for his death.

One of those years, after explaining the procedure once again but before I had time to crouch down and prepare myself, I suddenly realized that Don Miguel was kneeling at my feet, removing my sandal. He immediately began to wash my foot. I opened my mouth, and was just about to say, "Don Miguel, you haven't understood the instructions! I'm supposed to...!" I literally had the words on the tip of my tongue when I caught myself (thanks to my guardian angel). I stood there in absolute awe as this elderly man, kneeling on the earth that he had farmed all his life, washed my feet as if they were the feet of Jesus himself. My eyes filled with tears. To think that I was going to say to him, "Don Miguel, you haven't understood the instructions!" Not only had he understood the instructions; more important, he had understood the gospel. And thanks to humble Don Miguel, I was beginning to understand the gospel, too.

Don Miguel was not concerned about instructions or protocol. He *moved toward his neighbor* instinctively, naturally. The truth is, he hadn't understood "the *Padre*'s instructions." He was too busy trying to live the gospel. He who had never learned to *read* the gospel, understood it in the most profound way, surely far better than I. Don Miguel knew in his guts, in the depths of his heart, that the gospel is about serving one's neighbor, as the good Samaritan did, as Jesus did.

The call to leave our comfort zone, to leave home and move in the direction of our neighbor, is essential if we want to follow and experience communion with Christ. In the end it does not matter if one is a prodigal son, a good shepherd, a good Samaritan, or a woman who searches her house for the lost coin (Lk 15:4–10). If we respond by *moving in love toward our neighbor*, then we are following Christ. Archbishop Oscar Romero said in one of his homilies:

> There is a way to know if God is near to us or far away: everyone who is concerned about the hungry, about the naked, about the poor, about the disappeared, about the tortured, about the prisoner... will find God near.[27]

Can we not say with utter conviction that Jesus is the ultimate "good Samaritan"? Not only does he *give* us this marvelous parable; he *lives* it. It is Jesus, after all, who crosses over to *our* side of the road by being born in our world as God's incarnate Son. It is he who asks our beloved *Abba* for his part of the inheritance so that he can travel to the distant country in order to search us out, heal our wounds, and forgive our sins. Pope Francis, in his very first public audience in St. Peter's Square in Rome (March 2013), compares God with the good Samaritan. Both, he suggests, are willing to be disturbed and displaced by the cry of their neighbor:

God thinks like the Samaritan who does not pass near the victim, feeling sorry for him, or looking the other way, but coming to his aid without asking anything in return; without asking whether he is a Jew, or a pagan, or a Samaritan, if he is rich, if he is poor: he doesn't ask anything. He comes to his aid: this is God...*who moves toward us*, without calculating, without measure. God is like this; God always takes the first step...[28]

As the first of many brothers and sisters (Rom 8:29), Jesus is always ready to *bend down* and wash our feet, to enter into our lives and renew us with the gift of hope. He does not hesitate to plunge into our sinful world and into our wounded hearts. He is not afraid to get his hands dirty and to be wounded by love. He wears out more than a pair of shoes. In the end his bare feet will be nailed to a cross. His only concern is to show us the way back home to love, to the house of our *Abba*. The Italian Sacramentary celebrates Christ as the good Samaritan in one of its eucharistic prayers:

It is truly just to praise you and thank you in every moment of our life, in health and in sickness, in suffering and in joy, through Christ your Servant, our Redeemer. He spent his mortal life doing good and healing all who were prisoners of evil. Even today, as the Good Samaritan, he draws near to all who are wounded in body and spirit, pouring upon their wounds the oil of consolation and the wine of hope.[29]

Scripture scholar Amy-Jill Levine, reflecting on the parable of the Good Samaritan, analyzes the question, "Who is my neighbor?" Does this question lead us *toward* our neighbor, she asks, or is it an easy, indirect way to evade having to attend to him or her? In other words, do we truly want to reach out to our neighbor or are we bargaining for the path that requires minimum involvement?

According to Leviticus, love has to extend beyond the people in one's group. Leviticus 19 insists on loving the stranger...[so] to ask, "Who is my neighbor?" is a polite way of asking, "Who is *not* my neighbor?" or "Who does not deserve my love?"...The answer Jesus gives is, "no one." Everyone deserves that love—local or alien, Jew or Gentile...In Jewish thought, one could not mistreat the enemy, but love was not mandated. Proverb 25:21 insists, "If your enemies are hungry, give them bread to eat; and if they are thirsty, give them water to drink." ... Only Jesus insists on *loving* the enemy."[30]

Is the lawyer who approaches Jesus truly longing to reach out to his neighbor or is he seeking easy answers so that he does *not* have to alter his plans or shift his geography? Is he prepared to go to the "distant country" (the other side of the road) or is he trying to follow Jesus without getting his shoes dirty? Sooner or later he will have to learn that the way of discipleship usually leads to the cross, and it is most likely that a lot more than his shoes will get dirty if he follows that path.

Levine goes on to clarify a frequently misrepresented idea, regarding the options available to the priest and the Levite who pass by the man left half dead on the road.

> [Some] claim that the priest and the Levite passed by the man in the ditch, because they are afraid of contracting corpse contamination ... violating purity laws. But there is nothing impure about touching a person who is "half dead." Nor is there any sin involved in burying a corpse; to the contrary, the Torah expects corpses to be interred. The law, rather, required that both men attend to the fellow in the ditch, whether alive or dead, for one is to "love the neighbor" and "love the stranger" both ... Their responsibility was to save a life; they failed. Saving a life is so important that Jewish law mandates that it override every other concern, including the Sabbath (e.g., 1 Mac 2:31–41; 2 Mac 6:11).[31]

The fact is, then, that neither the Levite nor the priest has any excuse for not attending to the wounded man on the side of the road. Sadly, there is absolutely no movement on their part, save a glance of disinterested repulsion. There is no inner stirring of compassion, no praxis of faith. They both hurriedly walk past the lump of wounded humanity, looking the other way. Their religion seems to be about climbing a ladder, trying to get to heaven, fulfilling the requirements, getting saved. The phrase, "Who is my neighbor?" has not yet found its way into their mind and heart.

The encounter with the *other* is always about learning to love as God loves us, and love calls us to movement, to some kind of self-emptying action. This is the deeper meaning behind the prodigal Son's journey to the distant country. He sets off toward his neighbor in order to *pour himself out* in love. Is this not what we contemplate through the profound gesture of the woman who anoints Jesus' feet shortly before his death (Mk 14:3; Jn 12:3)? She, like the prodigal Son and the good Samaritan, spends her entire inheritance with utter gospel freedom. Guatemalan poet Julia Esquivel captures the power of her love that is always ready to pour itself out in response to the paschal love of Christ.

In Memory of Her

> Spell-bound,
> she savored, drop by drop,
> your whole heart
> —a chalice brimming with wisdom.
> Tranquil now, she felt
> the power of your resurrection
> that rescues us to joy.
> Intoxicated by your passion,
> she penetrated little by little
> the intimate secret
> of your total surrender
> and was transformed
> into an exquisite alabaster vessel
> overflowing with aromatic perfume.
>
> Liberated,
> she poured herself out without measure
> upon your pilgrim body,
> condemned by patriarchal powers
> to the ignominious torment of the cross.
>
> In love with life,
> and sensing your agony to come,
> she announced your impending end
> with the rare gesture of a free woman.
>
> She was harshly condemned
> by Judas and your friends,
> but in their presence you praised
> the extravagance of her tenderness,
> the highest approval
> that anyone could ever receive
> from your pure, fully human lips.

> In memory of your gospel
> that she lived,
> I beg you, Love of Loves,
> make of my clay
> a beautiful alabaster vessel
> and of my whole life,
> perfume of pure nard
> like the kind she used
> to anoint your weary feet,
> the daring one, blessed Mary of Bethany.[32]

Does the poor widow in the temple not do the same (Lk 21:1–4) when she questions the abuse of wealth and temple power through the total, uncalculated, and free gift of herself? Is it not what Don Miguel understood in the simplicity of his *campesino* heart? Is it not the freedom of spirit that is at the heart of the Beatitudes and Jesus' call to discipleship?

> As you go, proclaim the good news, "The reign of heaven has come near" ... *You received without payment; give without payment.* Take no gold, or silver, or copper in your belts, no bag for your journey, or two tunics, or sandals, or a staff ... Whatever town or village you enter, find out who in it is worthy, and stay there until you leave. As you enter the house, greet it. If the house is worthy, let your peace come upon it; but if it is not worthy, let your peace return to you. (Mt 10:7–13)

Jesus looks at the young lawyer in the eye and says, "Come and follow me. Only when you have gospel blisters on our feet will you know true freedom and finally glimpse the face of God." Sadly, the young lawyer is stuck. The other side of the road is far from his heart. His religion is about answers that are written in a book, and he has already read the book. Perhaps the greatest tragedy of all is to be *lost* without ever having set off.

6

The Table of Mercy

The family table

I was raised in a family of six: my mom, my dad, my three brothers and I. With four boys under one roof, we were a rather rambunctious group, to say the least. Given that our in-laws lived in other parts of the country, and that we only saw them every few years, *family* usually meant the six of us. Of course, I must not forget the ever-growing menagerie of pets: several dogs, a cat or two, three horses, turtles, parakeets, a few rabbits, and a couple colonies of gerbils (as far as I remember there was no *partridge in a pear tree*).

We did not have a perfect family by any stretch of the imagination, but I am aware today more than ever that "family" is an incredible gift, definitely not something to take for granted. God blessed me with a very human and very wonderful family. There is one important ritual that my family celebrated religiously every day, and which has played an enormous role in my formation as a human being and as a Christian. In fact, it is a source of great sadness for me to see that this ritual is becoming less and less part of the daily rhythm of many families in our times. I speak of sitting down at the same table to share a meal *together as family*.

Having said that, I quickly invite you to erase any mental picture that might tempt you to imagine a beautifully set dinner table with lighted candles, and four well-mannered boys, dressed as if on their way to church, eating quietly and conversing about the latest Shakespeare play that we were reading at school. The Pierce table was anything but that. Our family table was more like Grand Central Station —Texas style. We gobbled down bowls of cereal at that table before heading to school each morning, and we did our homework seated at that same table in the afternoons (when we weren't playing baseball or football with the neighbors or earning extra spending money delivering the local newspaper). When Mom called out, "Dinner's ready," it did not matter where we were or what we were doing. We knew that we had about three and a half minutes to get washed and be seated at the dinner table. There was no prearranged seating at our table, though we four boys usually tried to position ourselves closest to the dish that looked the most delicious. I always sat close to the dessert.

Every evening meal began with the same traditional Catholic grace: "Bless us, O Lord, and these thy gifts, which we are about to receive, from thy bounty, through Christ, our Lord. Amen." That prayer is still said every evening at our family table. For much of my life I did not even know what the phrase, "from thy bounty," meant, but that didn't matter; I knew it had something to do with God. No food entered anyone's mouth until we had finished the prayer, and made the sign of the cross: "In the name of the Father, and of the Son, and of the Holy Spirit. Amen." My Dad, who was a wonderful Christian man, though not a Catholic, would sort of mumble along with our Catholic piety, sometimes inventing his own words along the way.

What usually followed the "Amen" was pure, unmitigated chaos: four boys, ages ten, twelve, fourteen, and sixteen, fighting to fill their plates with food before anyone else could get to it. The closest metaphor that comes to mind is a school of swarming piranhas in the Amazon River. I think that mothers (and today many more fathers) deserve to be canonized as saints *and martyrs* for the perseverance they show through this ritual of producing a meal every day, only to watch it disappear in a matter of seconds, an innocent victim to the grinding and gnashing of teenage teeth.

As the meal got under way each evening, so did the conversation, and this, I dare say (with all due respect to my Mom's culinary creativity), was the most important part of our daily ritual. Not so unlike the eucharistic liturgy, where the sharing of word and bread make for a harmonious whole, our supper each evening provided a context for sharing the day's activities. We learned to dialogue at that table. I did not think much about this growing up, but now I see how important it has been in my human formation. You can be sure that there was nothing that even remotely resembled monastic table silence, the beautiful practice that I have learned to value greatly during my years accompanying our contemplative Dominican nuns worldwide. No, the image of a three-ring circus probably describes it best. I look back now and remember those years, seated at the same dinner table every evening, with great gratitude. The profound human and Christian values that we learned through osmosis around that table—over many, many years—continue to be some of the greatest pillars and gifts of my life, and a very important preparation for the many years of living in community with my brother Dominicans.

It is not possible to remember the details of eighteen or twenty years of table conversation, but what I *do* remember is that the table talk each evening was what enabled us to become family. It is what ancient Christian monasticism called *collatio*, roughly translated as "chewing on the Word." Our family *collatio* contained a little bit of everything: telling the stories of the day's happenings at school, asking for permission to go to a party or a Friday night football game, disagreeing about some burning life and death issue (like whose turn it was to wash dishes or feed the dog), the occasional sibling shouting match or explosion of anger, and, of course, the times when we would laugh until our sides hurt.

The dinner table was where we were reprimanded for fighting in the living room or for telling a lie. It was where we learned to say both "thank you" and "I'm sorry," and it was where pardon was granted. You didn't have to "go to confession" before sitting down for dinner; it all happened right there at the table, as we passed the mashed potatoes and gravy to the person sitting next to us. At table we were nourished in ways that I could never count. It was where love was expressed without necessarily having to say, "I love you." It was also the place where I sometimes wanted to get up, walk away, and never come back. (Yes, I, too, survived being a teenager.) I learned at that table that being *family* is not always easy, but it's family, and *family* is one of those things that you cannot buy with money. I also learned at that daily ritual, though I do not remember exactly how, that I was loved unconditionally. It is not that we went around saying those very words to one another, but when life's greatest challenges and crises came along—those moments in which a person *has to know* if, in fact, he or she is loved—there was no need to ask anyone. It was already there, right next to the salad, written on the very fabric of our hearts—in indelible ink.

When I read the gospels and see Jesus sitting at the table with his rather rag-tag bunch of friends and a scattering of questionable strangers, all I can do is smile and give thanks. I know just what's happening; I feel right at home in their company. I know what Jesus is trying to communicate. I know what it means to sit at the table with Jesus and the other disciples, with sinners and saints, because I have lived that marvelous, grace-filled mystery every day of my life. I know in the depths of my guts why it is a sin to turn someone away from the table, to throw someone out of the house. We are not there because we have passed a test and deserve to be there; we are there because God is good, and because, as human beings, we hunger for communion and for the mercy and compassion of God. We are there precisely *because* we are sinners and because it is for wounded people like us that Jesus has come to break bread and to break open his life, and in so doing, to show us the way home to God. We are there because one day Jesus said to his disciples, "Take this all of you and eat of it. This is my body."

Scripture scholar José Antonio Pagola delves into Jesus' table companionship with daring honesty.

> What is scandalous is not that [Jesus] associates with sinful and disreputable people, but that he sits with them at the dinner table. These meals with "sinners" are one of Jesus' most unique and surprising characteristics, perhaps the one that most distinguishes him from all his contemporaries and from the prophets and teachers of the past. Sinners are among his table companions; publicans and prostitutes are among his friends. Someone whom everyone considers a "man of God" would almost never do that. It is certainly a provocative action and an intentional one on Jesus' part... "Look, a glutton and a drunkard, a friend of tax collectors and sinners" (Lk 7:34; Mt 11:9).
>
> It is an explosive issue. To sit at table with someone is a sign of respect, trust, and friendship. One doesn't eat with just anyone; people eat with their own kind. Sharing the table means belonging to the same group... Gentiles eat with the Gentiles, Jews with Jews, men with men, women with women, rich with rich, poor with poor... Jesus surprises them all by sitting down to eat with just anyone. His table is open to everyone; no one feels left out. They don't have to be pure; they don't have to wash their hands... Everything will be different in God's reign: Mercy takes the place of holiness... God's reign is an open table where even sinners can sit down and eat...
>
> Jesus wants to show everyone what he experiences in his heart by sitting to eat with publicans, sinners, beggars, people recently cured of their illness, or people of doubtful morality ... [so] he tells them the parable of a man who held a great banquet and wouldn't stop until his house was filled with guests (Lk 14:16–24; Mt 22:2–13).[1]

Pagola reminds us of something that frequently gets lost in this sensitive discussion, namely, that God wants every single human being to find a place at the table of the Reign of God; there are no exceptions. Unfortunately, somewhere along the way, certain sectors of Christianity have decided that the "table of the Lord" needs to be protected from sinners. We speak of "following Jesus" and yet institute rules that have nothing to do with what Jesus himself did.

The world who God is

Many readers will be familiar with the name of Jean Vanier, the founder of L'Arche, a network of communities where persons with disabilities, along with their caregivers and friends, live together in community. There are few places in the world where one can glimpse the Reign of God so vividly. In a talk given at Harvard University in 1988, Jean said the following:

> For twenty-five years now I have had the privilege of living with men and women with disabilities. I have discovered that even though a person may have severe brain damage, that is not the source of his or her greatest pain. *The greatest pain is rejection*, the feeling that nobody really wants you "like that." The feeling that you are seen as ugly, dirty, a burden, of no value. That is the pain I have discovered in the hearts of our people...
>
> When we welcome people from this world of anguish, brokenness and depression, and when they gradually discover that they are wanted and loved as they are and that they have a place, then we witness a real transformation—I would even say "resurrection." ...As they discover a sense of *belonging*, that they are part of a "family," then the will to live begins to emerge.[2]

Jean Vanier has seen with his own eyes what happens when we follow in the footsteps of Jesus, embracing his vision of the Reign of God. Just as Jesus responded to pain and rejection, sin and violence in his own day by reaching out to *touch the untouchable*, incarnating in history God's gift of unconditional love, so has Jean Vanier tried to live his life, inviting others into the transforming experience of a community of unconditional acceptance and compassion. Little by little, in God's way and time, those who have known nothing but the pain of distance and rejection, those who barely survive on the margins of society taste—some for the first time—the healing joy of *belonging*. They truly discover what it means to "come to the water" (Is 55:1).

Once, when asked to define the theology of liberation, Gustavo Gutiérrez responded with another question: "How to say to the poor, the oppressed, the insignificant person, 'God loves you?' ...This is the question for our Christian commitment... Ultimately, we have no intellectual answers except to *be with* the poor."[3] Is that not what Jesus wants to express when he sits down to share a meal with tax collectors and sinners, telling stories about the lost being searched out and welcomed home? Jesus does not give intellectual answers to tell us who God is. He sits down with us and tells stories about the joy of finding our way back *home*, and of being enveloped in the eternal embrace of God's merciful love. As Jean Vanier said, "As they discover a sense of belonging, that they are part of a 'family,' then the will to live begins to emerge."

I have had the privilege of sitting at the dinner table on a number of occasions with Jean and his beloved brothers and sisters of L'Arche, experiencing the opening of my mind and heart to the ever-deeper meaning of Jesus' last supper words and gestures. Jesus is always present when we break bread in an environment of faith, love, and respect. Sometimes it is sacramental and at other times it is... just sacramental. In the end, it is God who feeds us, who gives his beloved Son to the world as bread, leaving no one left out. Says Gregory Boyle, "If we long to be in the world who God is, then somehow our compassion has to find its way to vastness, [by] the dismantling of barriers that exclude."[4] Gutiérrez reminds us that our fancy intellectual discourses break down when we sit down and share our bread with those on the margins of human existence. Is that not precisely the place where Jesus chooses to pitch his tent?

God really does love us. Can we give ourselves permission to believe this marvelous truth? In fact, God is so deeply and passionately in love with us that God is willing to spend eternity searching for the *last* of the lost sheep, the *last* prodigal daughter or son, the *last* coin that rolled under the refrigerator seven years ago—just so that the banquet table will be completely filled with God's beloved people. Would Jesus have told the parable of the great banquet (cf. Lk 14:15–24) if this were not precisely the deep longing of God's heart? When a woman is told that she cannot have her child baptized at the parish because she is not sacramentally married,[5] or when an elderly man dying of AIDS is denied Holy Communion because he *certainly must be a sinner*, does God not weep? Is the old *Abba*'s sprint through the village, calling for everyone to come to the extravagant *fiesta* in order to welcome home the lost son, not proof enough for us to finally let ourselves be converted to this God of wild and infinite love?

Jesus' motherly heart

Once, while making his way through the towns and villages along the Sea of Galilee, Jesus took a little detour and headed up a mountain, probably to rest awhile, or, as was his custom, to spend some time in prayer. Matthew, the evangelist, tells us that:

Great crowds came to him, bringing with them the lame, the maimed, the blind, the mute, and many others. They put them at his feet, and he cured them, so that the crowd was amazed when they saw the mute speaking, the maimed whole, the lame walking, and the blind seeing. And they praised the God of Israel. Then Jesus called his disciples to him and said, "I have compassion for the crowd, because they . . . have nothing to eat; and I do not want to send them away hungry, for they might faint on the way." The disciples said to him, "Where are we to get enough bread in the desert to feed so great a crowd?" Jesus asked them, "How many loaves have you?" They said, "Seven, and a few small fish." Then ordering the crowd to sit down on the ground, he took the seven loaves and the fish; and after giving thanks he broke them and gave them to the disciples, and the disciples gave them to the crowds. And all of them ate and were filled; and they took up the broken pieces left over, seven baskets full. (Mt 15:30–37)

It is the *motherly* heart of Jesus that gives itself away as healing love to the hungry, the sick, and the outcasts. He will turn stones into bread if it is necessary—*anything* to nourish the poor with new life and hope. He cannot stand by idly as the most vulnerable are pushed to the margins of the world's power structures. His maternal heart knows only tenderness and love.

Like a shepherd he feeds his flock;
in his arms he gathers the lambs,
Carrying them in his bosom,
and leading the ewes with care. (Is 40:11 NAB)

Jesus carries humanity in his arms like a mother who carries her baby. "I have compassion for the crowd," he says. "I do not want to send them away hungry, for they might faint on the way" (v. 32). These are clearly not the words of a religious zealot. Only a mother's heart would be concerned that no one faint on the way home.

Pope Francis employs a similar maternal image in his message for the 101st World Day of Migrants and Refugees: "The Church opens her arms to welcome all people, without distinction or limits, in order to proclaim that 'God is love' (1 Jn 4:8, 16) . . . The church without frontiers, Mother to all, spreads throughout the world the culture of acceptance and solidarity, in which *no one is seen as useless, out of place or disposable*. When living out this motherhood effectively, the Christian community nourishes, guides and indicates the way . . ."[6]

In 1864 a young, newly ordained French Dominican friar, Jean J. Lataste, was asked to preach a retreat at a women's prison in the town of Cadillac, in the Bordeaux region of France. Doubtful as to whether he had anything to offer these women, who were known locally as "the lost daughters," he accepted the invitation, but only in obedience. After many hours of hearing the women's confessions, the depth of their faith overwhelmed him. The following year he gladly accepted an invitation to repeat the experience. Lataste began to realize that these "lost daughters" were not only "being found" by Christ, but that they had a great capacity for holiness as well. Today the Dominican Sisters of Bethany, some of whom enter the congregation after serving prison terms, continue the apostolic work of their founder, sharing and announcing the unconditional mercy of Christ to all. Is this not what Pope Francis is trying to convey when he speaks of, "the Church without frontiers, Mother to all"?

This image of Jesus' *motherly* love brings to my mind a Mayan-Q'eqchí indigenous couple that I met some years ago at the beginning of a week of pastoral visits in the mountains of Alta Verapaz in Guatemala. In the first of the six or seven villages that we visited that week, this elderly couple had asked to speak with me about a problem within the family. I remember that we spoke for quite a while that evening, sitting next to the cooking fire in their simple thatched-roof hut. Eight days later, as Don Antonio, the catechist, and I were making our way down the mountain, exhausted from the week's long hikes and pastoral visits (I must confess that all I wanted at that moment was to take a warm shówer), we had to pass through some of the same villages that we had visited at the beginning of the week. As we were winding down the mountain, I noticed from a distance that two people were standing in the middle of the trail, about a hundred meters below us. What caught my attention was that they were neither going down the mountain nor coming up; they were just standing there.

As we drew closer, Don Antonio said to me, "*Padre*, I think that's the elderly couple that asked to speak with you when we came through this village a week ago." As we drew closer, I saw that it was, in fact, the same couple. When we reached the place, we greeted each other in the traditional Q'eqchí manner, "*Ma sa laa ch'ol?*" The elderly woman, who was barefoot, approached me, holding two bananas in her hands. With great reverence and respect, she gently placed the two bananas in my hands, saying in her Mayan tongue, "*Bantiox aaqwe Q'awa Padre*" ("Thank you, dear Father"). Having fulfilled their mission, they turned and walked away. The catechist later told me that they had been waiting for us since 7:00 in the morning. It was about 2:00 PM when we met them on the trail. They had waited the entire day in the hot sun for one reason only: to say, "thank you" and to give us nourishment for the journey. Is there any greater expression of love than this?

When I think back and remember that grace-filled encounter, I see in the profound gesture of this elderly indigenous couple the eucharistic and maternal heart of Jesus. They clearly understood that there is no distance between the practice of self-emptying love and the act of giving thanks. Does true loving kindness ever have limits? I felt almost embarrassed when I learned that they had waited all day to celebrate this "breaking of the bread" with us. I had worked in those villages enough by then to know that, for some families, a gift of two bananas involved great sacrifice. For them, though, to give of themselves, to say "thank you" was itself a profound spiritual and eucharistic act. I still remember their faces—poor and noble Mayan faces. Their eucharistic gesture moves me to this day, and in some ways has become one of my great moments of insight into the mystery of the paschal gift of Jesus himself.

This same self-giving love is celebrated thousands of times each day by the poor, who with great dignity always have room for unexpected guests at the table, regardless of their tribe or religion. They know in the depths of their compassionate, maternal hearts that the family table, like the Eucharist, must always be ready to welcome the unexpected guest. Mother Teresa of Calcutta was fond of urging people to "love until it hurts." I suspect that most parents understand that phrase very well. Mother Teresa tells the story of taking a bag of rice to a very poor Hindu family in India. She had barely given them the rice when suddenly the mother of the family poured half of it into an empty bag and set off in haste. Mother Teresa, when telling the story, says she was a bit shocked. When the woman returned a short time later, empty-handed, Mother Teresa asked her, "And the rice? What happened to the rice?" The Hindu woman responded, "They are hungry, too—a Muslim family—they also have many hungry children." Jesus' eucharistic love has no boundaries. The poor understand this intuitively, by faith.

The door to Jesus' motherly heart is always open, always ready to welcome those who come to him. They come bringing with them "the poor, the crippled, the lame, and the blind" (Lk 14:13), because they know that his heart is big enough to embrace the entire world. That is why, on the night before he dies, Jesus feeds his disciples with his own body and blood, like a mother who nurses her baby. Is this not the school where we learn to say "thank you"?

I pray for the grace to celebrate the Eucharist with a heart as pure and transparent as the hearts of that elderly Guatemalan couple. Their humble eucharistic gesture, their noble sacrifice of *giving thanks*, is the kind of priesthood I want to live. As Don Antonio and I walked the last kilometers down the mountain that afternoon, speaking very few words, I carried those two bananas in my hands as if I were carrying the Blessed Sacrament in a Corpus Christi procession. I had, in fact, touched the Body of Christ, and my life has never been the same.

Sitting at the table with Jesus

Many are familiar with the famous Rublev icon of the Trinity in which the three divine persons sit around a table that opens outward, inviting those of us who are outside to come in, to join in this banquet of love. My Dominican sister and friend, Sr. Claire Rolfe, comments that in the midst of the three persons in the icon, "there is a space, charged with tenderness and 'un-possessive generosity.' Jesus manifests to us a God of friendship. As we enter ever more deeply into union with God we are caught up in the immense movement of love which has its source and end in the heart of the Trinity. Says St. Catherine of Siena, 'With unimaginable love you looked upon your creatures... [and] fell in love with us. So it was love that made you create us.'[7] Through table fellowship and friendship, the life-blood of Trinitarian love circulates among us."[8]

Jesus realizes fairly early in his ministry that the only way to open his heart to the world, the only way to put his vision of community into practice is to stop *envisioning* it and start *practicing* it. As he begins to travel from village to village, preaching the Reign of God, one of the first decisions that he makes is to invite others to sit down with him at a table where they can share a meal and, with the meal, share their lives with one another. Simple, concrete, and liberating. He begins close to home, calling a group of rugged Galilean fishermen to join him in his new adventure (Lk 5:1–11). He knows that these folks are the salt of the earth, people who have learned to live day-to-day rooted in their trust in God. They also know how to put on a great fish fry, and that fits right into Jesus' strategy of bringing together good food, good people, and good news. Jesus is convinced that these simple fishermen will have no problem taking a risk and trusting in this new *Way* without needing all the answers beforehand. After all, doesn't a life dedicated to fishing teach one to trust in the graces and surprises of the present moment? Jesus is also aware that he, too, is still learning what it means to trust his *Abba*, confident that the *Way* forward will be revealed little by little. Maybe these well-tested fishermen can teach him a thing or two about trusting in God's providence, as well.

It is not long after calling the first disciples that Jesus takes an even bigger risk, inviting a tax collector to join him and his small band of disciples, as they continue their friendly visits to the towns and villages in the region of Lake Galilee.

> After this he went out and saw a tax collector named Levi, sitting at the tax booth; and he said to him, "Follow me." And he got up, left everything, and followed him. Then Levi gave a great banquet for him in his house; and there was a large crowd of tax collectors and others sitting at the table with them. (Lk 5:27–28)

Jesus is filled with joy as he shares table fellowship with Levi and his friends. He does not remember having laughed this much since his childhood days in Nazareth. The guests at Levi's house are as surprised as he is, and cannot stop commenting on the fact that a rabbi has accepted the invitation to come to one of their homes for dinner. They are amazed at the profound respect with which he treats them.

Accepting Levi's dinner invitation has opened a whole new chapter for Jesus, revealing to him new and deeper realms of his *Abba*'s heart. He thinks back to all those whom he met that unforgettable day on the banks of the Jordan River, and suddenly sees their hungry, searching faces reflected in those of the people gathered at Levi's house. Table friendship has suddenly become both political and mystical. Up to this point, everything has been preparation, listening, testing, and perhaps most of all, overcoming whatever obstacles might be preventing him from moving forward with great trust. "At last," Jesus says to himself, "I am finding my voice, trusting my intuition, listening to my own heart. It is in that listening that I hear the voice of my *Abba*."

This new moment, of course, has required that he take new risks. A few of Jesus' closest disciples struggle to understand this new path, realizing that it will require some radical adjustments if they are to comprehend their teacher's logic. They know that some of the tax collectors, for example, still have one foot caught in the cycle of sin and the attachment to money and power. Jesus himself is well aware that it will take time to teach them the new *Way*, the path to inner freedom. That they are open to hearing the good news is already a good sign.

One of the great blessings for Jesus has been the joy of discovering that sharing the bread of communion and friendship is a perfect setting for deepening communal trust in God.[9] He is not quite sure where all of this is going, but he keeps putting one step in front of the other—in simple trust—aware that this part of the journey is going to take some time. He knows that it will cause a few tensions in the surrounding towns and villages, but that is fine. There is a time for everything. Today he gives thanks to his *Abba* for the company of Levi and his new friends. They have shown genuine openness to learning the discipline of this new *Way*.

> In the ancient world . . . table fellowship, like hospitality, symbolizes spiritual unity (cf. 2 Jn 11). What does it signify for Jesus and the "kingdom of God" he proclaims if tax-agents and sinners are part of his fellowship? . . . Jesus understands himself as the physician who calls the sick to health. Like the physician, therefore, he must be where the sick are. His fellowship, we learn, is not one in which the "righteous" are separated from the sinners, as healthy people seek to protect themselves from the diseased, but one . . . of accessibility and availability . . . To drink the new wine offered at Jesus' banquet, to wear the new garment for his wedding feast, one must have a new heart, go through *metanoia*, a change of mind, such as that shown by tax-agents and sinners.[10]

Jesus puts his tired feet up close to the dwindling embers of the cooking fire and thinks back to the day that he rather unexpectedly called Levi to join his band of disciples. What still shocks him is not only Levi's response, but the spontaneity with which Jesus himself accepted Levi's invitation to dinner. He still cannot believe it: Dinner with tax collectors? Not in his wildest dreams would he ever have imagined being invited or accepting an invitation to such a party.

He knows that nothing will ever be the same after that dinner. In fact, things are likely to get more complicated, but that, too, is fine. He is convinced that his *Abba*'s promptings to reach out to those on the fringes is the only way forward. "In my *Abba*'s house there are many dwelling places" (Jn 14:2), he whispers to himself, chuckling again as he thinks back to the crazy unfolding of events at Levi's house that evening. Everything had been going so well. There was a wonderful atmosphere of camaraderie when suddenly the chaos broke out. It all started about the time that Levi and his wife, Miriam, started serving dessert. Jesus can still taste the toasted almonds and sweet dates that had just been served, along with some delicious freshly brewed tea, when suddenly the commotion began.

The guests were relaxed, enjoying their tea and conversation, when suddenly several of them jumped up and ran to the back of the house. There was pandemonium and shouting, when all of a sudden—surprise of surprises—they discovered a group of local Pharisees and scribes spying on the dinner party, caught with their hands in the cookie jar, hiding behind the palm tree next to Levi's neighbor's house.

As soon as they realized that they had been discovered, the intruders begin to shout violently at Jesus: "Blasphemer! How can you parade around town as a righteous man while eating and drinking with this filthy, sinful scum?" Levi and the other guests watched in dismay. Jesus listened calmly, and when they were finished, he spoke slowly and without a trace of anger: "Those who are well have no need of a physician, but those who are sick; I have come to call *not* the righteous but sinners to repentance" (Lk 5:27–32). The Pharisees were speechless. How do you argue with someone who says he has come to heal the sick? Is he not encouraging this despicable group of sinners in their wicked ways, though, and in the process, defiling himself at their table? Unable to respond and filled with anger, they turned and walked away, determined to put an end to such heresy.

Jesus' calm response to the verbal attacks that evening, along with the force with which he articulated his deep, inner convictions, reveals the inner journey that he has made in his obedient listening to the voice of his *Abba*. He is surprised that the Pharisees and scribes' accusations have not seemed to bother him much at all. The meal they shared that evening has truly opened up a new space deep within his being, helping him to understand as never before that sitting at table with friends can provide a space where God's grace, healing, and communion are discovered and shared.[11] It is an insight that will guide him for the rest of his life.

South African theologian Albert Nolan makes an important point, namely that "*Metanoia* (conversion) for Jesus is like accepting the invitation to a feast (Luke 14:15–17) or like discovering a treasure or a priceless pearl for which one happily sacrifices everything else (Mt 13:44–46)."[12] In other words, rather than being limited to the traditional idea that conversion is primarily a penitential way of life, as in the case of John's disciples, Jesus shows his followers that conversion requires a step into the radical practice of gospel joy. That is precisely why "Jesus gradually replaces [baptism] with communal meals as the ritual symbol of the coming of the Kingdom of God."[13]

Thanks to that unforgettable meal, Jesus feels much freer to give a definitive "yes" to his *Abba*'s unexpected plans and surprises. Getting to know Levi and his friends has helped him see the larger picture, clarifying for him the call to give priority to the poor and to marginalized sinners. He crosses a threshold that day, helping him to relax and trust his *Abba* more fully. Though he respects the deep faith of the Pharisees and scribes, which he knows is mostly sincere, he is convinced more than ever that he cannot be a pawn in their self-righteous version of religion. His *Abba*'s heart is too big for such childish games.

Jesus opposes the Pharisaic assumption that purity has to be *achieved* . . . "There is nothing outside a person, entering in, that can defile one, but what comes out from a person defiles the person" (Mk 7:15; also Mt 15:11). Washing does not make the produce of Galilee any purer than it already is and no amount of rinsing can cleanse the ... corruption of Capernaum ... Purity is a matter of the totality of one's being.[14]

As the embers of the fire begin to sputter and disappear, Jesus cannot help but smile as he looks back, recalling the unfolding of events that has brought him to where he is today. The mission gets a little clearer—and yes, a little more complicated—as they journey from village to village. Each stop, each person, each conversation, each shared meal opens his eyes more fully to this great and unexpected gift; there are new challenges almost daily. He blows out the candle and rolls into a blanket. "Thank you, *Abba*" are the last words he whispers before falling into a deep and restful sleep.

Erasing the boundaries

One of the longer voyages takes Jesus and his disciples north, along the Mediterranean coast, where they decide to rest for a few days in the region of Tyre and Sidon. The warm, salty air welcomes them with its healing embrace long before they enter the town. The next morning they are awakened by an unexpected knock on the door, accompanied by shouting:

> A Canaanite woman from that region came out and started shouting, "Have mercy on me, Lord, Son of David; my daughter is tormented by a demon." But he did not answer her at all. And his disciples came and urged him, saying, "Send her away, for she keeps shouting after us." He answered, "I was sent only to the lost sheep of the house of Israel." But she came and knelt before him, saying, "Lord, help me." He answered, "It is not fair to take the children's food and throw it to the dogs." She said, "Yes, Lord, yet even the dogs eat the crumbs that fall from their masters' table." Then Jesus answered her, "Woman, great is your faith! Let it be done for you as you wish." And her daughter was healed instantly. (Mt 15:21–28)

Until this unexpected encounter, Jesus has been focusing on what it means to seek out "the lost sheep of the house of Israel" (Mt 15:24). He knows that some of the "lost sheep" will require more patience than others. The project is likely to be difficult and dangerous. Few of the religious authorities will understand him, but ever since the dinner at the house of Levi and Miriam, he is dedicating his every ounce of energy to reaching out to the poor and dispossessed.

This new and unexpected dilemma, though, has radically shaken him. Jesus closes his eyes for a moment, which seems like a year, as he tries to listen to the voice of his *Abba*. A silent dialogue ensues:

> "But *Abba*, she is a *Canaanite, a Gentile*." He looks up to heaven, confused. "I can understand the lost sheep of Israel, the sinners, but a pagan?" Jesus is caught completely off guard. Just when he thinks that his heart has expanded as far as it can go, another challenge knocks at the door. "*Abba*," he calls out, searching for light and understanding, "tax collectors, prostitutes, Zealots, unjust land owners, even the guy at the fish market who rigs his scales to make extra money—they have all heard your word and are responding. It is wonderful. The lost sheep are coming home. But Gentiles? *Abba*, is there room in your house for Gentiles, too?"

Jesus hears no voice from heaven. In fact all he hears is the echo of the Canaanite woman's plea, as it quietly tears down the last walls that encircle his beautiful and tender Jewish heart. He is not lying when he tells her that his mission is to the lost sheep of Israel. He is, after all, the long-awaited Messiah, trying to respond to the voice of God. The desperate mother, however, is not there to talk theology. She needs action, which is why she politely invites Jesus to close his theology book and open his heart. He looks at her again, prostrate at his feet, while something like a sword pierces his heart. Her eyes are filled with such a deep faith. "But *Abba*, can a Gentile have faith?" he prays again. Suddenly, his own mother's face comes to mind: if *he* were sick, would she not do the same thing that this mother is doing? He looks up to heaven... "*Abba*, your will be done." Then he turns and looks deeply into the Canaanite woman's eyes, worn and tired from suffering, and says to her in a voice filled with awe and respect, "Woman, great is your faith! Let it be done for you as you wish" (Mt 15:28). She kisses his feet and leaves the house running. Jesus sits down and weeps for what seems like an eternity. He no longer knows who he is or what world he lives in, though he knows that gratitude is hidden somewhere amidst the tears. That day Jesus crossed over to the other side of the road... again.

> "[Jesus] had to listen in prayer and sensitize himself, walk in what light he had, try out something and fail, let go of his own plans in order to be available for the Father's, transcend his own limitations and step out in courageous unknowing..."[135]

The story of Jesus' encounter with the Canaanite mother is a marvelous gift to the Church, because it reminds us that he, like the rest of us, changes through his encounters with others. Jesus was born and raised in a Jewish world. For thirty years he has been growing into the consciousness of his mission as the long-awaited Messiah. It has not been an easy journey, and the most difficult part is still to come. Suddenly, though, he is being called to step into uncharted territory. Pope Francis sums it up beautifully:

> The Son of God "went forth" from his divine condition and came to meet us. The Church abides within this movement. Every Christian is called to go out to meet others, to dialogue with those who do not think as we do, with those who have another faith or who have no faith...No one is excluded from life's hope, from God's love. The Church is sent to reawaken this hope everywhere, especially where it has been suffocated by difficult and oftentimes inhuman living conditions; where hope cannot breathe it suffocates. We need the fresh air of the Gospel, the breath of the Spirit of the Risen Christ, to rekindle it in people's hearts. The Church is the home where the doors are always open, not only because everyone finds a welcome and is able to breathe in love and hope, but also because we can go out bearing this love and this hope. The Holy Spirit urges us to go beyond our own narrow confines and he guides us to the outskirts of humanity.[16]

Julia Esquivel captures the Canaanite woman's drama in this portion of her poem, "Lesson."

...Are they,
the permanently prostrated,
worthy "also" to receive all the gifts
of your unlimited grace?

The naked confession
of your amazement
makes my heart burst with joy:

Woman, how great is your faith!
You will have your desire.

Blessed are the nobodies
under the mountains
of patriarchal fear!

Because the hunger and thirst
of humanity
will be satiated.

Because our faith
moves mountains.

Because God groans within us,
pushing with force
in the work of giving birth![17]

The uniqueness of Jesus' mission is expressed powerfully through his ever-expanding table companionship. As we have seen, sometimes it even catches Jesus by surprise. First his meal with Levi and his friends, and now the encounter with the Canaanite woman, whose unbreakable faith *breaks open his heart*, helping him see and understand more fully that the bread of God's mercy is not reserved only for faithful Israel. She speaks the truth to him before he can even frame the question. It is becoming clear: God wants *everyone* to sit down at the table of love: saints and sinners, women and men, Jews and Gentiles, rich and poor alike. After all, is the table of his *Abba*'s heart not large enough to accommodate the whole world?

It will not be easy, though. People have never seen a rabbi sharing meals with such unorthodox folks. His words and actions are causing the ground to shift, angering the powerful, while sending refreshing winds of hope into the world of the poor and downtrodden. It is becoming a hot topic in town square conversations, along rural roads, and even in the sunbaked fishing boats on Lake Galilee.

In the midst of all of the complicated religious stuff that makes first-century Israel such a unique blend of colors and sounds, Jesus' heart never stops burning with passion and love for the people, especially the simple folk who are so often overlooked by the establishment. He refuses to give up his belief that, by living a new relationship with God and neighbor, we can help to heal the world's wounds. The dream has become real for him. Neither the path of slavery to the Law nor the path of hatred and violence can lead humankind to the fullness of God's Reign. He has friends on both sides of that treacherous divide, and he knows that it will take many meals and long conversations to explain his new vision and help them to see each other as brother and sister, but is that not what friendship is about? He is convinced in the depths of his heart that if we can sit down at a table and break bread together, if we can pray and laugh, dialogue and disagree, and still be able to embrace each other in the end, then we will find the way forward—the way to the fullness of the Reign of God—together.

Table of blessing, table of challenge

Theologian Karl Barth laments the unfortunate fact that the scribes and Pharisees never understand Jesus fully. They are unable to grasp the fact that "the messianic work of salvation does not consist in the coronation of righteous Israel but the blessing of sinful Israel. Jesus' eating with the publicans and sinners [is] a fulfillment of [that] blessing."[18] Jesus' actions are intentional and clear. Though he does not condone sin, he is not afraid to opens his arms—and the door of his heart—to sinners. No limits are ever placed on his free gift of mercy. Jesus embraces us in order to forgive us, to heal us and to heal our divisions. It is not the other way around. His embrace is never conditional.

Many of the religious authorities in Jesus' day had lost sight of the fact that every human being needs the assurance of this basic love of God in order to stay afloat in life. It is the ground that we stand on. The blessing of God's love is not a secret commodity destined for an elite few. It is the expansive and eternal gift of God's very own self, given freely to anyone who opens his or her heart to receive it. Joachim Jeremias reminds us that Jesus' inclusion of sinners at his table is one of the ways that he puts this unconditional love into practice.

> In Judaism ... table fellowship means fellowship before God, for the eating of a piece of broken bread by everyone who shares in the meal brings out the fact that they all have a share in the blessing which the master of the house had spoken over the unbroken bread. Thus Jesus' meals with the publicans and sinners, too, are ... not only an expression of his unusual humanity ... and his sympathy with those who were despised, but have an even deeper significance. They are an expression of the mission and message of Jesus (Mk 2:17), eschatological meals, anticipatory celebrations of the feast and the end-time (Mt 8:11 par.) ... The inclusion of sinners in the community of salvation, achieved in table-fellowship, is the most meaningful expression of the message of the redeeming love of God.[19]

Jeremias is pointing to something quite profound here: "Table fellowship means fellowship before God." In other words, when we sit at table "in the name of Jesus" (and this includes the table of the Eucharist) we are communing with God. We pray for this "communion" every time we recite the Lord's Prayer, with its simple, childlike request, "Give us this day our daily bread." The prayer itself releases a unifying spiritual energy, reminding us that the "us" is much bigger than just our particular ecclesial or spiritual community. The "Our Father" lets us *taste now*, even if in a limited way, the "spiritual communion" for which all of humanity so ardently longs.

Could that same profound intuition of communion have been the motivation behind Pope John Paul II's brave and gracious gesture in 2001, when he was the first pope to visit Greece in almost thirteen hundred years? After patiently listening to a list of grievances and apologizing for errors made by the Roman Catholic Church, John Paul II suddenly invited all present, including the Greek archbishop, to share in the praying of the Lord's Prayer, which he initiated in Greek. This happened during a historical visit to the Areopagus where Paul once preached before the altar "to an unknown god" (cf. Acts 17:16ff).

John Paul II's prophetic gesture was harshly criticized by some minority factions on both sides of the painful division, their reasoning being that it is not permissible to pray together as long as we are still divided. *O happy fault!*[20] Certainly a pope who learned the gospel in a world where to pray publicly could cost a person his or her life was not about to let religious protocol build yet another wall between Christians longing for the grace of communion. Is it not wonderful when God's grace occasionally sneaks in through our very tightly closed doors?

"Give us this day our daily bread" is undoubtedly one of the most human of all cries. Every child, even every animal, cries for food. When Jesus teaches the disciples to pray this most fundamental of prayers, he places at the heart of the prayer the longing for sustenance, the cry for life itself. Every living being needs and longs for nurturing. Jesus understands that this deep and primordial hunger has as much to do with spiritual sustenance as it does with physical survival. Begging for "our daily bread" frees us from the prison of our ego. It is a school of life where we become human, where we learn to depend on one another and on God. If someone is excluded from the table, then *Our Father* is no longer the *Abba* of everyone. This is what the older brother in the parable of the Prodigal Son simply cannot grasp. We journey to God *together*. We find God *together*. We help each other along the way. This is what it means to be the Body of Christ. For Jesus, the table is never a place for the perfect. It is the spaciousness of God's own heart, the place where we discover that we are "one."

Table of mercy

Understanding the table of the Lord as both a source of grace and a school of life is essential if we are to grasp the relationship between our celebration of the Eucharist and our lives as disciples of Jesus. We come to the table of God's word and the Body of Christ as hungry disciples, in need of God's love and mercy. We come as beggars.

It pains me deeply to have experienced in my years of ministry horrendous and, dare I say, sinful abuses of power in relation to the sacraments that are intended to be fountains of grace for God's people. One such story has already been referred to at the beginning of this book. What follows is another tragic story, one that I wish were not true. Unfortunately it really happened.

Several years ago I was approached by an elderly woman—a mother and grandmother—who asked me to help her find a way back home—to the Eucharist. In our conversation, which occurred outside of the context of the sacrament of reconciliation, this woman told me that she had been forced by her family to have an abortion when she became pregnant as a young, unwed teenager. Some years later she entered into a common-law marriage with a man and together they had several children. This all happened in the 1950s. Twenty-five or thirty years after the tragic experience of her abortion, she got up enough courage to approach the sacrament of reconciliation and seek absolution. She clearly understood at that point in her life that she had made a tragic mistake as a young teen. After hearing her story and discovering that she had never been married sacramentally in the Church, the priest told her that he could neither grant her the grace of absolution nor offer her holy communion, because she was "living in sin."

I heard the story *twenty* years after this woman's failed attempt to be reconciled with God, and by then she was a grandmother. After having been wounded in her one attempt to seek God's mercy, she had never again attempted to speak about it. In other words, forty or fifty years had passed since this woman's terrible teenage trauma, made only worse by a priest who, so lost in his own limited and fearful world of laws, had been unable to proclaim to this poor soul the absolute and unconditional mercy of God.

I asked the woman for permission to share her story with the bishop, and within an hour of our conversation, I had set an appointment to see him—urgently—the next day. When we met I explained the situation to him, asking for his pastoral support in my decision to offer this woman the sacramental absolution that she had been denied several decades before. I told him that due to certain family and immigration circumstances her marital status could never be resolved. I explained very clearly to the bishop that I could not, in conscience, deny absolution to this poor woman. After all, she had already carried this burden for way too many years. The bishop bowed his head in thought and prayer for a couple of minutes, and then, with tears in his eyes, he looked at me and said, "Brian, please hurry and take Christ's mercy to this daughter of God."

Though this story wrenches my heart every time I remember it, it also fills me with deep gratitude and hope, for thanks to this episode I was able to witness to God's abundant and gratuitous love. The first blessing came in the form of the elderly woman's exuberant joy and tears. After many years of wandering in a spiritual desert, she was able to experience in the depths of her being the mercy and freedom of Christ. Second, I can say that I know a bishop who was willing to recognize that the mercy of Christ is always greater that any limited law of the Church. Laws have their place in the Church, of course, as they do in any institution, but Moses was given God's Law not to be used as a tool of repression, but as a light on the pilgrim path of the people of Israel (Ps 119:105). On that unforgettable day, thanks be to God, the Light outshined the darkness.

Table of mission

At God's holy table we are called by the Holy Spirit to be Christ's body, a missionary community anointed to go out, break the bread of God's love that we have received, and share it with the world through our varied gifts and talents. We pray for this missionary grace at a particular point in the celebration of the Eucharist, namely when we invoke God to send the Holy Spirit upon the Body of Christ, as Dominican theologian, Paul Philibert, insightfully points out:

> In every Eucharist there are two critical invocations of the Holy Spirit: "O Lord, we humbly implore you: by the same Spirit graciously make holy these gifts we have brought to you for consecration, that they may *become the Body* and Blood of your Son our Lord Jesus Christ;" and after Christ's words of institution, [we pray]: "Grant that we who are nourished by the Body and Blood of your Son and filled with his Holy Spirit, may *become one body*, one spirit in Christ."[21]

In both invocations, the Holy Spirit's transforming/transubstantiating energy is released. The bread and wine *and* the people of God are transformed into Christ's Body.

> The Holy Spirit unites the wounded members of the body of Christ on earth with the risen body of Christ in heaven. In his broken body, death is overcome, life is restored and meaning returns to those whose lives are painful, broken or empty...

The Spirit who changes bread and wine into the Eucharistic body of Christ...is poured out as well on the missionary lives of those gathered at the Eucharist. When scattered again to transform the ethos of their homes, their neighborhoods, their work and their society, they carry the Spirit's energy to renew the face of the earth. The full power of the Eucharist does not detonate under the rafters of the parish church but "out there" wherever grace makes ordinary life incandescent with faith and love.[22]

As Jesus goes from village to village, eating with sinners and mixing with outcasts, many of his critics complain about his unorthodox table companionship; they are unable to comprehend his radical gestures of salvific love. They do not understand that by eating with sinners Jesus is not praising sin or blessing evil. On the contrary, he is healing the world with the balm of his mercy.

Through the outpouring of the Spirit, the Eucharist plunges our sinful selves into the abyss of God's mercy. We dare to say, "Lord, I am unfinished—have mercy...Lord, I am awakening to my true destiny, letting go of mistakes; I am poor, selfish, and hungry for you—have mercy."[23]

What is it that pushes so many religious people toward a harsh, fearful legalism that blinds them so that they do not recognize the liberating power of God's mercy present in the Eucharist? We *need* God's mercy; we hunger for it. God alone is whole and perfect; the rest of us are just a rag-tag bunch of hikers trying to find the trail that we have strayed from.

Many of Israel's religious leaders had forgotten that they, too, had a history of infidelity, and that God had embraced them with unconditional love and mercy. Are the scriptures not full of images of God as a potter who constantly fashions and refashions us in the divine image?[24] Are we not all fragile clay vessels in need of God's merciful, providential care (2 Cor 4:7)? If we throw all the sinners out of the Reign of God, what will there be left for the potter to do?

Jesus' free and relaxed camaraderie with his new and rather unorthodox group of friends does not mean that he cares little about how people live their lives. That may be the view of those who harshly criticize him, but it is not Jesus' view at all. "Strive to enter through the narrow door," he says (Lk 13:24), precisely because he is truly concerned with the life choices that the people he encounters along the way are making. Jesus is not just collecting a motley group of friends who are looking for a free ride to salvation. He is teaching the world about the gratuitous love of God and the responsibility that we have in responding to that gift.

Jesus, a faithful and practicing Jew, longs to see sinful, broken Israel turn toward God. Conscious of the fact that he has been anointed to help that happen, he is strengthened by his deep conviction that *community and friendship* form the ideal environment for passing on the good news. The shared table is a privileged place where we can glimpse the face of God. It is not by obediently following all the rules that we "win" entrance through the narrow door. We are ushered through that narrow door because God's love and grace are utterly amazing. In fact, it is the sudden awareness of that gratuitous love that opens our eyes to see the face of "Gentle Truth," to use one of Catherine of Siena's favorite titles for Jesus. The wonderful and utterly unexpected surprise, of course, is that he welcomes us with all of our bumps and bruises. The narrow door, open to all, is nothing less than the beginning of a great and never-ending adventure of love.

Jesus upsets the sacred status quo, of course, by choosing table friendship as a way of welcoming and rehabilitating sinners. In his new Way there is no "entrance exam" for joining the community, for taking a seat at the table; one need only be willing to take a step in the direction of grace, that is, enter though the narrow, open door. In the words of Timothy Radcliffe:

> He did not wait until they had repented before he invited them to the table. He did not say, "Look Joanna, once you have been off the street for a week, you can come to my party." He accepted them as they were...This yoke of Jesus' is easy and his burden is light because it is the offer of his friendship, and it can only be communicated in friendship...It is only side by side, sharing the struggle and the search, that we will [know that] this Word can never be a burden, only a gift.[25]

St. Paul reminds us that, "While we still were sinners Christ died for us" (Rom 5:8). Grace always takes the first step. We see this clearly in the case of Zacchaeus, who is both shocked and thrilled when Jesus looks up and sees him dangling from the sycamore tree (Lk 19:1–10). As we saw in chapter 1, the miracle of grace happens inside Zacchaeus's house as they break bread together at the table. Zacchaeus knows very well that such table companionship is absolutely forbidden by the authorities, but this day everything is different. No rabbi has ever offered him the time of day, much less proposed a friendly dialogue and accepted an invitation to join him and his wife for a meal. God suddenly seems real and true. Like the Rublev icon, Jesus' heart opens outward toward Zacchaeus and the entire world, announcing, "Blessed are you who are hungry now, for you will be filled" (Lk 6:21). There is no one to check passports at the threshold of grace. One need only step in that direction and say, "Lord, here I am."

For Jesus, the common table is the perfect venue for nurturing discipleship, a kind of rite of initiation, a first step for those who are searching for God and truth (as we have seen in the call of Matthew and his friends). It becomes clearer every day that Jesus is not simply *reforming* Israel's practice of faith, as one would do when patching an old garment. "He is turning the world, both Jewish and Gentile, upside down...[igniting] a social revolution, rather than a political one, a social revolution that calls for a deep spiritual conversion."[26] It is a revolution that begins with the words, "Blessed are you who are poor" (Lk 6:20).

> The Eucharist moves us beyond a unique focus upon the consecrated bread and wine (immense gift that it is) to the transformation of the world through the changed lives of those who become one body, one spirit in Christ.[27]

Sharing a meal together has the power of reminding us that we are not alone on the *Way*. It provides a context to hear the good news in many different and unique voices, voices that blend together to form a harmony, which, in turn, is a reflection of the Trinity. In Jesus' new community, where everyone is welcomed as brother or sister, the common table offers a place for story telling and dialogue, respectful listening and radical love of neighbor and enemy alike. The table becomes for Jesus and his disciples a reflection of the living God who welcomes us and calls every one of us by name. Each day Jesus sees the image of God with deeper clarity, a God whose arms are always open, anointing all who draw near with the healing balm of love. Is this not what Pope Francis suggests when he speaks of a Church with open doors?

> The Church is called to be the house of the Father, with doors always wide open. One concrete sign of such openness is that our church doors should always be open, so that if someone, moved by the Spirit, comes there looking for God, he or she will not find a closed door...Nor should the doors of the sacraments be closed for simply any reason. This is especially

true of the sacrament which is itself "the door": baptism. The Eucharist, although it is the fullness of sacramental life, is not a prize for the perfect but a powerful medicine and nourishment for the weak. These convictions have pastoral consequences that we are called to consider with prudence and boldness. Frequently, we act as arbiters of grace rather than its facilitators. But the Church is not a tollhouse; it is the house of the Father, where there is a place for everyone.[28]

Jesus is God's open door, God's heart that opens toward the world (cf. Rev 3:8; 4:1). This is the beauty of the incarnation. In Christ God moves *toward* the world, *toward* the sinner, *toward* those alienated from God's love. Exclusion from the table of God's infinite love is replaced by the open door of Jesus' pierced Sacred Heart—the total gift of himself. The prodigal Christ leaves home, through the door of the *Abba*'s infinite love, to search for us and lead us back home, through that very same door.

The table, rather than being a place of judgment, is where we are all welcomed back home. In fact, in the Roman law of Jesus' day a slave could be set free by his master's simple gesture of inviting him to the table to share a meal. Is this not what we celebrate every time we are welcomed to the eucharistic banquet of Christ's liberating love? Jesus himself tells us that, "Some are last who will be first, and some are first who will be last" (Lk 13:30). Though the words that Jesus speaks from the pulpit of the cross will be his final public preaching, is it any surprise to us that his final extended teaching, the last great discourse to his disciples, takes place at a table, during the paschal meal (cf. Jn 14–16)? Eating together, after all, has become perhaps his most important pulpit, the place where his word and bread are broken and shared with all.

The "scandal" of the Last Supper

On Holy Thursday night Jesus draws aside the veil hanging before the impenetrable mystery of the inner life of God to offer us a glimpse, partial yet captivating, of the Trinitarian banquet of love. He invites us to the feast.[29]

The Last Supper has been celebrated with reverence and devotion for two millennia. It has been and continues to be a fount of immeasurable grace and daily sustenance for followers of Jesus from every corner of the world. Precisely because I have experienced the Eucharist as a powerful fountain of grace, it is important (and also painful) for me to try to put into words what I feel compelled to write in the following paragraphs. I do so encouraged by Pope Francis' vision of a Church, "whose doors are always open...so that everyone can find welcome and breathe love and hope." It would do us all some good, I believe, to return to the gospels and read the Last Supper accounts again—with fresh attention—in order to renew our communal understanding of this deeply blessed sacrament of the Church.

To begin, it is important to remember that Jesus breaks the Bread of Life and pours himself out on the last night of his life in the midst of a group of disciples who are a rather complex mixture of saint and sinner, light and darkness, committed disciple and cowardly follower. This should not surprise us, of course, because we all find ourselves in one or another of these same categories at different times in our respective journeys of faith. We manage to come to the table of God's grace thanks to a very patient Good Shepherd, who never grows tired of setting off to look for us, even when we have wandered to some strange and faraway meadows. Given that we are all part of this mediocre herd of sheep (though occasionally there is a saintly exception to the rule), it is surprising how quickly we forget this truth and fall once again into the self-righteous sin of judging others as unworthy table companions.

There is no follower of Jesus whose mediocre faith has been judged and condemned so harshly as Judas Iscariot, "the betrayer."[30] Judas stands apart, in his own unique category, having been relegated to the role of evil incarnate, our much-needed scapegoat, the one we blame for the whole bloody mess. *His* terrible sin helps *us* feel less sinful. I say these words, of course, with great sadness. Is it not true that we rationalize this "demonization" of Judas because we need him, so that we can climb the ladder to heaven and, if necessary, step on his pitiful and sinful back in the process? How easily we forget that practically all those gathered with Jesus the night of the Last Supper abandoned him, except for some of the courageous women and the beloved disciple. Much has been written in the last twenty years on violence and the role of the scapegoat in society, following the profound and groundbreaking work of Rene Girard, James Alison, and others, so I will not delve into that rich bibliography here.

John's gospel tells us that, "Jesus knew that his hour had come to depart from this world and go to the Father. Having loved his own who were in the world, he loved them to the end. The devil had already put it into the heart of Judas son of Simon Iscariot to betray him..." (Jn 13:1–2). It is important for us to remember that Jesus excludes *no one* from the Passover meal, the ritual commemoration of Israel's liberation from slavery. There are no tollbooths at the door to the upper room, to use Pope Francis' image. All those called by Jesus are welcomed, without exception—including Judas. Albert Nolan suggests that Jesus learns this inclusive love by watching his *Abba*, who "makes the sun shine and the rain fall on the just and the unjust" (cf. Mt 5:44–45).[31] Though this all seems fairly clear and straightforward, it is not so simple. One need only read the "requirements for receiving Holy Communion" posted in some of our churches today to see how complicated this "table of love" has become.

> When the hour came, Jesus took his place at the table, and ... said to them, "I have eagerly desired to eat this Passover with you before I suffer; for I tell you, I will not eat it until it is fulfilled in the kingdom of God." Then he took a cup, and after giving thanks he said, "Take this and divide it among yourselves; for I tell you that from now on I will not drink of the fruit of the vine until the kingdom of God comes." Then he took a loaf of bread, and when he had given thanks, he broke it and gave it to them, saying, "This is my body, which is given for you. Do this in remembrance of me." And he did the same with the cup after supper, saying, "This cup that is poured out for you is the new covenant in my blood. But see, the one who betrays me is with me, and his hand is on the table." (Lk 22:14–21)

It is quite common in Europe to find ancient paintings and marble capitals of the Last Supper depicting the scene in which Jesus hands the eucharistic bread to Judas Iscariot (cf. Jn 13:26). It is a very powerful image, suggesting—and quite forcefully, I believe—that Jesus simply refuses to give up on this poor, tragic apostle. Is Jesus not prepared to travel to the other end of the world (or the other side of the table) to save Judas? The truth is, Jesus never gives up on *any* of us. What is amazing, though, is that the pure and unconditional love shown by Jesus toward Judas seems scandalously absent in conversations about the Last Supper over the centuries, up into our own times. When was the last time we heard a sermon preached about Jesus' merciful offering of his Body and Blood to Judas Iscariot? We almost take for granted that someone has to be excluded (sacrificed) from the table of the Lord.

At what point in history was the Eucharist robbed of its medicinal mercy and turned into a prize for the righteous? If Jesus had been as concerned about "public scandal" as some devout Christians today are, it is very likely that he would have had to eat the Last Supper alone. This is not said in a flippant way at all. Peter, the Rock, was seated at the same table as Judas Iscariot, and, lest we forget, his lantern was as low on oil that night as was Judas's. How can we possibly contemplate year after year this unbelievable paschal sacrifice of love, this gratuitous outpouring of mercy and forgiveness, and still conclude that we have the authority to turn a poor and hungry sinner away from the table of the Lord?

St. Thomas Aquinas, known for his great devotion to the Eucharist, was clearly and humbly aware that his own reception of the Body and Blood of Christ was possible only because God is infinitely merciful. In the following prayer, which tradition tells us Thomas used to pray before receiving communion, we see not only his great devotion to the holy sacrament of Christ's Body and Blood but, perhaps most important, we see that he clearly understands the Eucharist as the medicine of mercy for poor and destitute sinners:

> I come before you, O God, Source of all mercy. I am unclean, I beseech you to cleanse me. O Sun of Justice, give sight to a blind man...O King of Kings, clothe one who is destitute. Almighty, everlasting God, you see that I am coming to the sacrament of your only Son, our Lord Jesus Christ. I come to it as a sick man to the life-giving healer, as one unclean to the source of mercy...as one who is poor and destitute to the Lord of heaven and earth.[32]

Thomas, who knew he was a sinner, a "sick man," was not afraid to draw near to the fountain of God's grace, because he believed in the supremacy of God's infinite and healing mercy. It is that same radical trust in God's mercy and faithful love that accompanies Jesus in the celebration of the Last Supper.

> Jesus maintained his trust in the definitive reign of God, and emphatically reaffirmed it at the dinner where he bid farewell to his disciples, a few hours before he was crucified. This was the last of those festive meals that he had so joyfully celebrated in the villages and towns, symbolizing the ultimate banquet in the reign of God. How joyfully he had "anticipated" the final party in which God would share his table with the poor and hungry, with sinners and the impure, even with pagans outside Israel! This was his last festive meal in the world. Jesus sat at the table, knowing that Israel had not listened to his message. His death was near, but hope still burned in his grieving heart. The reign of God would come. God would triumph at the end, and Jesus with him, in spite of his failure and his death. God

would fulfill his reign, and invite Jesus to sit at the table to drink a "new wine" at the final banquet. This was his indestructible hope: "Truly I tell you, I will never again drink of the fruit of the vine until that day when I drink it in the kingdom of God."[33]

In the midst of that celebration of God's faithful love, Judas, along with all the others, is offered the Bread of Life. Could the meaning of Jesus' eucharistic gesture toward Judas be anything but a sign of his loving and steadfast hope for the salvation and rescue of this poor, broken brother? Certainly Jesus does not use the sacred Passover meal as an opportunity to "out" or humiliate a sinner in front of his companions. To suppose such a reading of this story is blasphemous. Jesus is clearly not saying, "Hey folks, the one I am about to pass the bread to is the bad guy, the evil one," though my sense is that sometimes we read the story in this way.

Does Jesus not direct himself to Judas precisely because he knows that it is never too late? Judas is, after all, the lost sheep for whose rescue Jesus has spent his *Abba*'s entire inheritance, is he not? Are we not that sheep, too? Is that not what Christ's coming into our sinful world is all about? Does God ever give up on us?

> When it was evening, he took his place with the twelve; and while they were eating, he said, "Truly I tell you, one of you will betray me." And they became greatly distressed and began to say to him one after another, "Surely not I, Lord?" He answered, "The one who has dipped his hand into the bowl with me will betray me. The Son of Man goes as it is written of him, but woe to that one by whom the Son of Man is betrayed! It would have been better for that one not to have been born." Judas, who betrayed him, said, "Surely not I, Rabbi?" Jesus replied, "You have said so." (Mt 26:20–25)

The gospel of Mark, the oldest gospel, omits Jesus' direct dialogue with Judas. In other words, there is no, "You have said so" response from Jesus. Says Mark, "When they had taken their places and were eating, Jesus said, 'Truly I tell you, *one of you* will betray me, one who is eating with me.' They begin to be distressed and to say to him *one after another*, 'Surely, not I?' He says to them, '*It is one of the twelve*, one who is dipping bread into the bowl with me'" (Mk 14:17–20). After Judas dips his hand into the bowl, Matthew tells us that Jesus addresses the entire group of disciples, "You will *all* become deserters because of me this night; for it is written, 'I will strike the shepherd, and the sheep of the flock will be scattered'" (Mt 26:31). There clearly is no doubt in Jesus' mind that *more than one* of the disciples will betray him on that sacred night. Peter's betrayal is no doubt as tragic as Judas' (Lk 22:54–62).

Then, as if to put salt into the wound, *a second* scandal interrupts the sacred meal. Some of the disciples begin to argue about who among them is the greatest (Lk 22:24), and this occurs *after* Jesus has shared his Body and Blood with them. These are the very apostles who will be the pillars of the new community of believers, and it seems as if they have understood nothing of what he has just done. Are we not shocked that Jesus shares his Body and Blood with any of them? Yet, that is precisely what he does. He shares the Bread of Life with Judas, and Peter, and the whole pitiful lot. And today he shares the Bread of Life with us, knowing that we, too, will contribute our own chapter to this history of lukewarm discipleship. "There is no greater love…"

Jesus knows who we are. He knows that he has called men and women made of clay to be his followers and, knowing this, he never condemns Judas (or us), though frequently the Last Supper scene is portrayed as if he does. He lets it be known that one of his close companions will betray him, and he clearly expresses his sadness and dismay that the disciples apparently have not understood much at all of what he has tried to teach them. "The kings of the Gentiles lord it over them; and those in authority over them are called benefactors. But not so with you; rather the greatest among you must become like the youngest, and the leader like one who serves" (Lk 22:25–26).

Jesus faces the situation with utter honesty, preparing them for the shocking events and scandals that will be unavoidable. It is a difficult moment that Jesus embraces with utter honesty, courage, and mercy. Having said that, though, it is heretical to suggest that Jesus ever uses the Eucharist as a tool for humiliating, excluding, or condemning a sinner. Any such reading of Christ's sacred celebration of the Passover meal would be a disgusting manifestation of violence.

I give you a new commandment

It is tragic that sometimes Jesus' unconditional and unfathomable love is lost in the fascination with Judas's sin. Have we given credence to the sensational versions of this story that thrive on the need to sacrifice a victim? Do we not have the responsibility to recover the real story, the story of grace and salvation, so that we can announce to the world the good news of Jesus' humble and nonviolent giving of himself on that most sacred of nights? Jesus does *not* throw Judas out of the upper room during the Last Supper. He does not point at him, ridicule him, or humiliate him. Instead, he reaches across the table to where Judas is sitting, cowering in the shadows of his own shame and self-hatred, and offers him the Bread of Life. Jesus will do anything to heal and save the soul of a human being. Through this tender gesture of mercy, Jesus calls out one last time to both Judas and Simon Peter, with the hope that they will hear God's voice of love and come back home. This is our story of grace, our story of salvation.

I am aware that these are difficult and complicated issues, but they are ones with which we must be willing to struggle, for at stake here is our faith in the eternal and universal love of Christ himself. Peter denied Jesus three times in the hours following the celebration of the Last Supper, and we know that Jesus continued to love him even after after his tragic denial. This is nowhere more evident than on the banks of the Sea of Tiberias, when the Risen Christ prepares breakfast for Peter and his companions (Jn 21:1–19). We can be certain that he would have done the same for Judas, had his tragic self-hatred not snatched him from their company.

Jesus offers his Body and Blood to all of his disciples for the same reason that he offers it to each of us—as an act of gratuitous and saving love. He calls to Judas from the depths of his shepherd's heart, "My brother, it is not too late, come home. Let us set off from this distant country of sin, for our faithful and compassionate *Abba* awaits us with open arms."

In the Last Supper Jesus begins the final extravagant spending of his *Abba*'s inheritance with his friends (Lk 15:13). It is a self-emptying that will become complete only on the cross. Looking evil and death in the face with utter freedom, he bends down and washes our feet, seats us at the table, looks into our eyes, and says, "This is my body. This is my blood. Eat and drink." Aware of the impending violence, he chooses to act preemptively and nonviolently, giving his life away in an act of total and perfect love, liberating the world from the stranglehold that violence has held on religious practice for millennia.

> You have heard that it was said, "You shall love your neighbor and hate your enemy." But I say to you, Love your enemies and pray for those who persecute you, so that you may be children of your Father in heaven; for he makes his sun rise on the evil and on the good, and sends rain on the righteous and on the unrighteous. (Mt 5:43–45)

In a 2002 article entitled "The Nonviolent Eucharist," Emmanuel Charles McCarthy reminds us that, "This new commandment of Jesus to 'love one another as I have loved you' is not a throwaway line or an arbitrary insertion...On the contrary, the new commandment is to be presented as the supreme and solemn summary of all of Jesus' teachings ...Poised between time and eternity and about to be pressed like an olive by religiously-endorsed violence, to which he knows he must respond with a love that is neither violent nor retaliatory...[Jesus] proclaimed, "I give you a new commandment: love one another. As I have loved you, so you also should love one another" (Jn 13:34).[34]

Jesus' outstretched and crucified arms are his last fully human embrace of a world wounded by sin—an embrace incapable of any form of exclusion. "No one has greater love than this, to lay down one's life for one's friends" (Jn 15:13). "*Abba*, forgive them; for they do not know what they are doing" (Lk 23:34).

> Aware that everything was now finished, in order that the scripture might be fulfilled, Jesus said, "I thirst." There was a vessel filled with common wine. So they put a sponge soaked in wine on a sprig of hyssop and put it up to his mouth. When Jesus had taken the wine, he said, "It is finished." (Jn 19:28–30 NAB)

7

There Is No Greater Love

In her book, *Death Comes for the Archbishop,* author Willa Cather describes a conversation between the retired Archbishop Latour and one of the younger priests. Seeing that the archbishop has caught a bad cold while returning in the rain from a pastoral visit, the young priest says to him, "You should not be discouraged; one does not die of a cold." The wise old archbishop smiles, and responds, "I shall not die of a cold, my son. I shall die of having lived."[1] Are these not the words of a person who is profoundly free? In a similar vein, Dominican friar Timothy Radcliffe once asked another friar, Chrys McVey, an American Dominican who had lived for forty years in Pakistan, how long he thought he would remain in Pakistan. McVey's response was, "Until I am tired of dying."[2]

There is an echo of great freedom in both of these responses. Both the archbishop in Cather's novel and my brother, Chrys McVey, lived good and fruitful lives. They both looked at death not as an enemy but as a friend. Can we not say the same of Jesus? Does he not also see death coming and embrace it freely, with great peace and with incredible love?

> For this reason the Father loves me, because I lay down my life in order to take it up again. No one takes it from me, but I lay it down of my own accord. I have power to lay it down, and I have power to take it up again." (Jn 10:17–18)

Jesus' inner freedom, rooted in his expansive love, is contagious. In fact, the whole movement of his life, symbolized in the prodigal Son's journey into the heart of broken humanity, is only possible because of his great inner freedom. Jesus is not afraid to love, to pour himself out, to cross over sacred borders that might cause a political uproar. Jesus dies "having lived" fully. Says Herbert McCabe:

As I see it, not Adam but Jesus was the first human being ...
the first human being for whom to live was simply to love—for
this is what human beings are for ... We resonate to him because he shows the humanity that lies more hidden in us—the
humanity of which we are afraid. He is the human being that
we dare not be. He takes the risks of love which we recognize
as risks and so for the most part do not take.[3]

This tremendous freedom confounds both the Jewish and Roman
authorities. Who is this man who loves life so deeply and freely, and yet
is not afraid of death? This Jesus is the one who calls us to follow him,
inviting us to pour our lives out in imitation of his self-emptying love.
In other words, "to die loving." As he himself proclaimed shortly before his death, "No one has greater love than this, to lay down one's
life for one's friends" (Jn 15:13). McCabe continues:

We recognize that our very nature calls us to something new
and frightening ... We are the kind of being that finds its fulfillment, its happiness and flourishing only in giving itself up, and
getting beyond itself. We need to lose our selves in love; that is
what we fear. We are summoned ... to venture into what is unknown, to abandon what is familiar and safe, and set out on a
journey or quest ... [and yet] we do not like to take risk(s) ...
We settle for the person that we have achieved or constructed;
we settle for our own self image because we are afraid of being
made in the image of God. This failure to respond to the sum-
mons into life, this failure of faith, is called sin ... Our greatest
talents and creative powers turn against us in destruction unless
they are in the service of love, unless they are used in obedience
to this mysterious call to transcend ourselves. We cannot live
without love and yet we are afraid of the destructive creative
power of love. We need to and deeply want to be loved and to
love, and yet when that happens it seems a threat, because we
are asked to give ourselves up, to abandon ourselves; and so
when we meet love we kill it ... Jesus had no fear of being
human because he saw his humanity simply as a gift from the
one he called "the Father."[4]

The furthest stretch of God's love

Death is robbed of its sting in Jesus' free gift of himself (cf. 1 Cor
15:55), making of his outstretched arms on the cross an icon of incredi-

ble love, reaching into every corner of the "distant country." Reflecting on the theology of Hans Urs von Balthasar, Robert Barron guides us through the inner workings of Jesus' paschal self-giving:

> The Incarnation of the Son in the human being, Jesus Christ, represents the furthest "stretch" of the Trinitarian love. By sending the Son into flesh, the Father embraces...not only the otherness of [creation] as such but more shockingly the radical otherness which is sin and rebellion. God looks into, takes on the abyss which is hatred of God, the darkness which is abandonment by God, the agony which is flight from God. And it is in this totally unexpected and gracious act...we glimpse the shocking super abundance of God's love...[which] shines forth nowhere more clearly than in this incarnational compassion for the sinner...The beauty and wonder of God is his embrace, in Jesus Christ, of the hopelessness of the sinful world.[5]

In the incarnation Jesus "stretches himself toward us." He comes to search for us, and as we saw in chapter 5, when he finds us on the side of the road, he bends down, heals our wounds, lifts us onto his shepherd shoulders and carries us to an inn, where—with water and oil and bread and wine—he restores us back to health (cf. Lk 10:34–35).

> The law of the Spirit of life in Christ Jesus has set you free... For God has done what the law...could not do: by sending his own Son in the likeness of sinful flesh...he condemned sin in the flesh, so that the just requirement of the law might be fulfilled in us, who walk not according to the flesh but according to the Spirit. (Rom 8:3–4)

Jesus, the prodigal Son, accepts in perfect obedience his *Abba*'s mission. The *Abba* knows of his people's suffering in the distant country. He loves them and longs to draw them to himself. By sending his Son he can rescue them so that they can be brought home from their long exile.

> St. Thomas Aquinas is very insistent that it is Jesus as a human being who does the work of salvation, acting of course through the grace of God and acting as the instrument of God, but acting as a human being, a saint. It is this loving obedience displayed finally on the cross that merits for Jesus his resurrection and the salvation of his followers. We are not saved by the intervention of a god but by the great sanctity of one of ourselves, a sanctity great enough for his prayer for us to be heard

...All our prayers are prayers only by sharing in the prayer of the cross, the exchange between Jesus and the Father in which Jesus offered the whole of his life to the Father and the Father raised him from the dead.[6]

As we have reflected earlier, we follow Jesus into the distant country, where we contemplate his face in the face of the poor and those who suffer. It is the poor Christ, the crucified Christ who will reveal to us the path of love, and in so doing, show us the face of our *Abba* (cf. Jn 14:8–9).

> In the Incarnate Son the Father unites himself with all who suffer, with all who have lost a sense of meaning, with all who walk in darkness, in order to show that their situation is not hopeless, that indeed it can become a place of springs...In Christ, the Father *stretches* out even to the limits of god-forsakenness in order to bring salvation. In sum, the Son is sent by the Father on a mission of glory and hope.[7]

This "stretch to the limits of god-forsakenness" is precisely what we contemplate in the prodigal Son's journey to the distant land, expressed sacramentally in the Last Supper:

> In the offering of bread and wine—and perhaps even more powerfully in the washing of the disciples' feet—the Christ speaks his identity as the one sent...Bending low in the humble gesture of washing, Jesus begins the "descent" into the lowly condition of the one alienated from God, a descent that will be completed only with his burial in the depths of the earth...In Mark's account, Jesus "falls to the ground" in prayer, overwhelmed...by the weight of sin...Balthasar quarrels with those who say that, as the second Person of the Trinity, Jesus could not have experienced the full psychological and spiritual agony of the damned ...Balthasar notices, throughout the tradition, this understandable tendency to "sanitize" the passion of Christ, to smooth its rough edges, but such "cleansing," he thinks, actually robs the incarnation of its salvific power.[8]

Is it not essential to do all we can to *not* sanitize the passion of Christ? Would sanitizing it not be the ultimate apostasy? In his short story, "A Woman of No Importance," Oscar Wilde tells the story of Mrs. Arbuthnot who, at age eighteen, fell in love with a man and got pregnant by him. Not wanting to marry her, he did offer to support the child. The play takes place twenty years later, when the child, Gerald, now a young man, has just discovered that he was born out of wedlock. He listens as his mother tries to explain how she feels toward him.

> To bear you I had to look on death. To nurture you I had to wrestle with it...Gerald, when you were naked I clothed you, when you were hungry I gave you food...You thought I spent too much of my time in going to Church...But where else could I turn? God's house is the only house where sinners are made welcome...For, though day after day, at morn or evensong, I have knelt in God's house, I have never repented of my sin. How could I repent of my sin when you, my love, were its fruit. Even now that you are bitter to me I cannot repent. I do not. You are more to me than innocence. I would rather be your mother—oh, much rather—than have been always pure ...Oh, don't you see? Don't you understand? It is my dishonour that has made you so dear to me. It is my disgrace that has bound you so closely to me. It is the price I paid for you—the price of soul and body—that makes me love you as I do... Child of my shame, be still the child of my shame![9]

Through this powerful story, Oscar Wilde leads us into the fortuitous and most amazing of all graces—the outpouring of one's life for no other reason than love. Our story of salvation does not end with a victory parade through Jerusalem. Can we not say, with profound faith, that Jesus would rather be our crucified friend and savior—who gave everything for love—than the triumphant warrior who gallops through town on a white stallion? "O *felix culpa*. Oh happy fault that earned so great, so glorious a Redeemer..."[10]

Maria Boulding, OSB, reminds us that Jesus does not skirt around suffering and shame; he goes through it, transforming it into love: "Jesus felt the full impact of evil to a degree of intensity the rest of us can scarcely conceive."[11] The bishop of Oran, Algeria, Pierre Claverie, who, as mentioned earlier, was assassinated three months after the brutal massacre of the seven Trappist monks from the Monastery of Our Lady of Atlas, knew that to truly follow in the footsteps of Jesus one must be willing to cross to the "other side" of the road and risk everything, pouring one's life out in loving service of others. Without giving oneself away in love, religion can easily be turned into a show:

> I believe that the Church dies in not being close enough to the cross of the Lord...The Church deceives itself and the world when it positions itself as a power among the rest, as a human-

itarian organization, or as a flashy evangelical movement. In this condition it can glitter on the outside—but it cannot burn with the fire of God's love, which is "as strong as death," as the *Song of Songs* puts it. It is truly a question of love, of love above all and of love alone...There is no greater love than to lay down one's life for one's friends.[12]

For Jesus, obedience to his *Abba* is not about having the correct answers for every existential or moral question; it is about being the living fire of God's love. Bishop Claverie was more focused on *being* a presence of gospel love and truth than on coming up with a successful evangelization campaign or having all the answers. Gregory Boyle reminds us that we cannot judge our Christian lives by measuring the success or failure of a given project. "All Jesus asks is, 'Where are you standing?' And after chilling defeat and soul-numbing failure, he asks again, 'Are you still standing there?'"[13]

Jesus is clearly standing with us, on fire with love. When religion loses this rootedness in radical love and compassion, then it can easily be turned into a battleground or a competition for orthodoxy. We can find ourselves, almost without realizing it, on fire with defending religion, while losing sight of Jesus' call to be an icon of the compassion of God. The Crusades and all forms of religious fundamentalism and violence are a sad example of this tragic phenomenon. Says Balthasar:

> This incarnation of God's solidarity with the poor (in every form) has, however, a catastrophic logic: if God takes this seriously, it will bring [Jesus] to the cross...because he now must really "be reckoned among those who have broken the law" (Lk 22:37)...Whoever puts himself at the head of the poor, in order to lead them along an unmarked path into the kingdom of God which is "near"...puts himself also at the head of the sinners, in order to lead them along, as the first of the "lost sons," to the Father who is drawing near and hastening to meet them.[14]

Jesus remains with us, standing with us and with all of humanity, until those who wield power in our world finally decide that his presence —his human presence—is too dangerous. His vision of the Reign of God, of the New Heavens and New Earth, threatens the worldview of those who live addicted to power and control. The decision is made: he must be eliminated. Says Herbert McCabe:

> My thesis is that Jesus died of being human. His very humanity meant that he put up no barriers, no defenses against those he

loved who hated him. He refused to evade the consequences of being human in our inhuman world. So the cross shows up our world for what it really is, what we have made it. It is a world in which it is dangerous, even fatal, to be human; a world structured by violence and fear. The cross shows that whatever else may be wrong with this or that society...there is a basic wrong, persistent throughout history and through all progress: the rejection of the love that casts out fear, the fear of the love that casts out fear...The cross, then, unmasks or reveals the sin of the world...It is when love appears nakedly for what it is that it is most vulnerable; and that is why we crucified Christ. Jesus was the first human being who had no fear of love at all; the first to have no fear of being human.[15]

The cross of Christ is not, as some may suggest, some strange masochistic fixation. It is an icon of love. Jesus does not ride a donkey into Jerusalem, wash the feet of his disciples, break his body into pieces of bread, and walk peacefully to the cross because he is a masochist. No, it is much simpler than that: he is in love with the world.

Despite being rejected, despite the incomprehensible, hellish abandonment in his last hour on the cross, there is no heart that overflowed with truer joy than the heart of Jesus...the joy in obeying, the joy that one may love to the point of giving oneself up, the joy that one may pour oneself out, a joy that is entirely "located" in God.[16]

The Lamb of God

Jesus sets off into the distant country of pain and brokenness for no other reason than to spend himself in love—pure unconditional love. He comes to pour his merciful love over the world, to wash the face of broken humanity. Says Jean Vanier, "It is forgiveness repeated seven times seventy-seven times—and even more—that gradually transforms...fear into trust...This is the secret of his mission, teaching us also to forgive...That is why he became the Lamb, the Lamb of God, to take away the sins of the world...He took into his flesh the violence of humanity, the accumulated violence of generations, in order to transform it into tenderness and forgiveness."[17]

In a terrible paradox, the divine Son is surrendered by the Father into the hands of his enemies; having "become" sin, the

Incarnate Son feels the...abandonment that accompanies the sinful rejection of God...the intensification and recapitulation of Abraham's willingness to sacrifice Isaac. What was interrupted many centuries before is now carried through to its awful conclusion...The divine Son, the eternal image of the Father, embraces from within the *feeling* of hopelessness and god-forsakenness. The only real 'word' from the cross...is the animal cry of abandonment: [18]

> At three o'clock Jesus cried out with a loud voice, "*Eloi, Eloi, lema sabachthani?*" which means, "My God, my God, why have you forsaken me?" (Mk 15:34)

God, as it were, from within the sinner's experience, [cries] out in the torment of being forsaken by God...It is not an angry and bloodthirsty God who "demands" the sacrifice of his Son; rather it is the loving Father who sends his Son to the limit of god-forsakenness, "sacrificing" him in order to show the mercy of God even to that furthest degree.[19]

"God cries out from within the sinner's experience." Can there be any "stretch" of incarnate love more radical than this? God hides inside the sinner, inside both victim and victimizer, and from this place of utter desolation, in the darkest corner of the distant country, God loves the world back into wholeness. Is this not the ultimate stretch of God's love?

> Jesus' ministry and his understanding of his vocation were directed to releasing human beings from all that constrained and cramped them in their response to love...He did it by allowing evil to mobilize a total onslaught on himself, and receiving it with love...In the most crushing physical unfreedom he was free. Evil had lost its power to constrain love, and the breakthrough to the new birth of his resurrection was the triumph of a love free to celebrate and express itself in him in every way that love can.[20]

In his novel, *Night*, Elie Wiesel tells the story of Juliek, a Jewish youth and a kind of "Christ figure" who manifests the power of love and beauty in the midst of the horrors of Nazism. To suggest that the Holocaust or the cross of Christ could have any semblance of "beauty" hidden in it sounds almost blasphemous. When seen through the lens of love, however, we find ourselves face-to-face with a gesture that is utterly pure and "beautiful." Wiesel describes the scene with incredible passion.

Night had fallen and the SS were ordering us to form ranks. We started to march once more. The dead remained in the yard, under the snow without even a marker... The cold was conscientiously doing its work. At every step, somebody fell down and ceased to suffer... Our eyes searched the horizon for the barbed wire of Gleiwitz... We saw the camp only when we stood right in front of its gate. The Kapos quickly settled us into the barrack... I was crushed under the weight of other bodies. I had difficulty breathing... Suddenly I remembered. Juliek! The boy from Warsaw who played the violin. "Juliek, is that you... are you all right?"

"All right, Eliezer... All right... Tired. My feet are swollen. It's good to rest, but my violin... " I thought he'd lost his mind ... "What about your violin?"... "I'm afraid... they'll break... my violin"... I could not answer him. Someone had lain down on top of me, smothering me... I succeeded in digging a hole in that wall of dead and dying people, a small hole through which I could drink a little air... [Suddenly] I heard the sound of a violin... was it a hallucination?... He was playing a fragment from Beethoven's Concerto. Never before had I heard such a beautiful sound... He was playing his life. His whole being was gliding over the strings. His unfulfilled hopes. His charred past, his extinguished future... I shall never forget Juliek. How could I forget this concert, given before an audience of the dead and dying?... I don't know how long he played. I was overcome by sleep. When I awoke at daybreak, I saw Juliek facing me, hunched over, dead. Next to him lay his violin, trampled, an eeringly poignant little corpse.[21]

Jesus, through his nonviolent and redeeming embrace of the inevitable, transforms the cross into an icon, a symphony of nonviolent love. His very body becomes the stones that will be used to rebuild this world, wounded by hatred and greed, making it into a peaceable kingdom for all.

Come to him, a living stone, though rejected by mortals yet chosen and precious in God's sight, and like living stones, let yourselves be built into a spiritual house... See, I am laying in Zion a stone, a cornerstone chosen and precious... He himself bore our sins in his body on the cross, so that, free from sins, we might live for righteousness; by his wounds you have been healed. For you were going astray like sheep, but now you have returned to the shepherd and guardian of your souls. (1 Pet 2:4–6, 24–25)

How, though, can the torture and murder of an innocent human become an image of love? I have had long conversations with my Buddhist friends, and I know how much they struggle with the image of the crucified Christ. I am aware of how this icon is seen from the outside. I sympathize with their struggle, because from a merely human point of view the cross truly is an image of violence. But it is much more than that. The cross, like the purity of Juliek's final concert, or like the seed sown into the ground in the springtime, is a paradox that shatters the respectable contours of good and evil, beauty and filth, life and death. The simple fact that Juliek, like Jesus, dares to create something beautiful in the midst of evil is an act of pure, gratuitous love, capable of healing our world.

Mother Teresa of Calcutta had a profound understanding of this mystery, as well. She did not conceive her call as one of transforming—through political advocacy—the unjust structures of society. She did that in an indirect way, though, by calling attention to the invisibility of the poor in our world. Mother Teresa's vocation was to embrace the crucified Christ with love, to "love Jesus in the distressing disguise of the poor." Her life was as pure as Juliek's final concert. Says Robert Barron:

> It is not an angry and bloodthirsty God who "demands" the sacrifice of his Son; rather, it is the loving Father who sends his Son to the limit of god-forsakenness, "sacrificing" him in order to show the mercy of God even to that furthest degree. And it is the Son who "sacrifices" himself, offering himself out of loving obedience, in order to fulfill the divine mission...Dead on the cross, Jesus' heart is opened by the soldier's lance, and blood and water gush forth...In God's unexpected and overwhelming embrace of that which is most opposed to God, life flows most abundantly. In his total gift of self in Christ, God opens his heart most fully...[while] from the pierced side of Jesus, the Church, the bearer of God's compassion, is born.[22]

James Alison, in a powerful article from the book entitled *Stricken by God*, leads us into the depths of Jesus' unbelievable inner freedom and love. In his embrace of the cross, Jesus fully and consciously inaugurates the New Creation.

> In St. John's Gospel (ch. 19)...Jesus is crucified on Thursday, not on Friday. On Thursday afternoon, he is going outside the walls to be killed at exactly the same time—three in the afternoon—when the priests in the temple were killing the lambs for the Passover feast (Jn 19:14–18). So, while they were killing the lambs, the real Lamb, the one who was identified as "the

Lamb of God," was going to the place of execution to be killed. But—bizarrely—he was going dressed in a "seamless robe," a priest's robe...So the high priest was going—the *Lord* was going—to "the temple" where he would be "the Lamb," for, as we are told, when they look upon him after he has died, they see that not a bone of his body was broken, alluding to the Passover lamb...

Jesus's cry on the cross in John's Gospel is, "It is finished," "It is completed." The atonement, and therefore the inauguration of creation, is completed...Immediately after this, at the resurrection, we are transferred to the garden. We are back to the "first day"...Peter and John come to look, then Mary Magdalene comes in. What does she see? Two angels! And where are the angels sitting? One at the head and one at the foot of the space that is open because the stone has been rolled away. What is this space? This is the Holy of Holies. This is the mercy seat, with the Cherubim present.

The *real* high priest was engaged in *being* the sacrifice, "the victim," the priest, the altar and the Temple on the city rubbish heap, at the same time as the corrupt city guys—which is how the ordinary Jews saw them at the time—were going through the motions in the corrupt Second Temple.[23]

Can there be any greater love than this? As Jesus hangs innocently on the cross in the final minutes of his life, embracing the world with his arms opened wide, the New Creation is born, flowing forth from his wounds like a river of life. Jesus cries out with a loud voice, "*Abba*, into your hands I commend my spirit" (Lk 23:46). Bishop Pierre Claverie, the martyred bishop of Algeria mentioned earlier, reminds us that, "There is no life without losing what we have, because there is no life without love...This is not a death wish, but a passion of love... Taking up our cross in the footsteps of Christ...means deliberately joining the gift of our life with his own."[24]

In Gethsemane Jesus was faced with the ultimate choice. He was asked to let go of everything, every other source of meaning ...His obedient dying was a Godlike act. Self-giving, self-emptying love, an ecstasy of unreserved giving in joy...It is the glory of God to give, holding nothing back...The resurrection is the Father's acceptance of the Son's gift, and the penetration by the Spirit of their mutual love into every fiber of Jesus's body and mind.[25]

Julia Esquivel, the Guatemalan poet mentioned in earlier chapters, in her poem "Siembra" ("The Sowing") reminds us that the New Creation can be born only from the fertile ground of Christ's paschal mystery, his total self-giving love that is transformed into new life:

Because you cannot kill death with death,
Therefore, sow life and kill death with life,
but to harvest life, which is infinite,
full and unending,

That'll have to happen through your own death,
loving with all you've got.
Because you can only sow life with life,
for life, like love, is stronger than death.[26]

Henri Nouwen, undoubtedly one of Christianity's greatest contemporary spiritual guides, reflects on his own spiritual journey in the light of the prodigal son. Following countless hours of meditation on Rembrandt's magnificent painting, depicting the father's embrace of the prodigal son, Nouwen invites us to know that we, too, are embraced and loved unconditionally by God:

When I began to reflect on the parable and Rembrandt's portrayal of it, I never thought of the exhausted young man with the face of a newborn baby as Jesus. But now, after so many hours of intimate contemplation, I feel blessed by this vision. Isn't the broken young man kneeling before his father the "Lamb of God that takes away the sin of the world?" Isn't he the innocent one who became sin for us? Isn't he the one who didn't "cling to his equality with God," but "became as human beings are?" Isn't he the sinless Son of God who cried out on the cross: "My God, my God, why have you forsaken me?" Jesus is the prodigal son of the prodigal Father who gave away everything the Father had entrusted to him so that I could become like him and return with him to his Father's home.[27]

Jesus is the prodigal son who gave away everything.

The father has not accomplished his will through any success of Jesus; Jesus is left with nothing but his love and his obedience, and this is the prayer to the Father to work through his failure. And, of course, the answer to that prayer is the resurrection.[28]

The last gift that Jesus freely gives to the world from the dark night of the cross is his final breath, so that we, the new Adam and the new Eve, might inhale his risen life—the mighty wind of the Holy Spirit—and begin to live the New Creation. As Alison says, the next scene is the great awakening, the homecoming. We find ourselves once again in the garden, contemplating the Lamb of God; it is the first day: "In the beginning was the Word..." (Jn 1:1). We have been created anew in the Spirit at the great banquet of God's mercy and compassion, at the table of Christ's Body and Blood. With all of creation we acclaim: "Behold the Lamb of God, behold him who takes away the sins of the world. Blessed are those called to the supper of the Lamb."[29]

> Despite being rejected, despite the incomprehensible, hellish abandonment in his last hour on the cross, there is no heart that overflowed with truer joy than the heart of Jesus...the joy in obeying, the joy that one may love to the point of giving oneself up, the joy that one may pour oneself out, a joy that is entirely "located" in God...Joy is then no longer psychological and something experienced...but becomes "ontological," essential, giving a foundation to being itself, transcendent and divinizing.[30]

Christ offers this joy to each of us, as well. It is what Pope Francis calls "the joy of the gospel," and we are reminded that it is what we will discover in the garden, on the first day of the week, when our prodigal journey leads us back home—to the God of surprises, the God of love.

8

The Descent into Hell

When he had spent everything, a severe famine took place throughout that country, and he began to be in need. So he went and hired himself out to one of the citizens of that country, who sent him to his fields to feed the pigs. He would gladly have filled himself with the pods that the pigs were eating; and no one gave him anything. When he came to himself he said, "How many of my father's hired hands have bread enough and to spare, but here I am dying of hunger." (Lk 15:14–17)

The prodigal Christ, who has spent his entire life journeying *downward* into the heart of the world now descends into the hell of human indignity and alienation. He is one of humanity's untouchables: a thief, a prostitute, a beggar, a tax collector, a sex offender, a drunk, a murderer, a drug-addict. The one they once called "Rabbi" is now mocked as a false prophet (Lk 23:36). He is a sinner, a disgrace in the eyes of his people: "Anyone hung on a tree is under God's curse" (Dt 21:23). Through his full and complete embrace of the human condition, there is nothing that Jesus does not experience or live through, and though he does not commit sin, his voluntary identification with sinners has landed him in the most God forsaken corner of the "distant country," in the company of sinners.

In the offering of bread and wine—and perhaps even more powerfully in the washing of the disciples' feet—the Christ speaks his identity as the one sent . . . Bending low in the humble gesture of washing, Jesus begins the descent into the lowly condition of the one alienated from God, a "descent" that will be completed only with his burial in the depth of the earth.[1]

143

The paschal meal that Jesus celebrated that last night with his disciples, though painful, rooted him once again in God's faithfulness toward the people of Israel. Their journey of liberation from slavery was real, and for Jesus, the act of remembering God's faithful love toward Israel proved to be a great light as he set off into his own long and dark night.

At no moment, though, does Jesus regret having faced sin head-on, looking it right in the eye and giving it a name. His parables about the wicked vineyard tenants (Mk 12:1–12) and the rich fool (Lk 12:13–21) were intended to be like mirrors held up before the people, hoping that by seeing the evil in their own faces they might be led to conversion. He called everyone to the hard work of conversion: "Let anyone with ears to hear listen!" (Lk 14:35). What he refused to do, though, was to fall into the trap commonly employed by other religious leaders, that is, to single out the poor and vulnerable as the scapegoats for an entire nation's sin.

> Woe to you, scribes and Pharisees, hypocrites! For you lock people out of the kingdom of heaven. For you do not go in yourselves, and when others are going in, you stop them.
>
> Woe to you, scribes and Pharisees, hypocrites! For you tithe mint, dill, and cummin, and have neglected the weightier matters of the law: justice and mercy and faith. It is these you ought to have practiced without neglecting the others. (Mt 23:13, 23)

Jesus knows very well that the powerful "wolves," dressed in pious sheepskins (Mt 7:15) and seated in the highest places of honor at synagogues and banquets, devour the poor and vulnerable without blinking an eye (Mk 12:39). He accepts his descent into the world of sin and hell in order to be a bearer of mercy for all. Preaching in El Salvador in 1978, Archbishop Oscar Romero made a passionate call for all sinners to repent, reminding them that the door to God's mercy is never closed:

> Brothers and sisters, I repeat again what I have said here so often, addressing by radio those who perhaps have caused so many injustices and acts of violence, those who have brought tears to so many homes, those who have stained themselves with the blood of so many murders, those who have hands soiled with tortures, those who have calloused their consciences, who are unmoved to see under their boots a person abased, suffering, perhaps ready to die. To all of them I say: no matter

your crimes. They are ugly and horrible, and you have abased the highest dignity of a human person, but God calls you and forgives you...The greatest criminal, once repented...is now a child of God.[2]

The prodigal Son has descended into our broken world in search of all of us: rich and poor, learned and uneducated, Jew and Gentile. His solidarity exposes him to the same despair and hunger for meaning and new life that we sinners experience. His heart reaches out in love as we cry out for mercy:

Be gracious to me, O Lord, for I am languishing;
O Lord, heal me, for my bones are shaking with terror.
My soul also is struck with terror,
while you, O Lord—how long?

Turn, O Lord, save my life;
deliver me for the sake of your steadfast love.
For in death there is no remembrance of you;
in Sheol who can give you praise?

I am weary with my moaning;
every night I flood my bed with tears;
I drench my couch with my weeping. (Ps 6:2–6)

Immersed in this terrible suffering of the poor and of sinners, the prodigal Son's mind wanders back home. He remembers and longs for the tenderness of his family's unconditional love. He sees the faces of neighbors and friends, the joy of the village, the children playing innocently, the meals with his disciples, meals where love flowed as fully and freely as the wine. Now it has all disappeared. Where are his friends? His disciples? What happened to the faithful voice of his *Abba*? "*Eloi, Eloi, lema sabachthani*?...My God, my God, why have you forsaken me?" (Mk 15:34).

There is perhaps no one who has written so poignantly about the pain of wandering lost in the land of sin as St. Augustine (354–430). Looking back on his own experience of exile from God, Augustine's *Confessions* record his prayer of longing to come home, and the joy of finally returning to the merciful embrace of God.

Late have I loved you, O Beauty, so ancient and so new, late have I loved you! And behold, you were within me and I was outside, and there I sought you, and in my deformity I rushed headlong into the well-formed things that you have made. You were with me, and I was not with you. Those other beauties held me far from you, yet if they had not been in you, they would not have existed at all. You called and cried out to me and broke my deafness; you shone forth upon me and you scattered my blindness; you breathed fragrance, and I drew in my breath and I now pant for you; I tasted and I hunger and thirst; you touched me, and I burned for your peace."[3]

Augustine, in his experience of overflowing joy and gratitude, reminds disciples of all ages that it is never to late to come home, to begin anew. This why the prodigal Son has made this journey into our unjust and sinful world, so that by repairing the broken road, he can show us the way back home.[4]

O marvelous disaster

In the letter to the Hebrews we read:

It was fitting that God, for whom and through whom all things exist, in bringing many children to glory, should make the pioneer of their salvation perfect through sufferings. For the one who sanctifies and those who are sanctified all have one *Abba*. For this reason Jesus is not ashamed to call them brothers and sisters . . . He had to become like [them] in every respect, so that he might be a merciful and faithful high priest in the service of God . . . Because he himself was tested by what he suffered, he is able to help those who are being tested. (Heb 2:10–11,17–18)

In the Apostles' Creed Christians profess that, after his death on the cross, "Christ descended into hell."[5] This phrase strikes our modern ears as rather repulsive, a remnant of an outdated theology. Does hell really exist? Does Jesus really *descend* into hell? Julian of Norwich, the fourteenth-century English mystic, tells us that,

When Adam fell, God's Son fell . . . God's Son could not be separated from Adam . . . Adam fell from life to death, into the valley of this wretched world, and after that into hell. God's son fell with Adam, into the valley of the womb of the maiden who was the fairest daughter of Adam . . . and powerfully he brought him out of hell . . . And so our good Lord Jesus has taken upon him all our blame . . . He was the servant before he came on earth, standing ready . . . until the time when [his *Abba*] would send him to do the glorious deed by which humanity was brought back to heaven.[6]

Every year, at the Easter Vigil celebration of Christ's resurrection, the Christian community gathers in the darkness of the night, with no light but that of the paschal candle, to remind us that the light and love of Christ have conquered death. An ancient Easter hymn, the *Exsultet*, is then intoned:

> "*O felix culpa!* Oh truly necessary sin of Adam,
>   destroyed completely by the death of Christ.
> *Oh happy fault* that earned so great, so glorious a Redeemer."[7]

It is not very common in our modern world to sing a hymn that glorifies death and praises sin. The purpose of the hymn's paradoxical language is to invite us to enter into the deeper levels of the paschal mystery. We certainly are not praising and glorifying God for sin or for the violent death of Jesus any more than we are thanking God for devastating hurricanes, or war, or terrorism, or the deaths of immigrants and refugees who die daily around the world in search of a better life.

The *Exsultet*'s opening phrase, "*O felix culpa,*" might be translated in a more modern way as, "*O marvelous disaster!*" It is supposed to shock us and force us to enter more deeply into the mystery of Jesus' salvific death. How, though, could we ever call murder "marvelous"? While Jesus' brutal crucifixion is a terrible, heart-sickening tragedy, we believe that it is also an inexplicable grace, the very path that leads us into an encounter with Love itself. Jesus dies loving—even his enemies (Lk 23:34), but not only that; the dead Christ continues his prodigal journey into hell, where he opens his arms in an offering of mercy, a salvific embrace of those whose lives of hatred, brokenness, and injustice seem to mean eternal damnation.

The paschal mystery of Jesus' total gift of himself on the cross is a paradox, one for which we "paradoxically" give thanks to God. Does that mean that God agrees with the brutal murder of Jesus? Does God just stand by and watch as the beloved Son dies innocently on the cross? Of course not. "Jesus nailed to the cross is God's entry into the shadow-side of our existence. It is the ultimate act of divine solidarity, the testimony that Jesus really is 'Emmanuel,' God-with-us (Mt 1:23)."[8] The *Abba* loves Jesus with a love beyond all telling—all the way to the end. Twice in the gospel, at his baptism and then later on the mountain of the transfiguration, we overhear the *Abba* express his great and tender love for the beloved Son: "This is my Son, the Beloved; with him I am well pleased; listen to him" (Mt 17:5). The *Abba*'s silence, as his beloved Son is being crucified, is the silence of a love that is greater than evil.

On May 21, 1996, Trappist monk Dom Christian de Chergé, OCSO, and six of his brother monks were brutally murdered and decapitated in Algeria, caught in the mindless violence of religious fundamentalism and the politics of power that continue to plague our world. Many months before being kidnapped, Dom Christian, the prior of the community, wrote a final testament, knowing that a violent death was very possible, given the political tensions that surrounded them. At the end of his last testament, he speaks directly to the person who one day could be his assassin. Like Christ on the cross, Dom Christian turns the hell of hatred into an opportunity for love, daring to see the image of God in his enemy:

> And also you, my last-minute friend, who will not have known what you were doing: Yes, I want this *thank you* and *goodbye* to be a "God bless" for you, too, because in God's face I see yours...[9]

Facing his own possible violent death, Jesus wrote a "final testament," as well, though not on paper. His "letter to the world" was written on his crucified, eucharistic body, which he gave to the world as spiritual food. This is signified in the Easter Vigil celebration when the paschal candle is *pierced* by nails in the form of a cross. We remember that hatred can be transformed into love and that darkness finally gives way to light. Before he gave his body and blood to his disciples, though, he prepared them by *bending down* to wash their feet. This outpouring of his love, this humble gift of himself to us, his brothers and sisters, shows us the depth of his love and prepares our feet for the pilgrimage back home to the house of his *Abba*, "who art in heaven..." (Mt 6:9).

> Jesus' abandonment on the cross represents God's final, absolute word of "no" to human evil...God in Christ descends as far as possible into the depths of human experience, even into its terrible God forsakenness, so as to become truly "God-with-us." The journey into the far country reaches its conclusion as Jesus goes down into the silent pit of death, deprived even of the Father's consolation. "God with us" yes: but he becomes also "God-without-God" for us and this is the event of our redemption.[10]

The Good News is proclaimed in hell

The frequent New Testament affirmations that Jesus was "raised from the dead" presuppose that the crucified one sojourned in the realm of the dead prior to his resurrection...[11] Jesus, like all [people], experienced death and in his soul joined the others in the realm of the dead. But he descended there as Savior, proclaiming the Good News to the spirits imprisoned there.[12]

An ancient homily for Holy Saturday, the day of the great silence, speaks of the journey that the crucified and dead Jesus, the Good Shepherd, makes to Hell, to visit and raise up Adam and Eve and "all those who have slept ever since the world began," all who have died with hope in God's gift of life:

> Today a great silence reigns on earth, a great silence and a great stillness. A great silence because the King is asleep... God has fallen asleep in the flesh and has raised up all who have slept ever since the world began... He has gone to search for Adam, our first father, *as for a lost sheep*. Greatly desiring to visit those who live in darkness and in the shadow of death, he has gone to free [them] from sorrow... he who is both their God and the son of Eve... "I am your God, who for your sake have become your son... I order you, O sleeper, to awake. I did not create you to be a prisoner in hell. Rise from the dead, for I am the life of the dead."[13]

Christ descends into the world and into hell with the same passion with which he lived his life: to search for the lost sheep. He finds more than lost sheep, though; he finds lost coins and lost sons and daughters, too. He even finds the rich man who ignored Lazarus at his gate (Lk 16:19–31). Can we not hope that, upon seeing the Risen Christ tending to the wounds of the poor, the rich man finally understands in hell what he ignored during his earthly life? Our hope makes us want to believe that he too follows Christ by *bending down* to assist Jesus in his mission of healing. Christ descends into hell singing the good news of salvation, for it is there that his final burst of salvific love is released:

> The gospel was preached even to the dead. [Jesus'] descent into hell brings the Gospel message of salvation to complete fulfillment. This is the last phase of Jesus' messianic mission, a phase which is condensed in time but vast in its real significance ... Christ went down into the depths of death so that "the dead will hear the voice of the Son of God, and those who hear will live." Jesus, "the Author of life," by dying destroyed "him who has the power of death, that is, the devil, and [delivered] all those who through fear of death were subject to lifelong bondage" ... so that "at the name of Jesus every knee

should bow, in heaven and on earth and under the earth" (cf. Phil 2:10).[14]

> Let this be recorded for a generation to come,
> so that a people yet unborn may praise the Lord:
> that he looked down from his holy height,
> from heaven the Lord looked at the earth,
> to hear the groans of the prisoners,
> to set free those who were doomed to die;
> so that the name of the Lord may be declared in Zion,
> and his praise in Jerusalem . . .
>   (Ps 102:18–21)

In the movie *Entertaining Angels*, based on the life of Dorothy Day, we glimpse again, through a contemporary lens, the mystery of Christ's self-emptying solidarity with broken and lost humanity. There is a scene toward the end of the movie when Dorothy's friend, Maggie, her life torn apart by alcoholism, steals from the meager savings of the Catholic Worker community in order to buy herself a drink. Dorothy walks in and surprises Maggie with her hand literally "in the cookie jar" (where the community kept their petty cash). When she asks Maggie what she is doing, Maggie unleashes the pent-up anger and violence of years of sickness and pain and physically attacks Dorothy, who controls her own almost instinctual reaction to strike back. Maggie falls to the floor, writhing like one of the demoniacs confronted by Jesus in his day. Dorothy looks deeply into Maggie's eyes and tells her that she sees light in her. Maggie cannot hear the words at first, and immediately denies that there could be any good in her sickened heart. She labels herself as a worthless drunk and whore. Dorothy does not move, nor does she summon the community to report the transgression. She stays put, kneeling faithfully at Maggie's side, cradling her head in her lap, soothing her with the unconditional mercy and love of God. It is raw, gospel compassion at its best.

Dorothy does what the prodigal Christ does. She *descends into Maggie's hell* in order to convey to Maggie the good news of salvation and the unconditional mercy of God. Her love for Maggie is a reflection of Jesus' love, for Jesus does not stand at a distance to lecture us about love; he *descends* into our brokenness and loves us. He *becomes* a leper in order to heal our leprosy. He *touches* the *untouchables*, and in so doing becomes an *untouchable* himself. He *becomes* an outcast so that he can welcome those pushed to the edge of society back into the family of God. He descends into hell in order to rescue those in hell. This downward movement of nonviolent, incarnate love, this preferential option for the poor, is repeated time and time again throughout the gospels. There is no greater love.

> O give thanks to the Lord, who is good;
> whose steadfast love endures forever.
> Let the redeemed of the Lord say so,
> those God redeemed from trouble
> and gathered in from the lands...
>
> Some sat in darkness and in gloom,
> prisoners in misery and in irons...
> Then they cried to the Lord in their trouble,
> and were saved from their distress;
> God brought them out of darkness and gloom,
> and broke their bonds asunder.
> Let them thank the Lord for his steadfast love,
> for his wonderful works to humankind.
>   (Ps 107:1–3,11–15)[15]

Renowned spiritual author Henri Nouwen suggests that "addiction" might be one of the words that can help us name the malaise that causes many to spiral down into a tragic spiritual death in our times. As we know, the tragic loss of life's deeper spiritual significance can happen in the midst of what outwardly seems to be a very successful life or career. Nouwen is not suggesting that everyone is an addict, but he does try to give a name to our world's compulsive search for happiness, often expressed by a reckless grasp for love and power. It is a frenetic search that leaves many people lost in a veritable hell, with no sense of how to find their way back home to freedom. Says Nouwen:

> "Addiction" might be the best word to explain the *lostness* that so deeply permeates society. Our addiction makes us cling to what the world proclaims as the keys to self-fulfillment: accumulation of wealth and power; attainment of status and admiration; lavish consumption of food and drink, and sexual gratification without distinguishing between lust and love... Our addictions condemn us to futile quests in "the distant country," leaving us to face an endless series of disillusionments while our sense of self remains unfulfilled. In these days of increasing addictions, we have wandered far away from our Father's home.[16]

Like Jesus' descent into hell, Dorothy's voluntary descent into Maggie's hell is an act of loving compassion. She sets off in search of the lost sheep, wanting nothing more than to welcome home the prodigal daughter of a loving God. Jesus' preferential love for the poor and for those condemned to a life of despair is not something easily explained within the limits of human logic. Jesus loves the unlovable and the broken-hearted unconditionally, and he invites us to follow him and learn this way of love. If we accept his invitation and follow him, then we must be willing to descend with him into the world's many versions of hell: war, oppression, addiction, domestic violence, gun violence, religious violence, hatred, greed, and so forth. We know the long list; they are words that we see every day in the headlines. Saint Andrew of Crete, in a Palm Sunday sermon, reminds us that:

> In his humility Christ entered the dark regions of our fallen world and he is glad that he became so humble for our sake, glad that he came and lived among us and shared in our nature in order to raise us up again . . . So let us spread before his feet, not garments or soulless olive branches, which delight the eye for a few hours and then wither, but ourselves, clothed in his grace, or rather, clothed completely in him. We who have been baptized into Christ must ourselves be the garments that we spread before him . . . "Blessed is he who comes in the name of the Lord. Blessed is the king of Israel."[17]

In her spiritual *Dialogue*, St. Catherine of Siena lets God know that she has finally understood this "crazy" and wonderful thing called "the love of God." Using pretty feisty language for a laywoman in the thirteenth century, Catherine says:

> If I turn to the earth, your mercy is everywhere. Even in the darkness of hell your mercy shines, for you do not punish the damned as much as they deserve . . . O mad lover! It was not enough for you to take on humanity: You had to die as well! Nor was death enough: You descended to the depths to summon our holy ancestors and fulfill your truth and mercy in them.[18]

When we Christians sing the *Exsultet* each year at Easter—"O marvelous disaster . . ."—we are not praising the murder of Jesus. We are, though, like Catherine of Siena, giving thanks to God for the gift of Jesus' unbelievable mercy and love. We give thanks for his total and free embrace of the cross, his final journey into Jerusalem, the heart-wrenching and love-filled celebration of the Last Supper, culminating in the tragic betrayal by Judas and Jesus' violent crucifixion and descent into hell.

This paschal self-emptying is not something that is easily "explained." Jesus, mad with love, accepts death that we might have life, and then he does the unthinkable: he descends into hell to search for all those who, in the course of human history, have chosen the path of hatred, violence, injustice, and all other forms of gospel infidelity. He journeys into the God-forsaken land of sin to offer us the gift of his reconciling love and then shows us the way back home to our beloved *Abba*.

Running in the "wrong" direction

My dear Dominican sister, Honora Werner, has a brother, named Roger, who died a few years ago after a long and blessed life. Roger was mentally challenged and lived much of his life in a home with other mentally challenged people. Roger was also on fire with the love of God. Though I never met Roger personally, I feel like I know him through Honora's wonderful stories. Whenever I see Honora I always ask her to tell me another "Roger story." I share here my favorite "Roger story":

> Roger was a great athlete and a regular participant in the annual Special Olympics—as a runner, and I understand, a pretty good one. One year Roger and one of his best friends were scheduled to compete in the same race. The pressure was on. The runners lined up, the gunshot sounded, and they took off with gusto. Roger, as usual, got off to an early lead, smiling as he gained distance from his competitors. On the final lap, clearly ahead of the rest of the pack, Roger glanced over his shoulder at those behind him and noticed that his good friend had stumbled and fallen on the track. Without blinking an eye, Roger made a 180° turn and began running against the traffic toward his good friend, smiling and waving to the other runners whom he passed on the way. When Roger reached his good friend, he helped him get up, and then the two of them, arm in arm, ran gloriously toward the finish line, completing the race together, crossing the finish line with their arms raised in victory! It was the triumph of a lifetime.

In the world's eyes, Roger and his friend came in last place. In the eyes of God, though, and in the upside-down logic of the Reign of God, Roger and his friend won much more than a race. They crossed the most important finish line of all, entering into the mysterious fullness of

God's world of unconditional love. Roger preached to the crowds that day. His prophetic gesture gives witness to the good news of salvation, which, like the Reign of God, often appears "upside-down."

In the Reign of God the prize is not about being the holiest, or the purest, or the most intelligent, or the most committed to the poor, or even the fastest runner. We are not awarded for being the first to reach heaven. The Reign of God, in fact, is not about competition at all. The Reign of God is about God's motherly heart that does not rest until all of the children have crossed the finish line. Roger understood that in a powerful and uncomplicated way.

Throughout his life, Jesus is constantly getting himself into trouble by running against the traffic and loving the wrong people. The religious authorities tell him time and time again to keep a safe distance from the tax collectors, and what does he do? He sits down and has dinner with them. They warn him not to hang out with prostitutes and lepers, and no sooner do they say the words, when on the very next page of the gospel we find him hugging them and calling them his friends! He is incorrigible.

We all know that, in the logic of the world, if you hang out with the wrong kind of people—the ones called "the losers"—you are not going to win any prizes. You are going to end up as just another loser. It is pretty clear, or at least it seems clear, as Jesus hangs helplessly on the cross, that his life ended without winning any prizes. We have no choice but to sing, "O marvelous disaster!"

Jesus is faithful to his *Abba*'s unconditional love all the way to the finish line. He continues to love even as he hangs dying on the cross: "Father, forgive them, for they do not know what they are doing" (Lk 23:34). Jesus does not stop there, though. After his death, as we have seen above, he turns around and runs against the traffic, against the flow of respectable humanity, with his eyes and arms and heart wide open, heading right back into the "distant country" of hell, just in case there is anyone who has been left behind. After all, how could Jesus cross the finish line knowing that someone has fallen and been left behind? St. Ambrose of Milan, writing around the year 390, said:

> Rise and run to the church ... The one who hears you pondering in the secret places of the mind *runs to you*. When you are still far away, he sees you and runs to you. He sees in your heart ... and embraces you.[19]

Is this not wonderful news for those of us who are trying to walk the path of God's love? Even though we are still far away, Jesus, the good shepherd, is already running toward us. He will run all the way to hell if necessary. He will not rest until the last sheep is found and brought home to the house of the *Abba*. God told St. Catherine of Siena to trust in the power of mercy, for no one is outside of the wide embrace of God:

> My daughter, see now and know that no one can be taken from me. Everyone is here as I said, either in justice or in mercy. They are mine; I created them, and I love them ineffably. And so, in spite of their wickedness, I will be merciful to them because of my servants, and I will grant what you have asked of me with such love and sorrow.[20]

Wise and wonderful Roger has finished his earthly race now; he has crossed the finish line. I am quite sure, though, that he is still running. I can almost see him, arm-in-arm with the prodigal Christ, looking over his shoulder to see who might have stumbled or fallen along the way of life. Roger understood the gospel call of unconditional love with a clarity and simplicity that is astounding. How can we claim "victory" if our brother or sister has fallen and cannot find the way back home? Could a person be so concerned about "being saved" that he or she might run right past a fallen neighbor with a scraped knee and see nothing (cf. Mt 25:31–46)? Would that not be the greatest blindness of all?

I am counting on Roger's help, not only to reach the finish line, but to help me learn to follow Christ. Something tells me that Roger understood a very profound piece of Jesus' teaching, a pearl of great price that we forget at our own peril. He reminds us that the "narrow door" (Lk 13:24) into God's eternal embrace has to be opened by *at least two people*. In other words, if we show up to that door alone, we will be in for a long wait. Jesus himself hinted at this when he said, "Where two or three are gathered in my name, I am there among them" (Mt 18:20). We are not saved alone; we are saved with our neighbor. I thank "Blessed Roger" for teaching me this great lesson in Christian discipleship.

The vow of the bodhisattva

We know through our gospel stories that two of Jesus' closest disciples also stumbled on the last lap of the race. In fact, tradition tells us that Peter fell *three times*! Judas' fall, as we know, left him seriously wounded, bloodied, lying on the edge of the track. There is hope, though. Word has it that Jesus, the "Good Shepherd," and his friend, Roger, the "Good Samaritan," have unexpectedly dropped out of first and second place in the race and are now running in the *opposite* direction, toward the "distant country," waving joyfully to all those who are racing feverishly to the finish line. Jesus and Roger stop when they reach Peter and Judas, both of whom are pretty badly wounded. And then the unexpected happens. Hundreds of children suddenly join them on the track to help in the rescue mission. Together they hoist the two apostles high into the air, and with shouts of joy, the entire group crosses the finish line together. Roger leads the pack with his arms lifted high in a sign of victory!

This is our story of salvation. Contrary to some versions, salvation is not some magic trick done behind a thick, heavy curtain up in heaven. There is no mysterious team handshake or secret password. It's all quite simple. God has chosen to use us, limited human beings, to help write this gospel love story. Christianity is only authentic—it only *works*—when we are concerned about the world's liberation, the world's salvation, and our neighbor's well-being more than our own. Roger and his friend, Jesus, have left us a great lesson. As Jesus himself said, "Many who are first will be last, and the last will be first" (Mt 19:30; Mk 10:31). It is Christian hope at its best.

In Buddhism, there is a special vow called the "vow of the bodhisattva." A bodhisattva is a kind of "Buddhist saint," one who makes a vow to *not* experience full enlightenment until the entire universe is enlightened. To put that in Christian parlance it would be like making a vow to *not* enter into the fullness of the Reign of God until the last sheep, the last sinner, the last runner in the race has been found, picked up into our arms and brought home.

> The *vow* of the bodhisattva is rooted in the experience of non-duality; it is oneness-in-suffering. For Christians this is *the key* to the practice of compassion. It is the willingness to lose one's separate self through communion with another's suffering ... "No one has greater love than this, to lay down one's life for one's friends" (Jn 15:13).[21]

A Christian bodhisattva understands that it is of no value to reach the Reign of God as long as there are still some people who have fallen on the way. Roger clearly knew what "oneness in suffering" meant that day at the racetrack. Maybe he learned it from the good Samaritan. What value is there in running to the temple if my neighbor is wounded on the side of the road? Why would I want to pray to God if my brother or sister is not with me (cf. Mt 5:23–24)?

The good Samaritan, as we saw in an earlier chapter, teaches us that to be a disciple of Jesus requires a willingness to change our geography; it requires *movement*. It is *not* about racing to see who gets to the temple first, or who reaches heaven first, or which church has the most members. As Roger teaches us so beautifully, the true Christian will always be the one who is running in the "wrong direction," moving *toward* the sinful, fallen world—not away from it. And it is not difficult to realize that if we are running *toward* the sinners, then we will very likely be accused, as Jesus was, of hanging out with tax collectors and sinners. *O felix culpa!*

Maybe the saints in heaven are something like Christian bodhisattvas who freely vow to remain on the racetrack, picking up fallen runners for as long as it takes, until every creature of God is safely home. I would not be at all surprised to find out that Roger is a captain of one of the bodhisattva squads. Word has it that another squad of saintly bodhisattvas are busy sweeping the dark alleys in a dangerous part of the city, helping the woman from Luke's parable (15:8) search *not* for a lost coin, but for a young teenage drug addict who was last seen curled up under an abandoned truck. Is this not what it means to follow Christ—to be prepared to go wherever he goes? When we live each day with trust in God's paradoxical paths, life itself is transformed into a parable of salvation.

Timeless communion

I have a good friend named Mel who is a Baptist minister. Mel lives in a large city that struggles with poverty, racism, hunger, and many of the woes of our modern world. When Mel is not preparing a Sunday preaching, he is usually in a meeting with other concerned ministers and rabbis, priests, imams, and ordinary committed citizens, looking for ways to reduce poverty and illiteracy in their city. One day Mel and I were speaking about heaven and the Reign of God and many other wonderful topics, when Mel said something that surprised me. I will try to reconstruct what he said:

> I wish we Baptists had the same understanding of the dead that you Catholics have. For us, when a person dies, we say goodbye to that person, celebrate the funeral, talk about all the good things that the person did, bury them, sing wonderful hymns and then it's all over. For us, there is a high wall of stone between us and them, between the living and the dead, as we wait for the second coming of Christ. You Catholics, on the other hand, don't have a wall separating you from the dead. It is just a fence. And that means that you can still reach through

the fence and touch the dead and communicate with them. There's something very profound in your relationship with the dead that I wish we had.

I must say in all honesty that Mel helped me understand and appreciate a dimension of my own Catholic faith in a very profound way that day. I think his metaphor of the fence is quite insightful. The saints are probably not up in heaven, sitting on big comfortable sofas, eating popcorn and watching Christian television programs! They are out on the battlefield of life, right next to *Abba*. They are also following Roger as he runs toward the distant country, bending down next to a fallen runner, showing all of us what it means to be a true disciple of Jesus. Thanks to God, the saints are like busy bodhisattvas doing full-time ministry on behalf of us fallen sinners, reaching their hands through the fence to help us stand up and continue the race. If that does not fill us with hope, then nothing will.

9

Resurrection
Fountain of Compassion

Early on the first day of the week, while it was still dark, Mary Magdalene came to the tomb and saw that the stone had been removed...She saw two angels in white...They said to her, "Woman, why are you weeping?" She said to them, "They have taken away my Lord, and I do not know where they have laid him." When she had said this, she turned around and saw Jesus standing there, but she did not know that it was Jesus. Jesus said to her, "Woman, why are you weeping? Whom are you looking for?" Supposing him to be the gardener, she said to him, "Sir, if you have carried him away, tell me where you have laid him, and I will take him away." Jesus said to her, "Mary!" She turned and said to him in Hebrew, "*Rabbouni!*" (which means Teacher)...Jesus said to her, "Go to my brothers and say to them, 'I am ascending to my Father and your Father, to my God and your God.'" Mary Magdalene went and announced to the disciples, "I have seen the Lord"; and she told them that he had said these things to her. (Jn 20:1, 12–18)

Later that same day, as the newborn Easter light begins to set, the disciples, gathered in the upper room, find themselves navigating the space between confusion and elation, between death and life.

Jesus came and stood among them and said, "Peace be with you." After he said this, he showed them his hands and his side. Then the disciples rejoiced when they saw the Lord. Jesus said to them again, "Peace be with you. As the Father has sent me, so I send you." When he had said this, he *breathed on them* and said to them, "Receive the Holy Spirit." (Jn 20:19–22)

The breath of new life that pours forth from Jesus sweeps through the entire house (cf. Gen 1:2), opening up not only the closed doors and windows of the upper room, but the closed and fearful hearts of the disciples, as well. As they breathe in the powerful Spirit that emanates from the Risen Christ, the long dark night of death suddenly gives way to a brilliant light and peace. The energy of a new creation floods into the room, filling them with hope: "In the beginning when...the earth was a formless void and darkness covered the face of the deep...God said, 'Let there be light;' and there was light...the first day" (Gen 1:1–5).

> At the beginning of the first creation story in Genesis, the Spirit hovered over chaos—the dark, lifeless chaos that was powerless even to await God's creative word before life came to be. But the cross was raised on Calvary over new chaos, the chaos of sin which had done its utmost to destroy God's Word incarnate in Jesus. In Christ's weakness, in his suffering and obedience, the mighty deed was done. At Easter the Spirit-breath of the risen Jesus inaugurated the new creation of grace...The mighty act was of God, but this time he would not act alone; he chose to empower fellow workers: "as the Father has sent me, so I send you." The Easter mission had begun.[1]

Stunned, yet overflowing with joy, the disciples feel their hearts being healed and stretched in ways never before imagined. Their crucified teacher and friend is here—*present*, alive, fully embodied, speaking to them.

> Suddenly the silence is no more the silence of absence...[it] is the place of a Word. That Word that they tried to silence now echoes anew. The Word is a promise of life...Frequently the emptiness is unpleasant, it frightens us, it offers no horizons. We begin to believe that nothingness, death, and anxiety could put an end to humanity forever...The tomb is empty: "He is not here." Nevertheless, they understand that this emptiness is not proof of an absence; on the contrary, it indicates that the One who was destroyed by death has parted. A new presence is born from the empty tomb...a presence that walks with them and gives them life. The silence is now inhabited by the Word. The emptiness is sustained by a dense presence of the One whom they loved and now can continue to love.[2]

In the midst of all the violence, most of the disciples have managed to stay rooted in the present moment. And now that the dust has begun to settle, they begin to weave together the pieces of this unbelievable story: "Yes, we saw him dead on the cross. This we know. Who, then, is this who stands before us, asking us for something to eat (cf. Lk 24:41)? How can this be?" The very disciples who were convinced that love had died forever suddenly find themselves bathed in a new and liberating light, witnesses to the birth of a new creation. The dark emptiness of the tomb has yielded to a new presence, accompanied by an ancient voice: "Let there be light and there was light" (Gen 1:3).

Soon thereafter two other disciples, both of whom had given up all hope, return to the community of believers in Jerusalem with unbelievable news: they too have seen Jesus. Though they did not recognize him at first, and thinking that he was just another pilgrim returning home from Jerusalem, they had invited him to rest for the night in their home. It was during the evening meal, at the moment of the breaking of the bread, that their eyes were opened, revealing that it was he (Lk 24:28–35). "But how can this be? We saw him dead on the cross. Our brother was dead and has come back to life, was lost and has been found" (cf. Lk 15:32).

> His obedient dying was a Godlike act. Self-giving, self-emptying love, an ecstasy of unreserved giving in joy...It is the glory of God to give, holding nothing back...The resurrection is the *Abba*'s acceptance of the Son's gift, and the penetration by the Spirit of their mutual love into every fiber of Jesus's body and mind.[3]

The wounds, though still very real and visible on the risen Jesus' body, appear almost luminous now. What had seemed grotesquely abhorrent on Calvary suddenly becomes a doorway into hope and healing. But how? Should they not be horrified by this gruesome reminder of violence and death? He is alive, though. Life has conquered death. Their teacher, the one who had called them "friends," has returned from the distant land of hatred, sin, and death. He who experienced abandonment on the cross now experiences the faithful and eternal embrace of his *Abba* and the joyful reunion with his beloved disciples. The cross has been transformed into an icon of immeasurable love; life is born from death. God, filled with joy at the beloved Son's resurrection, has thrown protocol to the wind and is dancing in the street!

> Like a woman with child, who writhes and cries out in her pangs when she is near her time, so were we because of you, O Lord; we were with child, we writhed...Your dead shall live, their corpses shall rise. O dwellers in the dust, awake and sing

for joy! For your dew is a radiant dew, and the earth will give birth to those long dead. (Is 26:17, 19)

The path of love

> Thomas (who was called the Twin), one of the twelve, was not with them when Jesus came. So the other disciples told him, "We have seen the Lord." But he said to them, "Unless I see the mark of the nails in his hands, and put my finger in the mark of the nails and my hand in his side, I will not believe." (Jn 20:24–25)

Much of Christian history has looked disapprovingly, almost with embarrassment, on Thomas's stubbornness. Could it be that we need to rethink our "doubting Thomas" aversion? Is he not, in fact, one of the most honest of all the disciples or do we simply relegate him, like Judas, to the category of scapegoat? Along with Mary Magdalene, who braves the night in search of her beloved teacher when everyone else has fled, Thomas does not accept easy answers in the face of the horror of the crucifixion. "You say he is alive? Then let me see the mark of the nails. I saw him die on the cross. His gospel is my life now. I refuse to let his story be whitewashed by easy religious answers." Thomas may be struggling with trying to understand his faith, but no one can "doubt" his rootedness in Christ. Precisely because they are willing to face the dark nothingness with nothing but bare faith, both Thomas and Mary Magdalene become great witnesses of the new creation that Jesus has come to inaugurate.

Is it not true that every honest believer must eventually face the dark night of faith? After all, it is not the cocky repetition of ancient beliefs that makes us disciples, but the obedient search for truth, the willingness to follow Christ in the midst of the dark "cloud of unknowing." Saul of Tarsus had to learn that lesson the hard way, letting himself be led like a child to Damascus and beyond, in fact, to a whole new life (Acts 9). "It is in the deepest darkness," says Thomas Merton, "that we most fully possess God on earth, because it is then that we are most truly liberated from the weak, created lights... [and] filled with his infinite light which seems pure darkness to our reason."[4] Only one who has risked the dark journey of discipleship, setting off with the prodigal Christ into the distant land of paschal love, can be counted among the "children of the light" (cf. Eph 5:8). Mary Magdalene and Thomas are tested guides on that dark path of faith.

Our encounter with the Risen Christ is not a competition to see who has the answer to the million-dollar question. It is not about winning the lottery or the national spelling bee. In fact, the key to this paschal faith is not about winning at all; it is about *losing*. Like the prodigal son, who returns home empty-handed, we discover the fullness of life by giving it away. "For those who want to save their life will lose it, and those who lose their life for my sake will save it" (Lk 9:24). The "winners," as Roger teaches us so well (ch. 8), are those who cross the finish line empty-handed, rooted in a love that is as "strong as death" (Song of Songs 8:6). These are the ones who taste true freedom. "No one has greater love than this, to lay down one's life for one's friends" (Jn 15:13).

Is this not what Jesus has been trying to teach us all along? Is this not why he says to Thomas, "Put your finger here and see my hands. Reach out your hand and put it in my side. Do not doubt but believe" (Jn 20:27)? Jesus is teaching Thomas (and us, too) that victory looks very much like failure. From the perspective of the crucified and risen Christ, life's failures and mistakes suddenly are infused with inexpressible hope. Jesus is calling us into true freedom, and he does so by reminding us that his defeat is our victory. Our poor, empty hands, like the empty tomb, are teaching us to hope and trust again. At last we begin to understand what he was trying to teach us that day on the mountaintop, when he said, "Blessed are you who are poor, for yours is the kingdom of God" (Lk 6:20).

In a profound and challenging article entitled, "Wound Made Fountain: Toward a Theology of Redemption," Jerome Miller leads us through this mystery of Christ's upside-down paschal journey, into the mystery of love.

> If, in the madness of divine irony, this *wound* is transformed into a fountain, then redemption flows...from it. The crucifixion...would simultaneously be murder and benediction, unbearable horror and transforming grace. If it is true that, in the historical Jesus of Nazareth, divinizing Love circulates without hindrance, this would mean that when my violence causes a fatal wound in him, there immediately flows from this wound, as from a fountain, a love that is directed toward me.[5]

Jesus invites Mary Magdalene, Thomas, and the other disciples to face head-on the evil caused by hatred, and to do so with nothing but the raw power of faith in Christ's risen, nonviolent love. One cannot live the paschal mystery from a safe distance. "Reach out your hand and put it in my side. Do not doubt but believe" (Jn 20:27). Miller continues:

If it had a million years, human intelligence would not be able to imagine the possibility that there is a kind of love capable of tenderly embracing the abhorrent... The love Paul describes, the love that embraces us "while we are still sinners" (Rom 5:8)—while we are unlovable—is, for us, morally unimaginable, logically inconceivable, historically impossible.[6]

Yet it is real. It is the only path of authentic Christian discipleship, the path that leads us into the mystery of radical nonviolent love. It is nothing less than the Risen Christ's gift to us, his disciples.

Nonviolence and the wounded Christ

Martin Luther King, Jr. understood in a very profound way what Jerome Miller calls "the madness of divine irony." King challenged an entire nation to embrace the active, nonviolent love espoused by Jesus, Gandhi, Franz Jägerstätter, Dorothy Day, the Dalai Lama, and others. King was convinced that only nonviolent resistance, what Gandhi called *ahimsa*, could transform the energy of hatred and violence into a creative force for change and a fountain of new life. Like the apostle Thomas, King reminds us that we must be willing to reach out and touch our world, mortally wounded by violence and social exclusion of all kinds, if we are to incarnate Christ's new creation. It is *not* accomplished by blaming the enemy, nor can we achieve it through military strength. It is possible only through the vulnerable and naked power of love. The struggle, as we know, was not easy for King. Many opposed him, and in the end he gave his life to enflesh his dream of peace. In his book, *Strength to Love*, King spells out his strategy of nonviolent social change, based on Christ-like love:

> To our bitterest opponents we say: We shall match your capacity to inflict suffering by our capacity to endure suffering. We shall meet your physical force with soul force. Do to us what you will, we shall continue to love you... Throw us in jail, and we shall still love you. Send your hooded perpetrators of violence into our community at the midnight hour and beat us, and leave us half-dead, and we shall still love you. But be ye assured that we will wear you down by our capacity to suffer. One day we shall win freedom, but not only for ourselves. We shall so appeal to your heart and conscience that we shall win you in the process, and our victory will be a double victory.[7]

I have a dear friend, Sheila, who served as a member of a Christian Peacemaker Team (CPT) during the Iraqi war that began with the US-led invasion in 2003. CPT teams are composed of committed peace activists dedicated to nonviolent witness and presence. After serving in this capacity for two years, Sheila returned to the United States. She continued to maintain contact with many of her friends back in Iraq, one of whom is the Iraqi Dominican friar, Yousif Thomas Mirkis, who now serves as the archbishop of Kirkuk in Iraq. In a letter that Fr. Yousif sent to Sheila after her return to the United States, which she later shared with me, he spoke of the difficult situation that they were facing, while reminding her that, despite the hardships, they had not lost their faith and trust in God. This is an excerpt from his letter:

> Yes, Sheila, we are in the middle of the storm, and the Lord seems to sleep, but he is here with us . . . It is so sweet to live as he suggests, in the foolish way of love of those who are around; it is not our choice but his. Be happy and count on my prayers.[8]

Fr. Yousif makes no attempt to protect himself from the consequences of following Christ. In fact, he freely chooses to embrace this "foolish way of love" with deep trust and inner freedom. Is it not with this same confidence in his *Abba*'s faithful, abiding presence that the beloved Son sets off into the distant country of sin and violence? Discipleship does not come with a divine immunization that protects us from suffering and failure. The opposite, in fact, is true. Following Christ leads us right into the middle of the storm; it is there that we learn to incarnate God's unconditional love for the world. Balthasar reminds us that this "foolish way of love" has profound implications:

> This incarnation of God's solidarity with the poor (in every form) has, however, a catastrophic logic: if God takes this seriously, it will bring [Jesus] to the cross . . . because he now must really "be reckoned among those who have broken the law" (Lk 22:37) . . . Those who put themselves at the head of the poor, in order to lead them along an unmarked path into the kingdom of God which is "near" . . . put themselves also at the head of the sinners, in order to lead them along, as the first of the "lost [children]," to the Father who is drawing near and hastening to meet them.[9]

The young Dutch Jewish philosopher and seeker, Etty Hillesum, who died a victim of Nazism in Auschwitz in 1943, clearly knew what it meant to walk the "foolish way of love." Etty had struggled intensely as a young adult in her search to understand the meaning of love, a search that broke her open in many ways, eventually leading her to God. Once she discovered God, Etty never looked back.

Following the Nazi invasion of Amsterdam in May 1940, Etty, like so many others, finds herself literally in "the middle of the storm," to use Fr. Yousif's phrase, one more victim of Hitler's fear-driven hatred. Rather than surrender to the poison of hatred, though, Etty opens herself to a love that transforms every fiber of her being, liberating her from inside out. Looking death in the face, she discovers the beauty and true meaning of life:

> I find life beautiful, and I feel free. The sky within me is as wide as the one stretching above my head. I believe in God and I believe in [humanity], and I say so without embarrassment...True peace will come only when every individual finds peace within him or herself...[transforming] hatred...into love.[10]
>
> Somewhere inside me the jasmine continues to blossom undisturbed, just as profusely and delicately as ever it did. And it spreads its scent round the House in which You dwell, oh God...Even if I should be locked up in a narrow cell and a cloud should drift past my small barred window, then I shall bring you that cloud, oh God, while there is still the strength in me to do so.[11]

Etty does not run from the chaos of war; instead, she faces the storm with courage and her profound faith in God and in life itself. She, like Fr. Yousif, finds God in the midst of the chaos—a discovery that sets her free and opens her to a love without limit. Following the path of the prodigal Christ, Etty walks into the distant land of suffering and evil with unbelievable faith and hope. Her journal entries attest to her deep freedom and love.

> This morning I said to Jopie, "It still all comes down to the same thing: life is beautiful. And I believe in God. And I want to be there right in the thick of what people call 'horror' and still be able to say: life is beautiful."[12]

It is noteworthy that in the days following his resignation in 2013, Pope Benedict XVI spoke of the courage and faith of two remarkable twentieth-century women, both of whom chose to share their lives with the poor: Etty Hillesum and the cofounder of the Catholic Worker movement, Dorothy Day. Pointing to the fact that both of these twenti-eth-century women chose the path of radical love in the midst of a world that easily runs from such dangerous demands, Pope Benedict says this of Etty Hillesum:

> I am also thinking of Etty Hillesum, a young Dutch girl of Jew-ish origin who died in Auschwitz. At first far from God, she discovered him looking deep within her and she wrote: "There is a really deep well inside me. And in it dwells God. Some-times I am there, too. But more often stones and grit block the well, and God is buried beneath. Then [God] must be dug out again" (*Diaries*, 97). In her disrupted, restless life she found God in the very midst of the great tragedy of the 20th century: the *Shoah*... Transfigured by faith, [she] became a woman full of love and inner peace who was able to declare: "I live in con-stant intimacy with God."[13]

Etty's rootedness in God sets her free. Once she discovers the foun-tain of life-giving water, her heart expands to embrace the entire uni-verse. Etty's love knows no boundaries. Writing in her diary, she says, "German soldiers suffer as well. There are no frontiers between suffer-ing people, and we must pray for them all."[14] Etty's deep interior peace confounds those who live in a world void of any semblance of transcen-dence. Sr. Jean Marie Dwyer says this about Etty's mystical journey:

> Etty knows the reality of the world around her and has no illu-sions of what is taking place... By living from within the truth and beauty of her inner chamber, Etty can face all the events of life with peace and stability... As [her] inward journey pro-gresses, there is also an increasing consciousness that this turn-ing inward is not introversion, but rather a broadening of her horizons... Fixing oneself in the God life within is the secret of peace and unchangeableness in the midst of life's vacillations.[15]

While the storm rages in the land of violence and sin, of war and injustice, Etty teaches us that it is possible to remain anchored in God, what Fr. Yousif calls "the foolish way of love." There is an inner peace that is greater than the fleeting ups and downs of the world. Says Balthasar:

> The "yes" to suffering and to the night receives its ultimate jus-tification from Christology, from a "yes" of the Son to the will

of the Father which can be spoken only in joy...One cannot dismiss the [fact]...that an element of joy dwells in the lowest depths of the abandonment by God, and that it is this joy which makes the abandonment possible.[16]

The journey into the distant country is not a picnic. The deeper significance of this paschal path, however, does not depend on us. The prodigal Christ has gone before us. He is the way, the truth and the life (Jn 14:4); we are his disciples. Our task is very concrete: to follow him.

Wound become fountain

The prodigal Christ's violent death, as we know, is not the end of the story. Jesus' risen body, marked with the mortal wounds of hatred and death, becomes a fountain. In a paradoxical way, the end of Jesus' life is only the beginning. Through his free and total identification with our human condition, Jesus imbues our fragile reality with a luminous gift of new life. Foolish love has the last word.

Then the soldiers came and broke the legs of the first and of the other who had been crucified with Jesus. But when they came to Jesus and saw that he was already dead, they did not break his legs. Instead, one of the soldiers pierced his side with a spear, and at once blood and water came out. (Jn 19:32–34)

The crucified and dead body of Christ has been transformed into a gushing spring of new life. This is what Etty Hillesum points to when she speaks of "the really deep well inside me."[17] Jerome Miller goes on to say that, "If forgiveness flows from the very wounds of the historical Jesus, then...forgiveness would not look past the evil I have done...It would be offered to the evil in me...What flows from the wound ...would then be a river of blood that baptizes me into grace."[18]

We who have been baptized and born anew in the river of the water of life that flows from the pierced side of the crucified Christ (Rev 22:1) are now sent into the distant country, following in the footsteps of our prodigal and now risen brother, Jesus. We are anointed to be a fountain of new life and to announce the dawning of a new day. Like Jesus, we must be prepared to give our lives away, to spend the *Abba*'s inheritance with the world, and to break and share the Body of Christ with all who "hunger and thirst for righteousness" (cf. Mt 5:6). This paschal paradox of death and life will mark us for the rest of our lives, for once we drink from the fountain of life that flows from the wounded side of Christ, we are sent to share his life-giving blood and his river of new life with the world.

> Then the angel showed me the river of the water of life, bright as crystal, flowing from the throne of God and of the Lamb through the middle of the street of the city. On either side of the river is the tree of life with its twelve kinds of fruit...and the leaves of the tree are for the healing of the nations...They will see his face, and his name will be on their foreheads. And there will be no more night; they need no light of lamp or sun, for the Lord God will be their light, and they will reign forever and ever. (Rev 22:1–5)

Jesus returns to his disciples on that glorious morning of the first day scarred by death, and yet he is very much alive. His presence sends shock waves through the community. Is this real or just a dream? "They were startled and terrified, and thought that they were seeing a ghost" (Lk 24:37). Looking around at each of his beloved followers, his friends, Jesus asks, "And Judas? Where is our brother, Judas?" (cf. Gen 4:9). They look at each other in utter shock and silence. No one knows where Judas is. No one has even dared to ask that question. Jesus looks at each of them with tenderness, and then asks the same question that he asked at Café Capernaum:

> Which one of you, having a hundred sheep and losing one of them, does not leave the ninety-nine in the wilderness and go after the one that is lost until he finds it? When he has found it, he lays it on his shoulders and rejoices. And when he comes home, he calls together his friends and neighbors, saying to them, "Rejoice with me, for I have found my sheep that was lost." (Lk 15:4–6)

"My friends, please excuse me, but I must return to the distant country; our brother, Judas, is lost. Remember, 'It is not the will of your *Abba* in heaven that one of these little ones should be lost' (Mt 18:14). I must go find our brother and bring him home. Keep the fire burning, and know that I am with you always" (cf. Mt 28:20). In the words of Pope Francis:

> An evangelizing community knows that the Lord has taken the initiative, [and] has loved us first (cf. 1 Jn 4:19), and therefore

we can move forward, boldly take the initiative, go out to others, seek those who have fallen away, stand at the crossroads and welcome the outcast. Such a community has an endless desire to show mercy, the fruit of its own experience of the power of the *Abba*'s infinite mercy... "You will be blessed if you do this." (Jn 13:17)[19]

Louis, my brother

When I entered the Dominican novitiate in the early 1980s, I was the youngest of the group of novices. I cannot help but smile as I look back on those days, aware now more than ever that I had no idea just what this new adventure would entail. In fact, had I known all that awaited me, I probably would have run in the opposite direction. O blessed ignorance!

I look back to that new beginning and realize that I was something like tiny Moses, being placed into the papyrus basket and pushed out onto a mighty river that would take me to places (interiorly and exteriorly) that I would have never dreamed would be part of my life. I had to learn to let go and trust the flow, usually having no earthly idea where this wild river would take me. I very likely would have abandoned ship that first year if it had not been for an elderly Dominican friar, named Louis, whose tender mercy pulled me out of the fast-moving waters on more than one occasion. "Fr. Louie," as we all called him, was a saint. The first person up every morning, he would drink his cup of black coffee and then sit for an hour in deep prayer in the dark chapel. I had never seen someone who could sit that still. I know without a doubt that I lived with a saint that very first year in the Order. My guess is that most every other friar who lived with Louie as a novice would echo my words. We all loved him.

Paradoxically, Fr. Louis was also a very wounded man, having gone through a vicious struggle with alcoholism. He was very open about his addiction and program of recovery, and though I did not have much experience with the disease of alcoholism, I learned a lot from this wise and wounded healer. Lou's honesty and vulnerability were precisely what made him so accessible to all of us. He was a true "brother" in every way. The humility and transparency that accompanied his struggle were a great teaching for all of us.

I entered the Order with lofty ideas of heroic holiness, convinced that one needed to become a great and holy athlete for Christ. And then I met Louie, whose vulnerable and humble life caught me completely off-guard. I knew intuitively that he was holy, even as my categories for defining "holiness" were being shattered before my very eyes. Though I did not understand it all at first, I clearly witnessed the compassion that flowed from every cell of his being. He was not afraid of our faults and our vulnerability, because he was so aware of his own *unfinishedness*. Some years later I read the following quote of Gerald May, and it was like hearing someone describe our dear brother, Fr. Lou.

> Although God calls us all toward a more perfect life, we cannot personally achieve the state of perfection. We can and should do our very best to move in that direction, struggling with every resource we have, but we must also accept the reality of our *incompleteness*... We need to recognize that the incompleteness within us, our personal insufficiency, does not make us unacceptable in God's eyes. Far from it... It is what draws us toward God and one another. If we do not fill our minds with guilt and self-recriminations, we will recognize our incompleteness as a kind of *spaciousness* into which we can welcome the flow of grace.[20]

My brother, Lou, not only taught me to embrace my own incompleteness, but he quietly revealed to me the wonder of my own inner *spaciousness*. It has been one of the greatest gifts of my life.

After my novitiate year ended, I was blessed to be able to see Louie about once a year at our annual provincial assembly; it was always like "coming home." I always looked forward to our "It's time-to-catch-up" chat. The first words out of his mouth each year were always the same: "How's my little brother doing?" As I write these words, tears are flowing freely down my face—tears of utter gratitude for the gift of this wonderful brother and mentor in my life. Some years later, Lou preached at my first Mass as a new priest, a blessing that I treasure to this day.

After finishing my theology studies I was called to be part of a new foundation that our Order was initiating in Central America. The continent that had so powerfully impacted me as a teenager was to become my home for many years to come. Thanks to the brothers with whom I lived and the many challenges and joys that we shared with the people of God, I still consider those years as some of the most formative years of my life. Living and working among the poor helped me to embrace my own poverty, awakening in me a profound sense of gratitude for the gift of life itself.

I saw less of my dear brother, Louie, during those years, though there are a few wonderful visits that still stand out in my mind. The last visit, though, just about broke my heart. I had heard that Lou's health was declining, but, worse yet, that he had fallen into a very deep depression. I sat for hours with Lou during that last visit, yet he was so lost in darkness that he could hardly acknowledge my presence. I tried to express how much I loved him, reminding him how grateful I was for his faithful, brotherly friendship over all the years, but he was unable to hear or believe in such words. That deep darkness was his companion until death.

I was not able to be present at Lou's funeral when, about a year after my last visit, he died. Sometimes I wonder if my beloved friend and mentor died crying out in the silence of his heart, "My God, my God, why have you forsaken me" (Mk 15:34)? For reasons that only God can know, Lou had been invited to enter deeply into the paschal mystery of the cross. Can such a mystery ever really be *understood*?

Wounded healer: A light shines in the distant country

> Is not this the fast that I choose: to loose the bonds of injustice, to undo the thongs of the yoke, to let the oppressed go free, and to break every yoke? Is it not to share your bread with the hungry, and bring the homeless poor into your house; when you see the naked, to cover them, and not to hide yourself from your own kin? Then your light shall break forth like the dawn, and your healing shall spring up quickly... Then you shall call, and the Lord will answer; you shall cry for help, and he will say, Here I am. (Is 58:6–9)

Isaiah, the prophet, reminds us that even in our darkest of nights, even in the midst of hunger, nakedness, and oppression God speaks a word of loving presence: "Here I am" (Is 58:9). This, of course, does not mean that one will always hear God's voice or experience that loving presence. When Jesus cries from the cross, "My God, my God, why have you forsaken me" (Mk 15:34), his cry, though obedient and faithful, seems to suggest that he had no *tangible* experience of his *Abba's* presence. His cry is in itself an act of faith. We know, of course, that God is not completely absent when Christ is crucified—a truth that becomes manifest in his resurrection from the dead. Still marked with the signs of violence and death, the risen Jesus returns to the disciples, very much alive and filled with the Holy Spirit's presence, to share a meal with them (cf. Lk 24:28–43). The chains of death have been broken, and our faith and hope are renewed. "In hope we were saved. Now hope that is seen is not hope...But if we hope for what we do not see, we wait for it with patience" (Rom 8:24–25).

Our dear brother, Lou, seems to have died in a similar state of desolation, without seeing or experiencing the light of the Risen Christ. Those who accompanied Lou to the end say that he struggled with tremendous darkness until the day he died. With unbelievable faith, he carried his cross through a wide and barren desert, all the way to the end. Lou's path of darkness and emptiness is a mystery that I hope to understand some day—a mystery that has always seemed tragic and unjust.

This was the only story of Lou's death that I knew—until a couple of years ago, when I happened to meet a Dominican sister who had worked closely with Lou during those last years of his life. When we discovered, after conversing a bit, that we both knew dear Louie, our eyes danced with joy, even as our hearts experienced an understandable heaviness of spirit. I said to the sister, "It still is a mystery to me that someone so loved and revered, so gifted and respected, could die in such darkness and desolation. I will never understand it." The Dominican sister nodded in agreement, confirming what we all felt regarding Lou. Then she continued, "But you know, Brian, doesn't it still amaze you that, even in his darkest days he never missed a day of visiting the people at the AIDS hospice downtown? I am still moved by his faithfulness to them until the end."

I am sure that my face, upon hearing her words, registered a look of utter shock. "What? Are you telling me that Lou continued visiting the people at the hospice during all that time?" She nodded her head: "Yes, every single day. He took public transportation downtown every day," she said, "and spent several hours, going from bed to bed, comforting the patients, praying with them, sitting next to them, holding their hands. Lou was the light that gave them hope in the midst of so much darkness."

I stood before this sister in utter shock. I knew that Lou had been ministering to people with HIV/AIDS in the last years of his life. Those were the early years of the epidemic, when many people were dying of the disease. Since I was not living in the United States during that time, though, I had no idea that Lou had continued to visit the hospice each day, even in the depths of his depression. I had somehow never heard this story. I was simply speechless. Again, in the words of Isaiah, the prophet:

Then your light shall break forth like the dawn, and your healing shall spring up quickly...Then you shall call, and the Lord

will answer; you shall cry for help, and he will say, Here I am.
(Is 58:6–9)

I listened to my Dominican sister's description of Lou's final years
and months in complete shock. Here was my dear friend and mentor,
plunged into his own darkness, struggling with serious depression, and
yet he got on a bus every day to go and share his loving and prayerful
presence with people dying of AIDS. Unable to glimpse even the slight-
est sliver of God's light and presence in his own heart, he was a beacon
of divine light and love for others. I simply could not believe what I
was hearing, certainly not because I thought that Lou was incapable of
such compassion; his whole life was about compassion. I just had no
idea that he had continued this ministry at a time of such darkness in
his own life.

Jerome Miller, writing as if he were speaking directly to Jesus, leads
us even deeper into this mystery of Christ's solidarity in the midst of
suffering, sin and evil.

> The Incarnation [describes] your will to "descend" into the
> world, [as] the flow of love...When You pour your love into
> history You hold nothing back...Your response to the wound
> that cries out to heaven is to divinize it...You embrace and
> pour yourself into the wound itself...This divinizing love does
> what would otherwise be not only impossible but unimagin-
> able and inconceivable: flooding the wound with love...
> [transforming] it into a fountain. What flows from this fountain
> is precisely the divine love that is poured into it. Toward whom
> does this love flow? It moves, with a kind of inexorable divine
> gravity, toward the place in the universe that most needs it.[21]

Using language very similar to that of the Rhineland mystics of the
thirteenth century, Miller leads us into the heart of the paschal mystery
by reminding us that God's love flows first through the wounds of the
crucified and risen Christ, and only then does it flow out into the world
like a healing balm (cf. Rev 22:1–2). Salvation does not happen only in
the end times. It is always happening. God is saving, healing, and loving
the world into wholeness here and now—today. Though it seems that
our dear brother, Lou, was not able to experience the fact that he was a
conduit for this powerful river of divine love, the truth is he was precisely that. His life, "hidden with Christ" (Col 3:3) and hidden beneath
the shadows of depression, was the instrument that God used to bring
the light of Christ to "the least of my brothers and sisters" (Mt 25:40).

To use an image from an earlier chapter, Lou's feet knew the path to the distant country, they knew how to cross to the other side of the road even when his mind and heart were lost and confused, plunged into the darkness of unknowing. St. Paul captures this mystery well, reminding us of God's marvelous capacity to do great things with our poverty and limitations:

> We have this treasure in clay jars, so that it may be made clear that this extraordinary power belongs to God and does not come from us. We are afflicted in every way, but not crushed; perplexed, but not driven to despair; persecuted, but not forsaken; struck down, but not destroyed; always carrying in the body the death of Jesus, so that the life of Jesus may also be made visible in our bodies. (2 Cor 4:7–10)

Our dear brother, Lou, and many like him, teach us that our incompleteness, our poverty and limitations are not the enemy. In fact, only a heart that is poor enough to receive the inflow of God's grace can in turn flow out into the world as a balm of divine healing. Lou's fragile and broken clay vessel was just the instrument that God needed to transmit the healing balm of God's compassion and mercy to the poor.

The prodigal Son who returns home, poor and tattered, wounded and empty-handed is not a victorious Super-Christ, mounted on a white horse, triumphantly galloping through town after conquering the enemy in the distant land. Suffering has changed him; love has transformed him. He returns home wounded, poor, barefoot, and scarred by the world's sin. "He was wounded for our transgressions, crushed for our iniquities . . . by his bruises we are healed" (Is 53:4).

Risen from the dead, Jesus does not hide his wounds or deny his defeat. He comes into the presence of his disciples marked by suffering and death, yet fully alive. He invites Thomas to touch his wounds: "Do not doubt but believe" (Jn 20:27). He is the same teacher of wisdom and truth that they have always known and followed, perhaps now more than ever. His feet, marked with the wounds of the crucifixion, still know the way to the other side of the road, where Lazarus sits waiting for a morsel of God's good news.

The compassion that flowed from the fountain of Lou's heart and soul during those final dark years was a source of blessing for many people. I know that to be true in my own life, and it is clearly the experience of those who met him in the AIDS hospice as he moved from bed to bed, allowing his own heart to be a channel for the unconditional love of Christ. Like Jesus, Lou was not afraid to touch broken and rejected humanity, to mix with those whom the world hides away in the "distant land" of quarantined rooms and hushed medical diagnoses. A beautiful and yet fragile earthen vessel, our dear brother Lou entrusted his incompleteness to Christ, allowing his own poverty to be transformed into an instrument of God's grace. In the darkness of faith, God freely poured him out as healing balm upon the wounds of others. I am profoundly blessed to have known a man in whom I saw the face—and touched the wounds—of the Risen Christ. He who once was lost in darkness has been found. I have no doubt that my beloved brother, Lou, has journeyed home with the Risen Christ, only to discover the open arms of the divine *Abba* waiting to welcome him home for all eternity. I can almost hear the children as they break into a glorious song of thanksgiving.

10

The Return of the Prodigal Son

I will *arise* and go to my father, and I will say to him, "*Abba*, I have sinned against heaven and before you; I am no longer worthy to be called your son; treat me like one of your hired hands." (Lk 15:18–19)[1]

The beloved Son, the one without sin (Heb 4:15), having embraced our broken, sinful world in loving solidarity, now sets off to return home to the Source, the great Wellspring of life: "I will arise and go to my father ..." (Lk 15:18). "The frequent New Testament affirmations that Jesus was "raised from the dead" presuppose that the crucified one sojourned in the realm of the dead prior to his resurrection."[2] We are reminded that it is not sin or hell that has the final word; love does. And it is precisely because of the victory of love that the prodigal Son, with his gentle shepherd smile, can call us to follow him back to the home of his *Abba*.

I do not call you servants any longer, because the servant does not know what the master is doing; but I have called you friends, because I have made known to you everything that I have heard from my *Abba*. (Jn 15:15)

For some in the distant land the thought of leaving behind the familiar and setting off into the unknown with Jesus is not as easy as one might think. Sometimes it is easier to maneuver within our familiar world of sin and alienation than it is to journey to a freedom that is unknown. The unknown, after all, is a mystery.

"Who is this 'Son' who calls us to follow him? What are his credentials? Does he realize that we are a pretty wretched group

177

of sinners? And he is inviting us to go home with him? And this place that he keeps calling his *Abba*'s *house*, where is it?" Jesus hears them expressing their fears and doubts. He knows that they are struggling to understand the meaning of God's unconditional mercy. He invites them in closer and recites to them part of an ancient psalm.

> The Lord does not deal with us according to our sins,
> nor repay us according to our iniquities.
> For as the heavens are high above the earth,
> so great is his steadfast love...
> As a father has compassion for his children,
> So the Lord has compassion for [us]. (Ps 103:10–11, 13)[3]

Sitting down in the cool shade of a large acacia tree, the gentle Shepherd speaks to them calmly, putting their minds at ease:

> "Do not let your hearts be troubled. Believe in God; believe also in me. In my Father's house there are many dwelling places. If it were not so, would I have told you that I go to prepare a place for you? And if I go and prepare a place for you, I will come again and will take you to myself, so that where I am, there you may be also. And you know the way to the place where I am going." Thomas said to him, "Lord, we do not know where you are going. How can we know the way?" Jesus said to him, "I am the way..." (Jn 14:1–6)

Pope Benedict XVI, during his final public celebration of the Eucharist as bishop of Rome, on Ash Wednesday 2013, reflected on what it means to "come home" in response to God's love.

> "Return to me with all your heart, with fasting, with weeping, and with mourning" (Joel 2:12). Please note the phrase "with all your heart"...means from the very core of our thoughts and feelings, from the roots of our decisions, choices and actions, with a gesture of total and radical freedom. But is this return to God possible? Yes, because there is a force that does not reside in our hearts, but that emanates from the heart of God and the power of His mercy.[4]

With tremendous inner freedom and confident of his *Abba*'s eternal mercy and compassion, the prodigal Christ sets off on the journey home with his new disciples and friends. Each and every step is a step into freedom, not just for this band of tattered friends, but for all of humanity. It is a path that leads from the dark tomb of death into the light of new life, from exile into the open arms of God.

> We have witnessed the great outward and downward "extension" of the Son [who]...now grasping the whole of finitude, the whole of rebellious humanity in his hands, journeys back to the Father in and through the Spirit...In this great Trinitarian act, the sinful world learns to hope again...[and] all those who are, for whatever reason, far from God are brought close.[5]

Homecoming

Pope Francis, speaking on the parable of the Prodigal Son in St. Peter's Square in October 2013, reminds us that God is always waiting for us, always ready to embrace us and welcome us home.

> You could say to me: but the Church is made up of sinners, we see them every day. And this is true: we are a Church of sinners; and we sinners are called to allow ourselves to be transformed, renewed, sanctified by God. There has been in history the temptation of some to say: the Church is only the Church of the pure, the perfectly consistent...This is not true! This is a heresy! The Church, that is holy, does not reject sinners ...She calls everyone to be enfolded by the mercy, the tenderness and the forgiveness of the Father...
>
> "I am a sinner, I have tremendous sins; how can I possibly feel part of the Church?" Dear brother, dear sister, this is exactly what the Lord wants, that you say to him: "Lord, here I am, with my sins"...In the Church, the God we encounter is not a merciless judge, but like the Father in the Gospel parable. You may be like the son who left home, who sank to the depths, farthest from the Gospel. When you have the strength to say: I want to come home, you will find the door open ...God is always waiting for you, God embraces you, kisses you and celebrates.[6]

Songwriter Joan Osborne has composed a song called "One of Us," in which she hints that maybe our journey home will not be as difficult and lonely as it might first appear. She invites us to pay attention, to contemplate the face of the "stranger" who, like us, is searching for the way back home. "What if," she asks..."What if the stranger we meet on the dusty road is Christ himself, trying to find his way back home to his *Abba*'s house?" The refrain in Osborne's song goes like this:

> What if God was one of us?
> Just a slob like one of us?
> Just a stranger on the bus
> Trying to make his way home?[7]

The beloved Son is "one of us," a pilgrim among pilgrims; he does not return to his *Abba*'s house alone. This is the best news of all for those of us who live here in the distant land. We have prayed with great fervor, "Give ear, O Shepherd of Israel, you who lead Joseph like a flock!... Stir up your might, and come to save us! Restore us, O God; let your face shine, that we may be saved" (Ps 80:1–3). Our cry has been answered mercifully in the person of Christ, the Good Shepherd.[8] Herein lies our hope. "He calls his own sheep by name and leads them out. When he has brought out all his own, he goes ahead of them, and the sheep follow him because they know his voice" (Jn 10:3–4).

> The Lord is my shepherd, I shall not want...
> He leads me beside still waters; he restores my soul.
> He leads me in right paths for his name's sake. (Ps 23:1–3)

The Good Shepherd, carrying the lambs in his bosom (Is 40:11), sets off for home with his rescued flock. It is a sight to be seen. Says St. Ambrose of Milan (ca. 340–397), "Christ carries you on his body, he who took your sins upon himself. The church seeks, and the father receives. The shepherd carries. The mother searches. The father clothes. First mercy comes, then intercession, and third reconciliation."[9]

We, the pilgrims who have wandered into the distant country of sin and injustice, of poverty and infidelity, are able to make the journey home precisely because we have experienced the mercy that flows from the heart of the prodigal Christ. We long to see the face of the beloved *Abba*, whom—thanks to the beloved Son—we have glimpsed dimly, as in a mirror (cf. 1 Cor 13:12).

> I have loved you with an everlasting love; therefore I have con-
> tinued my faithfulness to you... I am going to... gather them
> from the farthest parts of the earth... With weeping they shall
> come, and with consolations I will lead them back, I will let
> them walk by brooks of water, in a straight path in which they
> shall not stumble; for I have become a father to Israel... Set up

road markers for yourself, make yourself guideposts; consider well the highway, the road by which you went. Return, O virgin Israel. (Jer 31:3, 8–9, 21)

The Good Shepherd walks with us, leading us home into the open arms of the beloved *Abba*: "For you did not receive a spirit of slavery to fall back into fear, but you have received a spirit of adoption. When we cry, '*Abba! Father!*' it is that very Spirit bearing witness with our spirit that we are children of God, and if children, then heirs, heirs of God and joint heirs with Christ" (Rom 8:15–17). In the words of Pope Benedict XVI:

> He returns home, and he leads others home...He leads the way back from exile to the homeland, back to all that is authentic and true. Jesus, the true Son, himself went into "exile" in a very deep sense, in order to lead all of us home from exile.[10]

Not only does the Shepherd Christ lead us, his beleaguered flock, safely home to the house of his *Abba*; he is, in fact, the very *Way* by which we return. St. Catherine of Siena, the fourteenth-century lay Dominican mystic and prophet, was gifted with a vision from God, showing her that the crucified Lamb of God is the road by which the Shepherd's beloved flock is able to return home:

> By Adam's sinful disobedience the road was so broken up that no one could reach everlasting life...I wanted to undo these great troubles of yours. So I gave you a bridge, my Son, so that you could cross over the river, the stormy sea of this darksome life, without being drowned.[11]

Christ, crucified and raised from the dead, becomes a bridge by which we are able to cross from the distant world of sin and alienation back home, where our beloved God awaits us with an eternal embrace of love. "Look!" says God to Catherine of Siena:

> The bridge stretches from heaven to earth, joining the earth of your humanity with the greatness of the Godhead...The height stooped to the earth of your humanity, bridging the chasm between us and rebuilding the road...so that you might in truth come to the same joy as the angels. But my Son's having made of himself a bridge for you could not bring you to life unless you make your way along that bridge.[12]

The risen Shepherd, who has "stooped to the earth" to rescue us, now calls us to set off in faith. "You must all keep to this bridge...following in the footsteps of this gentle loving Word. There is no other way you can come to me."[13] Though we have been rescued by God's gratuitous and saving love, we must still respond in faith, following in the footsteps of the Risen Christ. Discipleship never ends, not even at death. Love never ceases to call us to a faith-filled response.

> This bridge has walls of stone so that travelers will not be hindered when it rains. Do you know what stones these are? ...These stones were hewn on the body of the Word, my gentle Son (I have told you that he is the bridge); he built them into walls, tempering the mortar with his own blood. That is, his blood was mixed into the mortar of his divinity with the strong heat of burning love...So you see, the bridge has walls and a roof of mercy. And the storehouse of holy Church is there to serve the bread of life and the blood, lest the journeying pilgrims, my creatures, grow weary and faint on the way.[14]

The journey home is like a great procession. It is Love that guides us: "For we do not have a high priest who is unable to sympathize with our weaknesses, but one who has similarly been tested in every way, yet without sin" (Heb 4:14–15). We make our way with Christ, the high priest, who longs to present us to his *Abba* as a spiritual sacrifice acceptable to God (1 Pet 2:5).

Timothy Radcliffe reminds us that, according to St. Thomas Aquinas, the moral life has to do with "the movement of one's whole life...Ethics is about becoming strong for the journey home... '*Virtus*' [virtue] means literally 'strength,' strength for the journey."[15] We are able to make the pilgrimage back home to God, following in the footsteps of the risen Shepherd of Israel, precisely because we are strengthened by and transformed into the *body of Christ* (cf. Rom 7:4). In the words of St. Ambrose cited above, "Christ carries [us] on his body."

As we journey home, our path illuminated by the newborn light of Easter morning, we find that we have been immersed in the river of new life that flows from the crucified and risen Son's pierced side. Like Moses, we are carried along by the dynamic flow of God's liberating love. That is not all, though, for also from his side flows the new wine of his love—the very wine that has been saved for the honored guests at the great wedding feast. We are shocked to discover that the best wine has been saved for the last (cf. Jn 2:9). Imagine! We, the least and the last of the tattered and tired pilgrims, are being welcomed home like special guests at the table of God's infinite mercy. Intuitively, without rehearsing at all, we break into song: *"Amazing grace, how sweet the sound..."*

Longing to see the face of God

> Timothy has just now come to us from you, and has brought us the good news of your faith and love. He has told us also that you always remember us kindly and long to see us—just as we long to see you. (1 Thes 3:6)

Israel's long pilgrimage of faith, marked by many displacements and itinerant journeys, is played out in a number of biblical stories, one of the most beautiful and powerful being the story of Joseph and his brothers from the book of Genesis. Betrayed by his older brothers and sold to the Ishmaelites for twenty pieces of silver (Gen 37:28; cf. Mt 26:15), Joseph is raised "in exile" as a servant in the house of Pharaoh. When, many years later, his brothers appear in Egypt in search of food because of the terrible famine back in Canaan, they are brought into the presence of their younger brother, Joseph—now an adult—though they do not recognize him. Holding back his tears during the emotional reencounter with his brothers, Joseph demands that his brother, Simeon, remain in Egypt as ransom until their youngest brother, Benjamin, is brought to Joseph in Egypt. While maintaining his anonymity, Joseph is teaching his brothers (and us, as well) a very important lesson, namely, that it is not possible to see the face of God if the least of our brothers and sisters is not with us.

The sons of Jacob, reduced to poverty and facing famine, have no other option but to agree to the unusual and risky conditions set by Pharaoh's servant, who happens to be their brother Joseph, whom they do not recognize. Though the brothers are aware that the deal struck with this servant of Pharaoh, if not carried out, could end in the tragic death of their brother Simeon, they have little choice. If nothing is done, they, their father, and their people will very likely die from starvation.

As the story unfolds, and as the brothers attempt to convince their father, Jacob, that the only chance for survival is for their youngest brother, Benjamin, to be taken to Pharaoh's governor in Egypt, they frequently repeat the conditions set by Joseph: "The man solemnly warned us, saying, *'You shall not see my face unless your brother is with you'*" (Gen 43:3).[16] This phrase, echoed several times in the story, is pregnant with biblical significance. It is, in fact, an echo of God's very own voice, heard repeatedly throughout the scriptures, frequently on the lips of Jesus. "Those who say, 'I love God,' and hate their brothers or sisters, are liars; for those who do not love a brother or sister whom they *have seen*, cannot love God whom they *have not seen*" (1 Jn 4:20). The gospel is unequivocal on this point: It is impossible to love God if we erect barriers that shield us from seeing and loving our neighbor.

This is the very same challenge that Jesus directed toward those dining at the house of Simon, the Pharisee, the day that the woman sat at Jesus' feet, bathing them with her tears (Lk 7:36ff). Jesus did not read a paragraph of theology to Simon, nor did he quote from some lengthy encyclical. He asked him a very simple and direct question: "Simon, do you see this woman?" (Lk 7:44). In other words, "Simon, if you cannot see this poor woman, crouched on the floor beneath your table, you will never be able to see God—no matter how many offerings you make at the temple."

The beloved Son understands more than ever now why he had to go on this mission of hope and salvation into the distant land of exile. Whether he set off fully aware of the universal consequences of his journey from the very beginning, we cannot say for certain. We can be sure, though, that by sending the Son into the world, gifted with his portion of the divine inheritance, the *Abba* clearly knew that he was sending "a part of himself" to us.[17] In other words, it is God himself who has come into our distant land, to visit us in and through the beloved Son. It is God who washes our feet with tears, and it is God's feet that we wash when we serve our neighbor. "Truly I tell you, just as you did not do it to one of the least of these, you did not do it to me" (Mt 25:45).

Jesus would certainly have been familiar with the ancient story of Joseph and his brothers, probably recounted to him many times by his parents. Now that he has seen the suffering of the world with his own eyes, he understands the stern demand of Joseph, his ancestor in faith, in a completely new way as it echoes forcefully in the depths of his being: "You shall not see my face unless your brother or sister is with you."

Jesus recognizes that it is his *Abba*'s voice speaking now: "My son, you shall not see my face unless your brothers and sisters are with you." Everything has finally become clear. The prodigal Christ grasps with greater insight now why his *Abba* blessed him and sent him into the land of desolation. He now understands that it was necessary that he be *sent* in order to restore to broken humanity the dignity that rightly belongs to us as children of God (cf. Acts 17:3).

Jesus is aware that his compassionate embrace of all of us, his new friends here in the distant land, not only communicates to us his *Abba*'s unconditional love, but it transforms his own consciousness as well, helping him to claim more fully his divine mission. As he looks at each one of us, his friends on the *Camino* called life, he understands why his own heart had to be wounded by love. He looks into the eyes of his *Abba* and says, "I thank you, Father, Lord of heaven and earth, because you have hidden these things from the wise and the intelligent and have revealed them to infants; yes, Father, for such was your gracious will" (Lk 10:21). The mission is clear now. Like a seed sown in the ground, his broken body and pierced heart have given birth to a story of unimaginable new life and love.

I am Jesus, your brother

The story of Joseph and his brothers culminates in a powerful and emotional encounter of healing and reconciliation. Seeing his younger brother, Benjamin, for the first time in many years, Joseph begins to weep uncontrollably, leaving him no choice but to reveal his true face to his brothers:

> "Come closer to me." And they came. And he said, "I am your brother Joseph whom you sold into Egypt . . . Do not be distressed or angry with yourselves . . . God sent me before you to preserve for you a remnant on earth, and to keep alive for you many survivors. So it was not you who sent me here, but God . . . Hurry and go up to my father and say to him, 'Thus says your son Joseph . . . Come down to me, do not delay' . . . Tell my father how greatly I am honored in Egypt, and all that you have seen. Hurry and bring my father down here." Then he fell upon his brother Benjamin's neck and wept, while Benjamin wept upon his neck. And he kissed all his brothers and wept upon them. (Gen 45:4–15)

The prodigal Son of God, now risen from the dead, enfolds us into that very same healing embrace of mercy. He who has come to search for us here in this distant land now draws near to us, calling each of us by name. "Come close to me; it is I, Jesus, your brother."

Preaching in 1294 on a letter of St. Augustine, Meister Eckhart makes reference to the prodigal son's return home to his *Abba*'s house, inviting us to open our eyes and recognize this *brother* as the Risen Christ himself:

> When [the parable] says "*your brother*," that means, Christ. They are unbelievable words, absolutely amazing . . . That is

why *we must celebrate and rejoice* ... because he who died has returned to life ... to live eternally ...

It is not necessary that God create a new world; he has done new things in this world. A man born of a virgin, risen from among the dead to live eternally in the heavens—that may be a more powerful work than "[re]creation of the world." And it is not surprising that what has been said in a literal sense about the prodigal, the unjust son, we explain about Christ.[18]

Letting ourselves be found

Everyone in the village knows that the old *Abba* has spent a good part of each day standing on the knoll at the edge of town, longing for his son's return. This, of course, has elicited more than a few sneers and jokes among the local villagers (cf. Lk 15:20). "When is the old man going to give up on that wretched son of his?" they mutter among themselves. The old *Abba* knows about all the talk, but he is not in the least concerned by what others may be thinking or saying. His thoughts, his hopes, his heart are set only on his son.

As we watch the unfolding of this beautiful story we are overwhelmed by the love flowing from the heart of the *Abba*. Suddenly the old man's face, though marked by suffering due to the long and "patient" wait for his son's return,[19] is resplendent with joy. From the knoll he has glimpsed his son on the horizon. We are shocked to see the old man start on a mad dash down the hill, his tunic tucked up under his arms and tears of exuberant love and joy flowing down his cheeks. As he runs, the old *Abba* feels that his heart is bursting open like a great geyser. In the words of St. Ambrose, "The father initiates the restoration of the son by running to [him], falling on his neck, and giving him the kiss of reconciliation."[20]

Says Balthasar, "The 'weakness' of the love in the heart of God becomes definitively visible in the figure of the father who runs to meet his lost son."[21] Kenneth Bailey quickly reminds us that if we want to feel the full impact of this parable we must keep in mind that, "Middle Easterners, wearing long robes, do not run in public. They never have ... [The *Abba*] humiliates himself before the village. Out of compassion he empties himself, assumes the form of a servant and *runs* to reconcile his estranged son."[22] Our joy only increases as we witness the *Abba*'s uncontrollable and marvelously scandalous love that breaks all the sacrosanct rules. Says Pope Francis:

God always thinks with mercy...like the father who awaits the return of his son and *goes out* to meet him, he sees him coming when he's still far off...What does this mean? That every day he went to see whether his son was coming home: this is our merciful Father. It is a sign that God was hoping for his return, with all his heart.[23]

The *Abba*, overwhelmed with joy and compassion, throws his arms around his beloved son and kisses him. Karl Barth, who repeatedly weaves the prodigal son into his theology of grace, says in a most wonderful way: "Jesus is hidden in the kiss which the father gives his son."[24] Then the son, his body still visibly scarred, marked by the wounds of hatred and violence, says, "*Abba*, I have sinned against heaven and before you; I am no longer worthy to be called your son" (Lk 15:21). The gentle *Abba* pauses, smiles, looking lovingly into his son's almond-shaped eyes, and says to his servants:

"Quickly, bring out a robe—the best one—and put it on him; put a ring on his finger and sandals on his feet. And get the fatted calf and kill it, and let us eat and celebrate; for this son of mine was dead and is alive again; he was lost and is found." (Lk 15:22–24)

In response, everyone begins to celebrate. The entire village is suddenly filled with activity and elation. The fire pits are started, food is prepared, musicians rehearse, and children run around filled with excitement. Everyone is busy helping in one way or another.

Everyone, that is, except the older brother, who has locked himself in his private cottage and pulled shut the curtains, furiously refusing to accept the unfairness of it all. *He*, after all, is the one who has stayed home, obediently following all the commandments, trying not to do anything to offend God. Filled with uncontrollable anger, he does all he can "to define the prodigal as a 'rebellious son.' If he can make that accusation stick, the prodigal will be stoned as required by the law set forth in Deuteronomy 21:18–21."[25]

When the *Abba* comes and knocks on the elder brother's door, he refuses to open it, shouting angrily from behind the door:

"For all these years I have been working like a slave for you, and I have never disobeyed your command; yet you have never given me even a young goat so that I might celebrate with my friends. But when this son of yours came back, who has devoured your property with prostitutes, you killed the fatted calf for him!" (Lk 15:29–30)

The great tragedy, of course, is that as long as the older brother understands salvation as "earning" his *Abba*'s love, he will always be a slave, living in a hell of his own making. He will always be lost. No one denies the fact that the older brother actually *is* a very good and responsible person. If only he could trust that his *Abba*'s love is generously poured out equally upon both sons, then everything would fall into place. Unfortunately, the river of love that flows from the *Abba*'s heart never has a chance to break through the ground of the older brother's soul because he is too busy digging a well, searching for water (cf. Jn 4:5–30).

The *Abba* tries to make clear to his older son how much he is loved: "Son, you are *always* with me, and all that is mine is yours. But we had to celebrate and rejoice, because this brother of yours was dead and has come to life; he was lost and has been found" (Lk 15:31–32). Tragically, the *Abba*'s plea falls on deaf ears.

Henri Nouwen, speaking with utter honesty about his own life and struggle to let himself be loved by God, invites us to see the drama of our lives from God's perspective:

> For most of my life I have struggled to find God, to know God, to love God...Now I wonder whether God has been trying to find me, to know me, and to love me. The question is not "How am I to find God?" but "How am I to let myself be found by God?"...God is looking into the distance for me, trying to find me, and longing to bring me home...It might seem strange, but God wants to find me as much as, if not more than, I want to find God...I am beginning now to see how radically the character of my spiritual journey will change when I no longer think of God as hiding out and making it as difficult as possible for me to find him...Wouldn't it be good to increase God's joy by letting God find me and carry me home?[26]

In the Eucharistic Prayer for Reconciliation II, from the Catholic Missal, we pray these grace-filled words: "When we ourselves had turned away from you on account of our sins, *you brought us back* to be reconciled, oh Lord, so that, converted at last to you, we might love one another through the Son, whom for our sake you handed over to death."[27] It is thanks to the utter faithfulness of God that we are not left to find our way back home on our own. God is always looking and watching for us; all we have to do is let ourselves be found. Once that happens, we can sing our glorious song of thanksgiving:

'Tis grace that brought us safe thus far
And grace will lead us home.[28]

The soul who triggered hope in God

Lifting us onto his shepherd shoulders, broken under the weight of the cross, the Risen Christ takes us with him back to his *Abba*. Says St. Bede the Venerable:

The entire divinely-arranged plan of our Redeemer's coming in the flesh is the reconciliation of the world. It was for this reason that he became incarnate, for this he suffered, for this he was raised from the dead—that he might lead us...back to God's peace by his act of reconciliation. Hence he was rightly given the name..."Prince of peace"...to you who were far off and peace to those who were near. (Eph 2:17)[29]

The *Abba*, having embraced his Son, suddenly looks down and sees the bloodied bare feet of his Son, who "emptied himself, taking the form of a slave" (Phil 2:7). In Middle Eastern culture only a slave goes barefoot. The *Abba* immediately calls out in a loud voice, "Quickly, bring out a robe—the best one—and put it on him; put a ring on his finger and sandals on his feet. And get the fatted calf and kill it, and let us eat and celebrate" (Lk 15:22–23). These words signal clearly that he welcomes him home *not* as a slave,[30] but as a son, the beloved Son who has returned home from the realm of the dead.

This is the good news that Jesus has come to announce to us. Life, says Thomas Aquinas, is an invitation to "friendship with God,"[31] an invitation to feast at the table of God's gratuitous love—a love that heals us, saves us, and sets us free. This is what Pope Francis alludes to in the first lines of his apostolic exhortation: "The joy of the gospel fills the hearts and lives of all who encounter Jesus. Those who accept his offer of salvation are set free from sin, sorrow, inner emptiness and loneliness. With Christ joy is constantly born anew."[32] The beloved Son is back home, born anew in the joy of God.

Jesus' parable has clearly turned the tables on what is considered proper in the realm of religion, forcing us to question certain sacred traditions, most importantly the manner by which we welcome sinners back home into the community of faith. As the older brother rages against his *Abba*'s "unjust mercy," the village children, playing in the doorways of their homes, applaud with joyful abandon and purity of heart as the old man throws open his arms in an embarrassingly public display of unconditional love. Dust swirls in the streets like confetti falling from heaven. The children "get it." They know instinctively why the old *Abba* is so happy, their innocence still untouched by the poison of a religion that loses sight of the God who loves us with the heart of a mother. Mercy breaks all the rules; it turns the world upside-down. This is what Jesus calls the Reign of God. Again, in the words of Pope Francis, who incarnates this parable in untold ways:

> The Church is...a "merciful mother" who understands...She never closes the door...She does not judge but offers God's forgiveness...[inviting] those of her children who have fallen into a deep abyss to continue on their way. The Church is not afraid to enter their darkness to give them hope; nor is the Church afraid to enter our darkness when we are in the dark night of our soul and...give us hope![33]

Charles Péguy, in his poem, "The Portal of the Mystery of Hope," publicly confesses his shock at the outpouring of mercy in Luke's three lost-and-found parables. How can a shepherd leave ninety-nine sheep behind to look for just *one* that is lost? And what about a good-for-nothing son who squanders the family inheritance? Amazed, though with a bit of humor, as well, Péguy confesses that, thanks to these parables, even God has learned to hope.

> What does this *one* have that makes him worth ninety-nine?
> It's unfair. Here is one soul (and it's precisely the one that was lost),
> who is worth as much, who counts as much, who causes as much joy
> as these poor ninety-nine others that had remained constant.
> Why...how?
> Here is one who weighs as much in God's scales as ninety-nine...
> It's this one, and no other, it's this sheep, it's this sinner, it's this penitent,
> It's this soul that God, that Jesus carries on his shoulders...
> God hoped, God waited for him.
> God, who is everything, had something else to hope for,
> From him, from this sinner. From this nothing. From us.

He was put in this position, he put himself in this position,
In the situation of having something to hope for,
To await something from this miserable sinner.
Such is the strength of the life of hope, my child...[34]

Jesus, the prodigal Son—Israel's younger brother—crucified as a sinner, crucified because of his free and dangerous love, is raised from the dead and called back to life by his *Abba*, who has waited and watched each day for his return. The "Author of life," says Luke, the one who was killed, is the very one "whom God raised from the dead. To this we are witnesses" (Acts 3:15).

> We had to celebrate and rejoice, because *this brother of yours was dead and has come to life*; he was lost and has been found. (Lk 15:32)

In a very moving sermon, St. Peter Chrysologus (406–450), speaking in the voice of Christ, throws open his arms to welcome home those longing to return to the house of God.

> I appeal to you by the mercy of God... because of God's desire to be loved rather than feared... You may run away from me as the Lord, but why not run to me as your father? Perhaps you are filled with shame for causing my bitter passion. Do not be afraid. This cross inflicts a mortal injury, not on me, but on death. These nails no longer pain me, but only deepen your love for me... Through them I draw you into my heart. My body was stretched on the cross as a symbol, not of how much I suffered, but of my all-embracing love... Come, then, return to me and learn to know me as your father, who repays good for evil, love for injury, and boundless charity for piercing wounds..."[35]

The prodigal Christ's journey is revealed as a mission of hope, a salvific hope that does not count the cost of loving, a hope that breaks the mold of worldly justice. Péguy continues:

This soul, who literally triggered hope in God,
Was the crowning of God's hope.
This soul who was dead, like Jesus (more dead than Jesus)...
is risen from the dead...
Remarkable virtue of hope, strange mystery,
She's not a virtue like the others...[36]

The circle is complete. God's sending of the divine Son into the world, into the distant country, heals the great divide that has kept us alienated from God and from one another. The bridge that stretches over the raging river, separating us from our true home in God, has been rebuilt, thanks to Christ's loving and free embrace of the cross. He has freed those lost in the realm of hatred, injustice, sin, war, racism, and hunger—that is, the realm of death.

> Now in Christ Jesus you who once were far off have been brought near by the blood of Christ. For he is our peace; in his flesh he has . . . broken down the dividing wall . . . that he might create in himself one new humanity in place of the two, thus making peace . . . So he came and proclaimed peace to you who were far off and peace to those who were near; for through him both of us have access in one Spirit to the Father. So then you are no longer strangers and aliens, but you are citizens with the saints and also members of the household of God, built upon the foundation of the apostles and prophets, with Christ Jesus himself as the cornerstone. In him the whole structure is joined together and grows into a holy temple in the Lord; in whom you also are built together spiritually into a dwelling place for God. (Eph 2:13–22)

Set free in God's love

The parable of the Prodigal Son is something akin to God's "Emancipation Proclamation,"[37] abolishing all forms of slavery and sin. Barbara Reid reminds us that the loving *Abba*, "is willing to pay the high cost to gather in all the children, none of whom have earned the right to this inheritance. All are sons and daughters through the lavish gift of God; none are slaves. To accept the love of God who acts like this is not only to restore right relation with God, but also to bring one into reconciled love with all people as brothers and sisters in God's family . . . This emphasis on the free, undeserved, gratuity of God's love is also a theme in Paul (2 Cor 5:17–21) . . . [who] clearly casts reconciliation as Christ's work, *not* something accomplished through the efforts of the lost."[38] In other words, we do not *earn* our way back home; it is God who runs toward us to set us free from all slavery. St. Athanasius, bishop of Alexandria (d. 373), echoes this good news of our freedom in Christ:

> [The prodigal's] father neither takes him in like a hired servant nor treats him like a stranger. Oh no, he kisses him as a

son. He accepts him as a dead man come back to life again. He counts him worthy of the divine feast and gives him the precious garment...Not only does he bring his son back from death...he begets him anew in the image of the glory of Christ.[39]

St. Paul, himself once a violent religious fundamentalist, becomes the great herald of our freedom in Christ: "For the law of the Spirit of life in Christ Jesus has set you free from the law of sin and of death. For you did not receive a spirit of slavery to fall back into fear, but you have received a spirit of adoption. When we cry, '*Abba*! Father!' it is that very Spirit bearing witness with our spirit that we are children of God, and if children, then heirs, heirs of God and joint heirs with Christ" (Rom 8:2, 15–17).

Cardinal Jorge Bergoglio, now Pope Francis, emphasizes that there are absolutely no limits to God's mercy. We are invited to taste this gratuitous outpouring of freedom each time we come home:

We are set free from all slavery and every kind of fear. We are free with the freedom that encourages us on the return from exile. We return in freedom, because we have understood the strength of the Word of God, and when we confess that we have sinned against heaven and against [God], a party is thrown! The *Abba*, from behind *our* wounded flesh, sees the Son, who has been wounded for us...Once we realize that we have been "welcomed home," we give more space to the Spirit.[40]

We, the prodigal sons and daughters of God, surrounded by the joy of the people of God, suddenly find ourselves held in the healing embrace of the Risen Christ. The victory has been won. Jesus, who faced death head-on in the distant country, has transformed it into a school of love. "Peace be with you," he says, as he breathes the Holy Spirit upon us (cf. Jn 20:21–22).

It is done! I am the Alpha and the Omega, the beginning and the end. To the thirsty I will give water as a gift from the spring of the water of life. (Rev 21:6)

O pilgrim, come home

Christ's rebirth from the realm of the dead is by no means the end of the story. His death and resurrection are, in fact, only the beginning.

As we are washed in the waters of new life (Rev 7:17), the Risen Christ once again anoints our feet for mission, sending us right back into the broken world from where we have come. Like Roger, we now find ourselves running in the other direction, toward the distant country, reminded that the Reign of God is not found at the finish line, but in our neighbor. "You cannot see my face unless your brother or sister is with you." Christ's return home is our beginning; his death is our life.

Jesus' mission will not be finished until every lost sheep and every lost daughter and son has been found and welcomed home. The Risen Christ anoints us, his prodigal sisters and brothers, breathing into our souls the power of the Holy Spirit: "I give you a new commandment, that you love one another. Just as I have loved you, you also should love one another" (Jn 13:34). His loving embrace of the world is now the model for our lives. Just as he lifted the lost sheep onto his tired shoulders, so too are we to do.

Henri Nouwen found in this magnificent parable a tremendous healing energy not only for himself but for the entire world, thanks to his chance encounter in 1983 with a poster of Rembrandt's painting, *The Return of the Prodigal Son*, pinned on someone's door. Though Henri later told friends that the initial experience was nothing terribly significant, the seed that fell into his heart that day set into motion an inner journey that would transform him radically.[41]

Henri eventually traveled to St. Petersburg in Russia to encounter the famous painting face-to-face. The experience of entering into visual communion with Jesus' parable, through the doorway of Rembrandt's powerful icon, was a life-transforming experience for Nouwen. Those contemplative days spent sitting quietly before this great work of art liberated Henri in many ways, eventually "becoming flesh" in the publication of his 1992 bestseller, *The Return of the Prodigal Son*. It is no surprise that in many Christian circles today, if one mentions the parable of Prodigal Son, most people immediately respond with the name of Henri Nouwen.

It is quite symbolic that Henri died unexpectedly on September 21, 1996, as he was preparing to set off to St. Petersburg to participate in a BBC commentary on the very painting that had radically changed his life. We might say that he died "coming home to the Father." Thomas Petriano, who knew Henri well, says quite frankly that, "Rembrandt indeed helped Henri find his way home."[42] In the book, *Remembering Henri*, a collection of memoirs about his life, Chris Glaser remembers Henri's funeral with a bit of nostalgic symbolism:

> That we gathered in an unfinished cathedral in Richmond Hill for our final farewell to Henri significantly illustrated his un-

derstanding that the church is not yet complete. Those gathered, many of whom represented various categories of contemporary outcasts, revealed Henri's deep yearning, not only for his own homecoming, the theme of his funeral mass, but of our own. Just as Rembrandt's *The Return of the Prodigal Son* served as an icon for Henri in his hunger to be welcomed by God the Father and Mother, so Henri's own icons—his books —say to us, "You can do this." They beckon us, in the words adapted from the wonderful hymn that is based on the parable of the prodigal:

> Come home, come home
> Ye who are weary, come home!
> Earnestly, tenderly, Jesus is calling,
> Calling, "O pilgrim, come home!"[43]

Aware that many people have read Nouwen's book, *The Return of the Prodigal Son*, I have chosen to pay tribute to his spiritual masterpiece by recalling a few of the profound insights into the parable that transformed his life. Nouwen finally discovered that, in the very depths of his being, he too was the prodigal son, embraced and loved unconditionally by God. That discovery set him free.

> I have to kneel before the father, put my ear against his chest and listen, without interruption, to the heartbeat of God. Then, and only then, can I say carefully and very gently what I hear. I know now that I have to speak from eternity into time, from the lasting joy into the passing realities of our short existence in this world, from the house of love into the houses of fear, from God's abode into the dwellings of human beings.[44]

> It seems to me now that these hands have always been stretched out—even when there were no shoulders upon which to rest them. Got has never pulled back his arms, never withheld his blessing, never stopped considering his son the Beloved One.[45]

> Our brokenness has no other beauty but the beauty that comes from the compassion that surrounds it.[46]

Nouwen, by sharing so profoundly his own journey into both Jesus' parable and Rembrandt's profound mystical encounter with the parable, helps us hear the voice of the Good Shepherd who calls each of us by name, inviting us to let ourselves be welcomed home.

I came to understand how from [Rembrandt's] brush there emerged the figure of a nearly blind old man holding his son in a gesture of all-forgiving compassion. One must have died many deaths and cried many tears to have painted a portrait of God in such humility.[47]

Receiving forgiveness requires a total willingness to let God be God and do all the healing, restoring, and renewing.[48]

And finally, Nouwen reminds us that the journey of life is not only the one that we walk with our feet. It is an inner pilgrimage, as well. The distant country and the house of the *Abba* are both outside and inside us. Sometimes the more treacherous portion of the journey is the inner part, where we frequently feel alone and lost. Whether *inner* or *outer*, though, it is here, in the pilgrimage of daily life, that we hear the faithful voice of the *Abba* calling us home.

The true voice of love is a very soft and gentle voice speaking to me in the most hidden places of my being. It is not a boisterous voice forcing itself on me...It is the voice of a nearly blind father who has cried...and died many deaths. It is a voice that can only be heard by those who allow themselves to be touched.[49]

Home is the center of my being where I can hear the voice that says: "You are my beloved, on you my favor rests"—the same voice that gave life to the first Adam and spoke to Jesus, the second Adam; the same voice that speaks to all the children of God and sets them free to live in the midst of a dark world while remaining in the light."[50]

Through many dangers, toils and snares,
I have already come;
'Tis grace that brought me safe thus far
And grace will lead me home.[51]

Epilogue

> When [the elder brother] came and approached the house, he heard music and dancing. He called one of the slaves and asked what was going on..."Your brother has come, and your father has killed the fatted calf, because he has got your brother back safe and sound." Then he became angry and refused to go in. His father came out and began to plead with him. But he answered his father, "Listen! For all these years I have been working like a slave for you, and I have never disobeyed your command; yet you have never given me even a young goat so that I might celebrate with my friends..." Then the father said to him, "Son, you are always with me, and all that is mine is yours. But we had to celebrate and rejoice, because this brother of yours was dead and has come to life; he was lost and has been found." (cf. Lk 15:25–32)

The festivities are in full swing, and everyone is taking turns toasting the son's return. The old man has not danced this much in years! The neighbors cannot help but be moved by the old *Abba*'s limitless love. This night is like no other.

At one point the *Abba* glances toward the window where the younger son is standing, looking out into the darkness. The *Abba* knows immediately what is going on. He knows that his son's heart cannot rejoice fully as long as there is still a lost sheep wandering in the distant country, especially when that lost sheep is his elder brother. The younger son looks over his shoulder and sees his *Abba* is watching him with deep, tender love. Though he knows that his *Abba*'s heart is filled with the joy of his return, both know that the joy is not complete and cannot be complete as long as a single child of his is still wandering, lost in the distant land. They look deeply into each other's eyes. The prodigal son smiles, and receives the gentle smile of his *Abba* in return. With a simple nod, the younger brother quietly slips out the back door. No one but his *Abba* sees him leave.

After a while the old *Abba* meanders over toward the window, purposely trying not to draw any attention to himself or to the fact that the younger son has been absent for almost an hour. He glances out the window and sees him—his tired and beautiful younger son—still standing alone before the door of his brother's house, waiting. Once again the younger son knocks softly on the closed door. Nothing. The *Abba*'s heart is breaking—again. The old man bows his head and closes his eyes, crying out from the depths of his heart, calling for his firstborn to come home. He imagines himself again on the hill on the outskirts of town, waiting and watching—*aching* for a lost son to be found.

After what seems like an eternity the old *Abba* opens his eyes. It is only then that he realizes that the music has died down and that all of the guests have gathered behind him, looking out the window over his shoulders. Tears are flowing down the faces of most of them. There, before the old *Abba* and the entire village, are two brothers dancing and laughing beneath the stars of a night as new and pure as the night into which God spoke the first words of creation.

> In the beginning God said, "Let there be light,"
> and there was light. (Gen 1:1–3)

I, the author of this story, attest to its authenticity. You, the reader, may ask how can I make such a statement regarding a text of sacred scripture. The answer is rather simple. I am the older brother that you saw dancing under the stars that night. When my brother died a violent death at age thirty-three, I made a promise that I would never let his story be forgotten. May his story, that has become my story, too, live in our hearts forever. Amen.

Notes

Introduction

1. Schillebeeckx, Edward, *Jesus: An Experiment in Christology* (New York: Seabury Press, 1979), 156–57.

1. Incarnation

1. *Adam* literally means "earthling," from Hebrew—*adamah*—earth.

2. Meister Eckhart (1260–1327) builds on Aquinas's theological movement of *exitus-reditus* (the dynamic flow of divine energy and being out of and back into God). Eckhart formed part of the Rhineland mystical renewal, called the "Friends of God," that included many Dominican friars and nuns and independent beguines, all of whom were delving into the depths of mystical experience. Two of Eckhart's Dominican disciples, John Tauler and Henry Suso, followed in his footsteps, furthering the work of their renowned teacher. The beatification process of Eckhart continues to go forward, thanks to the clarification of Cardinal Ratzinger (later Pope Benedict XVI) that Eckhart does not need to be "rehabilitated," given that he was never condemned by the Church.

3. Meister Eckhart, OP, *The Complete Mystical Works of Meister Eckhart*, trans. and ed. by Maurice O'C. Walshe and revised by Bernard McGinn (New York: The Crossroad Publishing Co., 2009), Sermon 51, p. 270.

4. John Tauler, OP, *Johannes Tauler: Sermons* (New York: Paulist Press, 1985), 36. Italics added.

5. Robert Barron, "The Christian: Missionary of Hope," *Chicago Studies* 33, no. 2 (August 1994): 140. Italics added.

6. Latin for "image of God."

7. Barron, "The Christian," 140. Meister Eckhart made this same link to the divine *flow* of love from the Holy Spirit in another of his sermons: "The first emanation is that of the Son from the Father, which occurs in the way of birth. The second emanation is that of the Holy Spirit...this emanation is by love." See Meister Eckhart, *The Complete Mystical Works*, Sermon 23, p. 155. Italics added.

8. Donagh O'Shea, OP, "Today's Good News," *Living with Christ* (August 2011): 136.

9. Pope Benedict XVI, *Jesus of Nazareth: The Infancy Narratives*, trans. Philip J. Whitmore (New York: Image, 2012), 41–42.

10. Donald Goergen, OP, *The Mission and Ministry of Jesus*, Theology of Jesus, vol. 1 (Collegeville: The Liturgical Press, 1992), 42.

11. Maria Boulding, *The Coming of God*, 3rd ed. (Conception, MO: The Printery House, 2000), 56–58.

12. Goergen, *Mission and Ministry*, 45.

13. Pope Benedict XVI, *Jesus of Nazareth*, 68.

14. This phrase appears dozens of times in the Bible. Here are some texts: Gen 26:24, Gen 28:15, Josh 3:7, Is 41:10, Jer 1:8, Jer 1:19, Jer 15:20, Jer 30:11, Mt 28:20, Jn 14:25, Acts 18:10, 1 Cor 5:4.

15. From the "Final Message" of the Synod on the Word of God in the Life and Mission of the Church, convoked by Pope Benedict XVI (Vatican City: en.radiovaticana.va/: Oct. 24, 2008), n. 4.

16. The literal meaning of the Greek text is: "The Word became flesh and pitched his tent among us" (Jn 1:14).

17. Kathy Coffey, "Our Heart's Delight," from *Give us this Day: Daily Prayer for Today's Catholic* (Collegeville, MN: The Liturgical Press, November 2014): 121.

18. Pope Francis, "A Big Heart Open to God," an interview with Pope Francis conducted in Rome by Antonio Spadaro, SJ, editor in chief of *La Civiltà Cattolica*. Cited in *America* (September 30, 2013): 24.

19. Pope Francis, apostolic exhortation *Evangelii Gaudium* (Vatican City: Libreria Editrice Vaticana, November 24, 2013), n. 67.

20. *The Dialogue of St. Catherine of Siena*, trans. Suzanne Noffke, OP (New York: Paulist Press, 1980), 68–69, n. 28–29.

21. Herman Hendrickx, *The Parables of Jesus: Studies in the Synoptic Gospels* (Makati, Philippines: St. Paul Publications, 1987), 152.

22. Barbara E. Reid, OP, *Parables for Preachers* (Collegeville, MN: The Liturgical Press, 1998), 59.

23. Ibid., 59.

24. Kenneth E. Bailey, *Jacob and the Prodigal: How Jesus Retold Israel's Story* (Downers Grove, IL: Inter-Varsity Press, 2003), 138.

25. Ibid., 102.

26. Joseph Fadelle, *A Price to Pay: A Muslim Risks All to Follow Christ* (San Francisco: Ignatius Press, 2012).

27. Bailey, *Jacob and the Prodigal*, 146. Italics added.

28. Ibid., 110.

29. Sandra Schneiders, *Women and the Word* (New York: Paulist Press, 1986), 47.

30. The term *ousia* (translated as "inheritance" or "property" but more accurately meaning "being" or "nature") used to denote what the son requests of his father in the parable of the Prodigal Son is found in the Nicene Creed, where Christ is described as being "consubstantial" or "one in being" (Gr. *ho-*

moousios) with the Father. The Beloved Son has no need to ask for a share of the Father's *ousia*; it is always his.

31. Frère Pierre Marie, founder of the Fraternity of Jerusalem, suggests that the greatest inheritance of all is the blessed knowledge that one is a son or daughter of God. See Henri J. M. Nouwen, *The Return of the Prodigal Son* (London: Darton, Longman and Todd, Ltd., 1992), 56–57.

32. Pope Francis, apostolic exhortation *Evangelii Gaudium*, n. 40.

33. Maria Boulding, *The Coming of God*, 3rd ed. (Conception, MO: The Printery House, 2000), 58.

34. Pope Francis, "A Big Heart Open to God," 24. Italics added.

35. Bailey, *Jacob and the Prodigal*, 80–81.

36. Ibid., 82.

37. Pope Francis, Address to the Participants in the Plenary Assembly of the Pontifical Council for Promoting the New Evangelization (Vatican City: en.radiovaticana.va/: Clementine Hall of the Apostolic Palace, October 14, 2013). Italics added.

2. Amazing Grace

1. John of the Cross, "The Dark Night," *The Collected Works of St. John of the Cross*, trans. Kieran Kavanaugh, OCD, and Otilio Rodriguez, OCD (Washington, DC: Institute of Carmelite Studies: 1979), 296.

2. The song, "Amazing Grace," one of the most well-loved African American spirituals, was composed by John Newton (1725–1807). It is the story of his conversion from slave trader to abolitionist.

3. Who Is This Man?

1. Kenneth E. Bailey, *Jacob and the Prodigal: How Jesus Retold Israel's Story* (Downers Grove, IL: Inter-Varsity Press, 2003), 13. I am greatly indebted to Professor Bailey for his profound insights into this parable.

2. Bailey, *Jacob and the Prodigal*, 61–62.

3. Charles Péguy, *The Portal of the Mystery of Hope*, trans. David Louis Schindler, Jr. (Grand Rapids, MI: William B. Eerdmans Publishing Co., 1996), 91–93.

4. Cyril of Alexandria, *Commentary on Luke*, Homily 106, cited in *Ancient Christian Commentary on Scripture*, "New Testament III: Luke," ed. Arthur A. Just, Jr. (Downers Grove, IL: Inter-Varsity Press, 2003), 243.

5. Gregory Boyle, SJ, *Tattoos on the Heart* (New York: Free Press, 2010), 75. Italics added.

6. Ibid., 82. Italics added.

7. Oscar A. Romero, the archbishop of San Salvador from 1977 to 1980,

was assassinated while celebrating the Mass on March 24, 1980. He was beatified as a martyr on May 23, 2015.

8. Archbishop Oscar A. Romero, Homily of February 18, 1979, *Mons. Oscar A. Romero: Su Pensamiento, Vol. VI* (San Salvador: Arzobispado de San Salvador, 2000), 157–59. Italics added.

9. See José Antonio Pagola: *Jesus: An Historical Approximation*, trans. Margaret Wilde (Miami: Convivium Press, 2014), 152. I have incorporated what Pagola and Schillebeeckx both consider a more exact translation of verse 47. In other words, the woman's great love flows from her experience of having been forgiven. Says Schillebeeckx: "The measure of forgiving is the measure of the responsive love, and not vice versa." Edward Schillebeeckx, *Jesus: An Experiment in Christology* (New York: The Seabury Press, 1979), 208.

10. Schillebeeckx, *Jesus: An Experiment in Christology*, 208.

11. Pagola: *Jesus: An Historical Approximation*, trans. Margaret Wilde (Miami: Convivium Press, 2014), 195–96, slightly adapted into the present tense.

12. Barbara E. Reid, OP, *Parables for Preachers* (Collegeville, MN: The Liturgical Press, 1998), 182–83. See also Donald Goergen, OP, *The Mission and Ministry of Jesus*, Theology of Jesus, vol. 1 (Collegeville: The Liturgical Press, 1992), 89–91.

13. Pagola: *Jesus: An Historical Approximation*, 197, slightly adapted into the present tense.

14. Albert Nolan, OP, *Jesus Today: A Spirituality of Radical Freedom* (Cape Town: Double Storey Books, 2006), 53–54. (Also published by Orbis Books in the United States.)

15. Albert Nolan, OP, *Jesus Before Christianity* (New York: Orbis Books, 1978), 30, slightly adapted into the present tense. See also Nolan, *Jesus Today*, 49, 33.

16. E. P. Sanders, *Jesus and Judaism* (Philadelphia: Fortress Press, 1985), 181, 192. Sanders has rectified some formerly erroneous notions regarding sin and impurity in the time of Jesus.

17. Schillebeeckx, *Jesus: An Experiment in Christology*, 208–12. Italics added. To facilitate the reading of the text, several of the scripture citations quoted by Schillebeeckx have been left out and appear here: Mt 22:1–14; Lk 14:16–24; Lk 15:1–8; 19:10; Mt 9:36; 15:24.

18. Ibid., 212.

19. Joachim Jeremias, *New Testament Theology: The Proclamation of Jesus* (New York: Charles Scribner's Sons, 1971), 119, 121. Italics added.

20. Barbara E. Reid, OP, *Parables for Preachers* (Collegeville, MN: The Liturgical Press, 1998), 183–84.

21. Pope Francis, words spoken at the recitation of the Angelus (Vatican City: Libreria Editrice Vaticana, November 9, 2014).

22. Goergen, *Mission and Ministry*, 101–2.

23. Pope Francis, "A Big Heart Open to God," an interview with Pope Francis conducted in Rome by Antonio Spadaro, S.J, editor in chief of *La Civiltà Cattolica*. Cited in *America* (September 30, 2013): 24.

24. Pagola: *Jesus: An Historical Approximation*, 195.

25. Interestingly, as I write these pages, the world is scrambling to care for those infected with the highly contagious Ebola virus. Though quarantining patients is essential, no one is suggesting that these people be put on an abandoned island and left to die.

26. Christopher Hayden, *Praying the Scriptures: A Practical Introduction to Lectio Divina* (London: St. Paul's, 2001), 68–69.

27. Nolan, *Jesus Before Christianity*, 78–79.

28. John Riches, *The Oxford Companion to the Bible*, ed. Bruce M. Metzger and Michael D. Coogan (New York: Oxford University Press, 1993), 588.

29. St. Paul uses the word "saints" to refer to the followers of Jesus.

30. Laurence Freeman, OSB, *Jesus: The Teacher Within* (New York: Continuum, 2002), 95.

31. Eugene LaVerdiere, SSS, *Luke* (Wilmington, DE: Michael Glazier, Inc., 1980), xiii. Italics added. This quote has been changed to present tense for better fluidity with the rest of the chapter.

32. Hayden, *Praying the Scriptures*, 70. This quote has been changed to present tense for better fluidity with the rest of the chapter.

33. N. T. Wright, *Luke for Everyone* (Louisville: John Knox Press, 2004), 183.

4. Jesus the Prodigal Son

1. Maria Boulding, *The Coming of God*, 3rd ed. (Conception, MO: The Printery House, 2000), 57–58.

2. Karl Barth, *Church Dogmatics IV*, "The Doctrine of Reconciliation," Vol. 2 (Edinburgh: T. & T. Clark, 1958), 23. Italics added.

3. Ibid.

4. Ibid.

5. Albert Nolan, *Jesus Today: A Spirituality of Radical Freedom* (Cape Town: Double Storey Books, 2006), 191. (Also published by Orbis Books in the United States.)

6. Henri J. M. Nouwen, *The Return of the Prodigal Son* (London: Darton, Longman, Todd, 1994), 106–107.

7. Lk 9:59, 14:27, 18:22. The phrase "follow me" and its variations appear dozens of times in the four gospels and throughout the New Testament.

8. Thea Bowman, *Thea Bowman: In My Own Words*, ed. Maurice J. Nutt, CSsR (Liguori, MO: Liguori Publications, 2009), 41–42. Italics added.

9. Francesca Ambrogetti and Sergio Rubin, *Pope Francis: Conversations with Jorge Bergoglio* (New York: G. P. Putnam's Sons, 2013), 82–83.

10. José Antonio Pagola, *Jesus: An Historical Approximation*, trans. Margaret Wilde (Miami: Convivium Press, 2014), 99–100.

11. The story of the life and tragic death of the Trappist monks of the Monastery of our Lady of Atlas in Algeria is powerfully presented in the film, "Of Gods and Men."

12. Jean Jacques Pérennès, OP, *A Life Poured Out: Pierre Claverie of Algeria* (New York: Orbis Books, 2007), 243–44.

13. Shigeto Oshida, OP, *Takamori San: Teachings of Shigeto Oshida, Zen Master*, ed. Claudia Mattiello (Buenos Aires: Ed. Continente, 2005), 70. Translation slightly altered.

14. Pérennès, *A Life Poured Out*, 164–65.

15. Jerome A. Miller, "Wound Made Fountain: Toward a Theology of Redemption," *Theological Studies* 70 (2009): 546.

16. A segment from the "Paschal Proclamation" (*Exsultet*), cited from the English trans. and chants of *The Roman Missal* (International Commission on English in the Liturgy, 2011), 355.

17. Pope Francis, "A Big Heart Open to God," an interview with Pope Francis conducted in Rome by Antonio Spadaro, SJ, editor in chief of *La Civiltà Cattolica*. Cited in *America* (September 30, 2013), 24.

5. Becoming a Neighbor

1. St. Catherine of Siena, *Catherine of Siena: Passion for Truth, Compassion for Humanity*, ed. Mary O'Driscoll, OP (New York: New City Press, 1993), Prayer n. 9, p. 63.

2. *The Dialogue of St. Catherine of Siena*, trans. Suzanne Noffke, OP (New York: Paulist Press, 1980), 54, n. 15.

3. Herbert McCabe, OP, *Faith within Reason* (London: Continuum, 2007), 156–57.

4. Timothy Radcliffe, OP, *I Call You Friends* (London: Continuum, 2001), 56–57.

5. John Tauler, OP, *Johannes Tauler: Sermons* (New York: Paulist Press, 1985), 36.

6. Pope Francis, Message for Lent 2015, "Make your hearts firm" (Vatican City: en.radiovaticana.va/: February 27, 2015).

7. Pope Francis, homily preached at Holy Thursday Mass, St. Mary of Providence of the Don Gnocchi Foundation in Rome (Vatican City: en.radiovaticana.va/: April 17, 2014).

8. Gregory Boyle, SJ, *Tattoos on the Heart* (New York: Free Press, 2010), 70–72. Italics added.

9. Pope Francis, apostolic exhortation *Evangelii Gaudium* (Vatican City: Libreria Editrice Vaticana, November 24, 2013), n. 47. Italics added.

10. Cardinal Walter Kasper, "The Message of Mercy," *America* (September 15, 2014): 18. Italics added.

11. Pope Benedict XVI, "Message for Lent 2013" (Vatican City: Libreria Editrice Vaticana, October 15, 2012), n. 3.

12. Archbishop Oscar Romero, homily preached on March 23, 1980, in Scott Wright, *Oscar Romero and the Communion of Saints* (New York: Orbis Books, 2009), 130.

13. *Jesus I Trust in You: Selected Prayers of Saint Faustina* (Krakow: Misericordia Publications, 2008), 17–18.

14. Pope Francis, Homily in St. Peter's the day after naming twenty new cardinals (Vatican City: Libreria Editrice Vaticana, February 15, 2015).

15. "Amazing Grace," John Newton (1725–1807), slightly adapted.

16. W. H., *These Were My Realities: The Prison Journal of an Incarcerated Sex Offender* (a self–published book, copyrighted in 2006, ISBN number 978-1-4243-1477-5), 321.

17. Donald Goergen, OP, *The Mission and Ministry of Jesus*, Theology of Jesus, vol. 1 (Collegeville: The Liturgical Press, 1992), 30–31, slightly adapted into the present tense.

18. Laurence Freeman, OSB, "Christian Meditation Newsletter" 27, no. 3 (August 2003): 3–4. Italics added.

19. N. T. Wright, *Luke for Everyone*, (Louisville: John Knox Press, 2004), 105.

20. Karl Barth, *Church Dogmatics IV*, "The Doctrine of Reconciliation," Vol. 2 (Edinburgh: T. & T. Clark, 1958), 23.

21. Etienne Charpentier, *How to Read the New Testament* (New York: Crossroad, 1984), 37.

22. This translation of v. 36, from *La Nueva Biblia Española*, is, according to Gustavo Gutiérrez, the most faithful rendition of the Greek word, *gegonénai*. Cited from Gustavo Gutiérrez, OP, author's translation, "Seguimiento de Jesús y Opción por el Pobre," *Paginas*, n. 201 (October 2006): 7.

23. Gutiérrez, "Seguimiento de Jesús," *Paginas* 201, 6–21.

24. Pope Francis, First General Audience of his Pontificate (Vatican City: Libreria Editrice Vaticana, March 27, 2013).

25. *Campesino* is the Spanish word for "rural peasant."

26. An endearing way to say "the dear *Padre*," literally, *"the little Padre."*

27. Oscar Romero, *Daily Meditations*, trans. Irene B. Hodgson (London: Darton, Longman and Todd Ltd., 2006), 33. From a homily preached on February 5, 1978.

28. Pope Francis, First General Audience of his Pontificate (Vatican: Libreria Editrice Vaticana, March 27, 2013). Italics added. Slightly revised into the present tense.

29. Cited from the Sacramentary of the Mass, Italian Episcopal Conference, "Common Preface VIII." My translation.

30. Amy-Jill Levine, "Go and Do Likewise: Lessons from the Parable of the Good Samaritan," *America* (Sept. 29, 2014): 17. Italics added.

31. Ibid.

32. Julia Esquivel V., *Algunos Secretos del Reino/Secrets of God's Reign*, trans. Kathy Ogle, Cecilia M. Corcoran, FSPA, and Judith Noone, MM, with a minor translation adjustment (Washington, DC: Epica, 2002), 80–83.

6. The Table of Mercy

1. José Antonio Pagola: *Jesus: An Historical Approximation*, trans. Margaret Wilde (Miami: Convivium Press, 2014), 197–99. Pagola's credentials are impressive; he studied scripture at both the Papal Biblical Institute in Rome and the École Biblique in Jerusalem.

2. Jean Vanier, *From Brokenness to Community* (New York: Paulist Press, 1992), 13–15. Italics added.

3. "An Interview with Gustavo Gutiérrez," by Mev Puleo, *St. Anthony Messenger* (February 1989): 10. Italics added.

4. Gregory Boyle, SJ, *Tattoos on the Heart* (New York: Free Press, 2010), 66, 75.

5. This example was used by Pope Francis during a daily Mass at Casa Santa Marta: "Think about a single mother who goes to the [parish] secretary and says: 'I want my child baptized.' And then this Christian says: 'No, you cannot because you're not married!' But look, this girl who had the courage to carry her pregnancy and not to return her son to the sender, what is it? A closed door! This is not zeal! It is far from the Lord! It does not open doors! Jesus instituted the seven sacraments … and we are establishing the eighth: the sacrament of pastoral customs! … Jesus is indignant when he sees these things!" (Vatican City: Libreria Editrice Vaticana, May 25, 2013).

6. Pope Francis, Message for the 101st World Day of Migrants and Refugees (Vatican City: Libreria Editrice Vaticana, September 23, 2014). Italics added.

7. St. Catherine of Siena, OP, *The Dialogue of St. Catherine of Siena*, trans. Suzanne Noffkee, OP (New York: Paulist Press, 1980), 49.

8. These words from Sr. Claire are from a personal letter sent to me in the 1990s.

9. The term "table companionship" is a marvelous phrase, meaning "to share bread with." See Joachim Jeremias, *The Parables of Jesus* (New York: Charles Scribner's Sons, 1972), 132.

10. Luke Timothy Johnson, *Sacra Pagina: The Gospel of Luke*, ed. Daniel J. Harrington, SJ (Collegeville, MN: The Liturgical Press, 1991), 98–100.

11. See Eugene LaVerdiere, SSS, *Luke* (Wilmington, DE: Michael Glazier, Inc., 1980), 84–85.

12. Albert Nolan, OP, *Jesus Before Christianity* (New York: Orbis Books, 1978), 94.

13. Bruce Chilton, *Rabbi Jesus: An Intimate Biography* (New York: Image Books, 2000), 60. See also Nolan, *Jesus Before Christianity*, 27. Though there is a reference to Jesus employing the baptismal ritual (Jn 3: 22–26), it does not appear to have lasted very long at all.

14. Chilton, *Rabbi Jesus*, 85, 87. Italics added.

15. Maria Boulding, *The Coming of God*, 3rd ed. (Conception, MO: The Printery House, 2000), 73.

16. Pope Francis, Address to the Plenary Assembly of the Pontifical Council for Promoting the New Evangelization (Vatican City: Libreria Editrice Vaticana, October 14, 2013).

17. Julia Esquivel, *Algunos Secretos del Reino/Secrets of God's Reign*, trans. Kathy Ogle, Cecilia M. Corcoran, FSPA, and Judith Noone, MM (Washington, DC: Epica, 2002), 54–56, with minor translation adjustments.

18. Karl Barth, *Church Dogmatics IV*, "The Doctrine of Reconciliation," Vol. 2 (Edinburgh: T. & T. Clark, 1958), 22.

19. Joachim Jeremias, *New Testament Theology: The Proclamation of Jesus* (New York: Charles Scribner's Sons, 1971), 115–16.

20. A segment from the "Paschal Proclamation" (*Exsultet*), sung every year at the Easter Vigil, from the English translation of *The Roman Missal* (Collegeville, MN: Liturgical Press, 2011), 363.

21. Paul Philibert, OP, "Finding Mercy at the Table," *Celebration* (February 2015): 4. Italics added.

22. Ibid.

23. Ibid.

24. Cf. Is 29:16; 45:9; 64:8; Jer 18:16; Sir 33:13, etc.

25. Timothy Radcliffe, OP, "Our Burden to be Shared," *The Tablet* (19/26 December 2009): 13.

26. Nolan, *Jesus Today: A Spirituality of Radical Freedom* (Cape Town: Double Storey Books, 2006) 50. (Also published by Orbis Books in the United States.)

27. Philibert, "Finding Mercy at the Table," 4.

28. Pope Francis, apostolic exhortation *Evangelii Gaudium* (Vatican City: Libreria Editrice Vaticana, November 24, 2013), n. 47.

29. Gregory Collins, OSB, "Some Fruit from the Tree of Thy Passion," *Spirituality* 15, no. 77 (March–April 2008): 81.

30. The words "betrayer" and "betrayed" appear more than a dozen times in reference to Judas in the gospels.

31. Nolan, *Jesus Today*, 71.

32. St. Thomas Aquinas, Prayers I and II in *Piae preces*, Appendix in *Opuscula alia dubia*, III, *Opera Omnia* (Parma: 1869), 24:241–42.

33. Pagola, *Jesus: An Historical Approximation*, 119.

34. Emmanuel Charles McCarthy, "The Nonviolent Eucharist," *Celebration* (January 2002): 37–38.

7. There is No Greater Love

1. Willa Cather, *Death Comes for the Archbishop* (New York: Vintage Books, 1971), 267.

2. Timothy Radcliffe, OP, "Mission to a Runaway World" (Rome: public talk given at SEDOS, December 5, 2000).

3. Herbert McCabe, OP, *God Matters* (Springfield, IL: Templegate, 1987), 93.

4. Ibid., 94–95.

5. Robert Barron, "The Christian: Missionary of Hope," *Chicago Studies* 33, no. 2 (August 1994): 140–41. Italics added.

6. McCabe, *God Matters*, 99.

7. Barron, "The Christian," 141.

8. Ibid., 142.

9. Oscar Wilde, "A Woman of no Importance," *Collins Complete Works of Oscar Wilde* (Glasgow: Harper Collins Publishers, 1994), 508–9.

10. A segment from the "Paschal Proclamation" (*Exsultet*), *The Roman Missal* (Collegeville: Liturgical Press, 2011), 355.

11. Maria Boulding, *The Coming of God*, 3rd ed. (Conception, MO: The Printery House, 2000), 57.

12. Pierre Claverie, OP, in Jean Jacques Pérennès, OP, *A Life Poured Out: Pierre Claverie of Algeria* (New York: Orbis Books, 2007), 244.

13. Gregory Boyle, SJ, *Tattoos on the Heart* (New York: Free Press, 2010), 172–73.

14. Hans Urs von Balthasar, *The Glory of the Lord: A Theological Aesthetics* (San Francisco: Ignatius Press, 1989), 7:138.

15. McCabe, *God Matters*, 97, 95.

16. A. Frank-Duquesne, "Joie de Jésus-Christ," *Etudes Carmélitaines* (1947), cited in Hans Urs von Balthasar, *The Glory of the Lord*, 537, n. 3.

17. Jean Vanier, *The Broken Body: Journey to Wholeness* (New York: Paulist Press, 1988), 107–8.

18. Barron, "The Christian," 143–44.

19. Ibid., 143–45.

20. Boulding, *The Coming of God*, 59.

21. Elie Wiesel, *Night*, new trans. by Marion Wiesel (New York: Hill and Wang, 2006), 92–95.

22. Barron, "The Christian," 145–46.

23. James Alison, "God's Self–Substitution and Sacrificial Inversion," *Stricken by God: Nonviolent Identification and the Victory of Christ*, ed. Brad Jersak and Michael Hardin (Grand Rapids and Cambridge: William B. Eerdmans Publ., 2007), 170–71.

24. Claverie, in Pérennès, *A Life Poured Out*, 237.

25. Boulding, *The Coming of God*, 75–76.

26. Julia Esquivel, "Siembra" (Guatemala, *Algunos Secretos del Reino/Secrets of God's Reign* (Guatemala and Washington, DC: EPICA, 2002), 28–29, translation slightly adapted.

27. Henri J. M. Nouwen, *The Return of the Prodigal Son* (London: Darton, Longman and Todd, Ltd., 1992), 56.

28. McCabe, *God Matters*, 100.

29. Taken from the Communion antiphon of the Celebration of the Lord's Supper.

30. Frank-Duquesne, "Joie de Jésus-Christ," 23–27.

8. The Descent into Hell

1. Robert Barron, "The Christian: Missionary of Hope," *Chicago Studies* 33, no. 2 (August 1994): 142.

2. Archbishop Oscar Romero, *The Violence of Love: The Pastoral Wisdom of Archbishop Oscar Romero*, compiled and trans. James R. Brockman, SJ (San Francisco: Harper & Row, 1988), 109–110.

3. St. Augustine of Hippo, *The Confessions* (n. 27), in *Light from Light: An Anthology of Christian Mysticism*, ed. Louis Dupré and James A. Wiseman, OSB (New York: Paulist Press, 2001), 62–63.

4. Catherine of Siena reminds us that Christ crucified is the bridge that allows us to return home. Cited in *The Dialogue of St. Catherine of Siena*, trans. Suzanne Noffke, OP (New York: Paulist Press, 1980), 58–59, n. 21.

5. *Catechism of the Catholic Church*, United States Catholic Conference, Inc. / Libreria Editrice Vaticana (Liguori, MO: Liguori Publications, 1994), no. 631.

6. Julian of Norwich, *Showings*, trans. Edmund Colledge, OSA, and James Walsh, SJ (New York: Paulist Press, 1978), 274–75.

7. This phrase, referring to the fortuitous graces that flow from the cross of Christ, comes from the "Paschal Proclamation" (*Exsultet*), cited from the English trans. and chants of *The Roman Missal* (International Commission on English in the Liturgy, 2011), 355.

8. Gregory Collins, OSB, "Some Fruit from the Tree of Thy Passion," *Spirituality* 15, no. 77 (March–April 2008): 84.

9. Christian Salenson, *Christian de Chergé: A Theology of Hope* (Collegeville: Liturgical Press, 2009), 201.

10. Collins, "Some Fruit from the Tree of Thy Passion," 86.

11. Cf. Acts 3:15; Rom 8:11; 1 Cor 15:20; Heb 13:20.

12. Ibid., *Catechism of the Catholic Church*, n. 632. See also 1 Pet 3:19; Acts 3:15; Rom 8:11; 1 Cor 15:20; cf. Heb 13:20.

13. *Catechism of the Catholic Church*, no. 635. See also Rev 1:18 and Phil 2:10. Italics added.

14. Ibid., *Catechism of the Catholic Church*, nos. 634–35.

15. Ps 107 has been slightly altered to be more inclusive.

16. Henri J. M. Nouwen, *The Return of the Prodigal Son* (London: Darton, Longman and Todd, Ltd., 1992), 42–43. Italics added.

17. From a Sermon by St. Andrew of Crete, Bishop, *A Short Breviary—Liturgia Horarium* (Collegeville, MN: St. John's Abbey Press, 1975), 299.

18. St. Catherine of Siena, *The Dialogue*, 72, n. 30.

19. St. Ambose of Milan, *Exposition of the Gospel of Luke* (7. 229–230), cited in *Ancient Christian Commentary on Scripture*, "New Testament III: Luke," ed. Arthur A. Just, Jr. (Downers Grove, IL: Inter-Varsity Press, 2003), 250. Italics added.

20. St. Catherine of Siena, *The Dialogue*, 56–57, n. 18.

21. Brian J. Pierce, OP, *We Walk the Path Together: Learning from Thich Nhat Hanh and Meister Eckhart* (New York: Orbis Books, 2005), 154.

9. Resurrection

1. Maria Boulding, OSB, *Gateway to Resurrection* (London: Burns and Oates, 2010), 12.

2. Bruno Cadoré, OP, Master of the Order of Preachers, Easter Letter to the Order of Preachers: "Christ, the Lord, has Risen!" (This is an internal letter, written to the worldwide Dominican Order, 2012), 1.

3. Maria Boulding, *The Coming of God*, 3rd ed. (Conception, MO: The Printery House, 2000), 76. The word "father" has been changed to *Abba*.

4. Thomas Merton, *New Seeds of Contemplation* (New York: A New Directions Book, 1961), 135.

5. Jerome A. Miller, "Wound Made Fountain: Toward a Theology of Redemption," *Theological Studies* 70 (2009): 547–48. Italics added.

6. Ibid., 548.

7. Martin Luther King, Jr., *Strength to Love* (Cleveland: William Collins / World Publishing Co., 1963), 47.

8. Excerpt from a personal letter sent to Sheila Provencher from Fr. Yousif, OP, Iraq (May 2006).

9. Hans Urs von Balthasar, *The Glory of the Lord: A Theological Aesthetics* (San Francisco: Ignatius Press, 1989), 7:138, slightly altered into the plural form.

10. Etty Hillesum, *An Interrupted Life and Letters from Westerbork* (New York: Henry and Holt & Co., 1996), 144–47.

11. Ibid., 179.

12. Ibid., 226.

13. Pope Benedict XVI (Vatican City: Libreria Editrice Vaticana, February 13, 2013). See also Hillesum, *An Interrupted Life*, 44.

14. Hillesum, *An Interrupted Life*, 156.

15. Jean Marie Dwyer, OP, *The Unfolding Journey* (Toronto: Novalis, 2014), 44, 46.

16. Balthasar, *The Glory of the Lord*, 537.

17. Hillesum, *An Interrupted Life*, 44.

18. Miller, "Wound Made Fountain," 549.

19. Pope Francis, apostolic exhortation *Evangelii Gaudium* (Vatican City: Libreria Editrice Vaticana, November 24, 2013), n. 24. "Father" has been replaced by *Abba*.

20. Gerald G. May, MD, *Addiction and Grace* (San Francisco: Harper & Row Publishers, 1988), 31. Italics added.

21. Miller, "Wound Made Fountain," 546–47. This quotation has been slightly altered into the present tense.

10. The Return of the Prodigal Son

1. I use the word "arise" here (Lk 15:18), taken from the King James Version of the Bible, as it captures well the parable's resurrection imagery.

2. *Catechism of the Catholic Church*, United States Catholic Conference, Inc.—Libreria Editrice Vaticana (Liguori, MO: Liguori Publications, 1994), n. 632. Cf. Acts 3:15; Rom 8:11; 1 Cor 15:20; Heb 13:20.

3. Slightly altered to be more inclusive.

4. Pope Benedict XVI, Homily at St. Peter's Basilica, Ash Wednesday Mass (Vatican City: Libreria Editrice Vaticana, February 13, 2013).

5. Robert Barron, "The Christian: Missionary of Hope," *Chicago Studies* 33, no. 2, (August 1994): 147–48.

6. Pope Francis, Vatican City, "Catechesis on the Creed," given during his weekly General Audience (St. Peter's Square, Vatican City: Libreria Editrice Vaticana, October 2, 2013).

7. "One of Us," a song written by Eric Bazilian (of the Hooters) and originally released by Joan Osborne on the album *Relish* (1995), is the theme song for a television series in the United States called *Joan of Arcadia*.

8. This juxtaposition of the New Testament parable told by Jesus and the Old Testament imagery of the Good Shepherd is intended to show the literary and spiritual unity between the Old and New Covenants. Though the parable does not explicitly speak of the prodigal Son returning home with others, we know that biblically speaking Christ the Good Shepherd brings all of redeemed humanity home to God.

9. St. Ambose of Milan, from *Exposition of the Gospel of Luke* (7. 207–208), cited in *Ancient Christian Commentary on Scripture*, "New Testament III: Luke," ed. Arthur A. Just, Jr. (Downers Grove, IL: Inter-Varsity Press, 2003), 243.

10. Pope Benedict XVI, *Jesus of Nazareth: The Infancy Narratives*, trans. Philip J. Whitmore (New York: Image, 2012), 111–12.

11. *The Dialogue of St. Catherine of Siena*, trans. Suzanne Noffke, OP (New York: Paulist Press, 1980), 58–59, n. 21.

12. Ibid., 59, n. 22.

13. Ibid., 60, n. 23.

14. Ibid., 66, n. 27.

15. Timothy Radcliffe, OP, *What is the Point of Being a Christian?* (London: Burns and Oates, 2005), 41–42.

16. Genesis 43:3 is correctly translated from the original Greek as, "You shall not see my face," though sometimes it is rendered as, "You shall not appear in my presence" (NAB, NJB).

17. To say that God sends "a part of himself," though somewhat awkward theologically, is a way of reminding us that God is *completely present* in the incarnate Son, Jesus Christ.

18. Meister Eckhart, "Sermo Paschalis" ("On the Day of the Resurrection," 1294), *Parisius Habitus, Lateinische Werke*, ed. L. Sturlese. Cited in Marie-Anne Vannier, *De la Résurrection à la naissance de Dieu dans l'âme: Retraite avec Maître Eckhart* (Paris: Les Éditions du Cerf, 2008), 69–71. Italics added. I am grateful to the Dominican nuns in Saint-Maximin-la-Sainte-Baume in France for directing me to this sermon of Eckhart.

19. The word "patient" comes from the Latin *patientia*, meaning "suffering."

20. St. Ambrose of Milan, cited in *Ancient Christian Commentary on Scripture*, "New Testament III: Luke," ed. Arthur A. Just, Jr. (Downers Grove, IL: Inter-Varsity Press, 2003), 247.

21. Hans Urs von Balthasar, *The Glory of the Lord: A Theological Aesthetics* (San Francisco: Ignatius Press, 1989), 7:137–8.

22. Kenneth E. Bailey, *Jacob and the Prodigal: How Jesus Retold Israel's Story* (Downers Grove, IL: Inter-Varsity Press, 2003), 109. See Joachim Jeremias, *The Parables of Jesus* (New York: Charles Scribner's Sons, 1972), 130.

23. Pope Francis, First General Audience of his Pontificate (Vatican: Libreria Editrice Vaticana, March 27, 2013). Italics added.

24. Karl Barth, *Church Dogmatics IV*, "The Doctrine of Reconciliation," Vol. 2 (Edinburgh: T. & T. Clark: 1958), 22.

25. Bailey, *Jacob and the Prodigal*, 183.

26. Henri J. M. Nouwen, *The Return of the Prodigal Son* (London: Darton, Longman, Todd, 1994), 106–7.

27. Eucharistic Prayer for Reconciliation II, *The Roman Missal* (Collegeville: Liturgical Press, 2011), 768.

28. "Amazing Grace," composed by slave trader John Newton (1725–1807), altered into the plural form.

29. St. Bede the Venerable, *Homilies on the Gospels*, Book Two (*Cistercian Studies*, Vol. 111), 79–80.

30. Bailey, *Jacob and the Prodigal*, 172.

31. See Thomas Aquinas, *Summa Contra Gentiles*, Book IV, Chapter 22.

32. Pope Francis, apostolic exhortation *Evangelii Gaudium* (Vatican City: Libreria Editrice Vaticana, November 24, 2013), 1.

33. Pope Francis, Weekly General Audience (Vatican City: Libreria Editrice Vaticana, September 18, 2013).

34. Charles Péguy, *The Portal of the Mystery of Hope*, trans. David Louis Schindler, Jr. (Grand Rapids, MI: William B. Eerdmans Publishing Co., 1996), 79. Italics added.

35. From a sermon by St. Peter Chrysologus, Bishop, *A Short Breviary— Liturgia Horarium* (Collegeville, MN: St. John's Abbey Press, 1975), Sermon 108, 354–55.

36. Péguy, *The Portal of the Mystery of Hope*, 79–80.

37. United States president Abraham Lincoln issued his "Emancipation Proclamation" on January 1, 1863, as the northern and southern states entered into their third year of a terrible, bloody civil war. The proclamation stated that "all persons held as slaves are, and henceforward shall be free." Lincoln was assassinated two years later while attending a play at Ford's Theatre in Washington, DC.

38. Barbara E. Reid, OP, *Parables for Preachers, The Gospel of Luke, Year C* (Collegeville, MN: The Liturgical Press, 1998), 65, 67. Italics added.

39. St. Athanasius, "Festal Letter no. 7," cited in *Ancient Christian Commentary on Scripture*, "New Testament III: Luke," ed. Arthur A. Just, Jr. (Downers Grove, IL: Inter-Varsity Press, 2003), 251.

40. Jorge M. Bergoglio (Pope Francis), *Mente Abierta, Corazón Creyente*, trans. Brian J. Pierce (Madrid: Editorial Claretiana— Publicaciones Claretianas, 2013), 204. Italics added.

41. Thomas Petriano, "Henri, Rembrandt and Vincent," in *Remembering*

Henri, ed. Gerald S. Twomey and Claude Pomerleau (New York: Orbis Books, 2006), 108.

42. Ibid., 117.

43. Chris Glaser, "Henri's Legacy," in *Remembering Henri*, ed. Gerald S. Twomey and Claude Pomerleau (New York: Orbis Books, 2006), 144.

44. Nouwen, *The Return of the Prodigal Son*, 17.

45. Ibid., 44.

46. Ibid., 35.

47. Ibid., 21.

48. Ibid., 53.

49. Ibid., 40.

50. Ibid., 37.

51. From the song, "Amazing Grace," composed by John Newton (1725–1807).

Index

215